The Bread

and Bread Machine

Cookbook

The **Bread**

and Bread Machine Cookbook

Christine Ingram
and Jennie Shapter

LORENZ BOOKS

First published by Lorenz Books in 2003

© Anness Publishing Limited 2003

Lorenz Books is an imprint of Anness Publishing Limited
Hermes House, 88–89 Blackfriars Road, London SE1 8HA

This edition distributed in the UK by The Manning Partnership Ltd,
tel. 01225 478 444; fax 01225 478 440; sales@manning-partnership.co.uk

This edition distributed in the USA and Canada by National Book Network,
tel. 301 459 3366; fax 301 429 5746; www.nbnbooks.com

This edition distributed in Australia by Pan Macmillan Australia,
tel. 1300 135 113; fax 1300 135 103; customer.service@macmillan.com.au

A CIP catalogue record for this book is available from the British Library.

Publisher: Joanna Lorenz
Managing Editor: Judith Simons
Project Editor: Sarah Ainley
Jacket and Text Design: Chloë Steers
Text Editor: Jenni Fleetwood
Typesetting: Jonathan Harley
Illustrations: Angela Wood
Recipes: Christine Ingram and Jennie Shapter
Indexer: Helen Snaith
Production Controller: Darren Price

1 3 5 7 9 10 8 6 4 2

NOTES
Bracketed terms are intended for American readers.
For all recipes, quantities are given in both metric and imperial measures
and, where appropriate, measures are also given in standard cups and spoons. Follow
one set, but not a mixture, because they are not interchangeable.
For greatest accuracy, use metric measures when baking in a bread machine.

Standard spoon and cup measures are level.
1 tsp = 5ml, 1 tbsp = 15ml, 1 cup = 250ml/8fl oz

Australian standard tablespoons are 20ml. Australian readers should use 3 tsp
in place of 1 tbsp for measuring small quantities of gelatine, flour, salt, etc.

Medium (US large) eggs are used unless otherwise stated.

Where the loaves are made automatically you will usually find three separate
lists of ingredients, each relating to a different size of machine. The small size is
recommended for bread machines that are designed for loaves using 350–375g/
12–13oz/3–3¼ cups of flour, the medium size for machines that make loaves using
450–500g/1–1¼lb/4–5 cups of flour and the large size for bread machines that are
capable of making loaves using up to 675g/1½lb/6 cups of flour. Refer to your
manufacturer's handbook if you are not sure of the capacity of your machine.
If only one set of ingredients is given for a loaf that is to be baked automatically, relate
these to the size of your machine to make sure it is suitable for the job.

CONTENTS

INTRODUCTION

There is something undeniably special about bread. The flavour and unmistakable scent of a freshly baked loaf combined with contrasting textures of soft crumb and crisp crust, is a sensuous experience. Most people have their own particular favourite: ciabatta, rich with olive oil; dark, malty rye; honeyed Challah; or a Middle Eastern bread, redolent of herbs and freshly ground spices. Whatever the shape or texture, bread has a special place in our affections.

Most people today have varied diets that include potatoes, pasta and rice. However, in some countries, such as the southern and eastern Mediterranean regions of Europe, bread is the most popular of the carbohydrates, eaten with every meal and often with every course.

Bread forms the basis of breakfast for many of us. The aroma of a freshly baked loaf – so easy to achieve with a bread machine – is a wonderful wake-up call, as is the prospect of tucking into warm freshly-baked croissants or a bagel with cream cheese. Sandwiches get us through the working day, and bread in some guise or other is the basis of some of our favourite snacks, from hamburgers, hot dogs and pizzas to the more sophisticated offerings of city cafés, such as olive focaccia, burritos or hot beef on rye.

Perhaps the best thing about bread is that it goes so well with other foods. It can be cut into slices or broken into rough chunks to be eaten with a meal – to mop up soups and sauces or to eat with cold meats, pâtés and cheese. Breads from the Middle East can be split and stuffed with meats and salads, and those from northern Europe taste delicious spread with strongly flavoured cheese or topped with smoked fish or pickled vegetables.

The types of bread for which there are recipes are endless. They range from evenly crusty breads, such as baguettes, to round cobs or Italian country loaves, known as "oven bottom-baked", which means they have been baked without tins (pans) or containers on the sole of the oven or on flat sheet trays. Loaves, such as the traditional English farmhouse, baked in metal tins, characteristically have a golden top with thinner crusts on the sides. Rolls or breads baked up against each other have even softer sides and are described as "batch-baked" because one baking produces many breads. Sourdough breads are made without yeast – they use a natural leaven instead – and are often labelled "yeast-free" breads or "naturally leavened". There are many varieties of sourdough bread. Some are made entirely from wheat, some from rye, others from a blend of both of these or other cereals. They are normally heavier than the average leavened yeast loaf, with a dense texture and pleasant and distinctive tart flavour.

The tradition of bread making has never stood still. In recent years there has been a huge upsurge in the popularity of home-baked bread. Much of this is a result of the increased use of easy-to-operate bread machines. These machines produce bread that looks and tastes as if aching effort went into its making, but in fact nothing could be further from the truth. Bread machines can bake a wide range of breads, both sweet and savoury, using different grains and flavourings, simply by the touch of a few buttons. The dough for many shaped breads, such as plaits, croissants and breadsticks, can even be made in a bread machine using the "dough only" setting. It is then shaped by hand and baked in an oven in the usual way. Bread machines take the hard work out of bread making while ensuring that all the pleasure is retained.

This book will provide the bread maker with everything he or she needs to know about handmade and machine-made bread. In it you will find recipes for a selection of breads made entirely by hand, as well as others made by machine. There are also instructions in the reference section to show you how to convert a favourite recipe for handmade bread into one to be made in a bread machine. So, whatever your choice of method, this comprehensive book will inspire you to bake more delicious home-made bread.

BAKING BREAD

Whether baking by hand or by machine, a good basic knowledge of bread-making ingredients and techniques will ensure success. This chapter guides you through the correct equipment for accurate measuring and successful baking, as well as explaining what bread machines are. The ingredients, and how they react with one another in the bread-making process, are explained in detail before a complete guide to using yeasts, bread preparation, finishing and baking. There are also tips for using bread machines and adapting traditional recipes for use in a bread machine. The chapter concludes with a troubleshooting section, which suggests ways of improving your baking skills when something goes wrong.

Equipment & Utensils

B read making is not an exact science and you do not need a fully equipped kitchen with state-of-the-art utensils if you decide to have a go. If you are using a bread machine the most expensive item will be the machine itself, and the essential items of equipment for bread making using a machine are primarily concerned with accurate measuring.

SCALES/WEIGHTS

Sets of balance scales are more accurate but spring balance scales are easier to use and more convenient. For bread making, you will probably be using large quantities of dry ingredients, and will therefore need large scales with a deep bowl.

For machine-made bread, electronic scales give the most accurate results and are well worth investing in.

MEASURING JUGS

Heatproof glass jugs (cups) are the most convenient. The measurements should be clearly marked on the outside. Be sure to buy jugs with both imperial and metric measurements so that you can follow any recipe with ease.

MEASURING SPOONS

Smaller quantities of dry ingredients, such as sugar, salt and, most importantly, yeast, need to be measured carefully, especially when baking bread in a machine. A set of spoons usually measures from 1.5ml/¼ tsp to 15ml/1 tbsp. Level off the ingredient in the spoon for an accurate measure.

SIEVES

It is worth having at least one large sieve for flours, plus a smaller sieve should you wish to add ground spices or dust loaves with flour or icing (confectioners') sugar after baking them.

BOWLS

It is not possible to make handmade bread without at least two good-sized mixing bowls. Choose a bowl with a wide mouth that is still deep enough to contain the batter or dough. A smaller china or glass bowl is useful for making up dried yeast.

FOOD PROCESSORS AND MIXERS

Most food processors are able to mix and knead dough extremely efficiently and in a fraction of the time it would take by hand. An electric mixer fitted with a dough hook will knead dough in a time similar to that taken to knead by hand but with much less effort. For machine-made bread always check the instructions in the instruction booklet, since only the larger machines can handle large amounts of dough, and you may need to knead the dough in batches.

ROLLING PIN

Some doughs need to be rolled out, and you will need a large rolling pin for this job. A wooden rolling pin that is long and smooth without separate handles is ideal.

DOUGH KNIFE OR SCRAPER

This is an extremely handy piece of equipment when kneading dough by hand. The rectangular piece of flexible steel on a wooden handle is very useful in the early part of kneading, for lifting and working sticky or difficult doughs.

PLASTIC SCRAPER AND SPATULA

Use these tools to help remove dough that is stuck on the inside of the bread machine pan. Make sure they are pliable. The scraper also comes in handy for lifting and turning sticky dough, and dividing dough into pieces for shaping into rolls.

KNIVES AND SCISSORS

You will need a sharp knife or pair of scissors for slashing the dough – either during rising or just before baking. This adds a decorative finish.

PASTRY BRUSH

This is essential for glazing loaves and rolls. Choose a good, wide brush made from natural fibres; nylon will melt if used for brushing hot loaves during cooking.

BREAD PANS

It is worth having a selection of bread pans. These are readily available in all sizes. Include a 450g/1lb and preferably two 1kg/2¼lb pans so that you can make loaves in a variety of shapes and sizes. If the pans are labelled with their dimensions, rather than their capacity, look out for 18 × 7.5cm/7 × 3in (equivalent to 450g/1lb) and 23 × 13cm/9 × 5in (equivalent to 1kg/2¼lb). Other useful sizes are 30 × 10cm/12 × 4in and 25 × 10cm/10 × 4in. Heavy-gauge baking pans are best, because they are less likely to distort in the oven.

Focaccia and deep-pan pizzas bases are usually cooked in a large, shallow, round cake pan, with a diameter of 25–28cm/10–11in, or a 25cm/ 10in pizza pan. Aside from their obvious use, muffin pans with 7.5cm/3in cups are ideal for making elaborately shaped rolls. Tall, narrow speciality breads like Panettone and Sally Lunn are usually baked in a deep 15cm/6in cake pan.

MOULDS

There are various sizes of brioche mould for the traditional fluted brioche. A kugelhopf mould is a fluted ring mould essential for making Kugelhopf or the Viennese Gugelhupf. A savarin mould is a straight-sided ring mould. If you do not have the correct mould, it is sometimes possible to improvise. Boston brown bread, for example, should be baked in a special mould, but the heatproof glass jar from a cafetière coffee jug can be used instead.

BAKING SHEETS

Buy baking sheets that are either completely flat or have a lip on one long edge only. This makes it easier to slide bread or rolls on to a wire rack. Strong, heavy baking sheets distribute the heat more evenly.

DISHTOWELS AND CLEAR FILM

Use a clean dishtowel or clear film (plastic wrap) to cover the dough during proving.

WATER SPRAY BOTTLE

To achieve a crisp crust use a water spray bottle to mist the oven.

WIRE RACK

The hot cooked bread should be turned out on to a wire rack and left to cool before being stored or sliced.

BREAD MACHINES

A bread machine is designed to take the hard work out of making bread. Like most kitchen appliances, it is a labour-saving device. It will mix the ingredients and knead the dough for you, and allows the bread to rise and bake at the correct temperature and for the correct time. There are many different models, but all operate in much the same way.

For most breads, all you will need to do is to measure the ingredients for your chosen recipe, put them into the pan in the correct order, close the lid, select a suitable baking programme and opt for light, medium or dark crust. You may also choose to delay the starting time, so that you have freshly baked bread for breakfast or when you return from work. Press the Start button and in a few hours you will have a beautifully baked loaf, the machine having performed the kneading, rising and baking cycles for you.

Bread machines always offer a selection of programmes to suit recipes using different types of flour and varying levels of sugar and fat. You can explore making a whole variety of raw doughs for shaping

sweet and savoury breads, sourdough breads, mixed-grains, Continental-style breads and many more.

All bread machines work on the same basic principle. Each contains a removable non-stick bread pan with a handle, into which a kneading blade is fitted. When inserted in the machine the pan fits on to a central shaft which rotates the blade. A lid closes over the bread pan to contain the ingredients within a controlled environment. The lid includes an air vent and may have a window for checking the progress of your bread. The machine is programmed using the control panel.

The shape of the bread pan determines the size and shape of the bread. There are two shapes currently on the market: one rectangular and the other square. The rectangular pan produces the more traditional shape, the actual size varying from one manufacturer to another. The square shape is mostly to be found in smaller machines and produces a tall loaf, which is similar to a traditional rectangular loaf that has been stood on its end. The vertical square loaf can be turned on its side for slicing to give smaller slices of bread.

The size of the loaf ranges from about 500g/1¼lb to 1.3kg/3lb, depending on the machine, with most large machines offering the option of baking smaller loaves as well. One of the machines available makes small, medium and large loaves.

BUYING A BREAD MACHINE

There is plenty of choice when it comes to selecting a bread machine to buy. Give some thought to which features would prove most useful, and then shop around for the best buy available in your price range. Consider the size of loaf you would like to bake, which may be governed by the number of people in your family and how many of you take sandwiches for lunch. A large bread machine will often make smaller loaves as well but not vice versa. Consider whether the bread shape is important, and choose a machine with a square or rectangular bread pan.

Are you likely to want to make breads with added ingredients? If so, an audible signal known as a raisin beep is very useful. Does the machine have speciality flour cycles for wholemeal (whole-wheat) loaves, and would this matter to you? Another feature, the dough cycle, adds a great deal of flexibility, as it allows you to make hand-shaped breads. Extra features on some bread machines, such as jam-making and rice-cooking facilities, are extremely specialized and only you know whether you would find them worth having.

One important consideration is whether the manufacturer offers a well-written manual and an after-sales support system or help line. If these are available, any problems or queries you might have can be answered quickly, which is particularly useful if this is your first bread machine.

A bread machine takes up a fair amount of room, so think about where you will store it, and buy one that fits the available space. If it is to be left on the work surface and aesthetics are important to you, you will need to buy a machine that will be in keeping with your existing appliances. Most bread machines are available in white or black, or in stainless steel.

Jot down the features that matter to you, listing them in order of preference. Use a simple process of elimination to narrow your choice down to two or three machines, which will make the decision easier.

BUILT-IN SAFETY DEVICES

Most machines include a power-failure override mode. If the machine is inadvertently unplugged, or there is a brief power cut, the programme will continue as soon as the power is restored. The maximum time allowed for loss of power varies from 10 to 30 minutes. Check the bread when the power comes back on; depending on what stage the programme had reached at the time of the power cut, the rising or baking time of the loaf may have been affected.

An over-load protection is fitted to some models. This will cut in if the kneading blade is restricted by hard dough and will stop the motor to protect it. It will automatically re-start after about 30 minutes, but it is important to rectify the problem with the dough first. Either start again or cut the dough into small pieces and return it to the bread pan with a little more liquid to soften it.

Types of Flour

The largest single ingredient used in bread is flour, and the right flour is the key to good bread making. Wheat is the primary grain used for grinding into flour. Apart from rye, it is the only flour with sufficient gluten to make well-leavened bread. For extra flavour, texture and manageability, wheat is often mixed with other grains.

Wheat Flours

Wheat consists of an outer husk or bran that encloses the wheat kernel. The kernel contains the wheat germ and the endosperm, which is full of starch and protein. It is these proteins that form gluten when flour is mixed with water. When dough is kneaded, gluten stretches like elastic to trap the bubbles of carbon dioxide, the gas released by the action of the yeast, and the dough rises. Wheat is processed to create many sorts of flour.

Plain White Flour

This flour contains about 75 per cent of the wheat kernel. The outer bran and the wheat germ are removed to leave the endosperm, which is milled into a white flour. It is multipurpose flour, and contains less protein and gluten than bread flour. The main use for plain white flour is in quick teabreads, when chemical raising agents such as baking powder are added to give a light, airy crumb. It can also be used for soda bread.

American all-purpose flour is a medium-strength flour, somewhere between the British plain and strong white flour. Soft flour, sometimes known as American cake flour, is made from soft wheat and has been milled very finely. It gives sponge cakes and similar baked goods a crumblier texture than when standard plain or all-purpose flour is used.

Unbleached White Flour

Flour that is unbleached is creamier in colour than other white flours, which have been whitened artificially. Bleaching, which involves treating the flour with chlorine, is becoming increasingly rare because of health concerns, and the majority of white flours are unbleached, although you should check the packet to be sure. In Britain, flour producers are required by law to add or fortify their white flours with certain nutrients such as vitamin B1, nicotinic acid, iron and calcium. These are often added in the form of white soya flour, which also has a natural bleaching effect.

Strong White/White Bread Flour

For almost all bread making, the best type of flour to use is one which is largely derived from wheat that is high in protein. This type of flour is described as "strong" and is often labelled "bread flour", which underlines its suitability for the task. Proteins in the flour, when mixed with water, combine to make gluten, and it is this that gives dough its elasticity when kneaded and allows it to trap the bubbles of carbon dioxide given off by the yeast. Soft flour produces flat loaves that stale quickly; conversely, if the flour is too hard, the bread will have a coarse texture. A balance is required and most millers blend hard and soft wheats to make a flour that produces a well-flavoured loaf with good volume. Most strong white flours have a lower protein content than their wholemeal (whole-wheat) equivalent, and a baker would probably use a flour with a protein level of 12 per cent. The protein value of a flour can be found listed on the packet under "Nutritional Value".

FINE FRENCH PLAIN FLOUR

French bakers use a mixture of white bread flour and fine plain flour to make baguettes and other specialities. Fine French plain flour is called *farine fluide* in its country of origin because it is so light and free-flowing. Such is the popularity of French-style baked goods that this type of flour is now available in supermarkets the world over.

WHOLEMEAL FLOUR

This flour is made using the whole of the wheat grain and is sometimes called 100 per cent extraction flour: nothing is added and nothing is taken away. The bran and wheat germ, which are automatically separated from the white inner portion if milled between rollers, are returned to the white flour at the end of the process. For making bread you should use strong wholemeal (whole-wheat) bread flour, with a protein content of around 12.5 per cent. Loaves made with 100 per cent wholemeal bread flour tend to be very dense. The bran inhibits the release of gluten, so wholemeal doughs rise more slowly. For these reasons, many bread recipes recommend blending wholemeal flour with white bread flour.

STONEGROUND WHOLEMEAL FLOUR

This wholemeal flour has been ground in the traditional way between two stones. The bran and wheat germ are milled with the rest of the wheat grain, so there is no separation of the flour at any stage. Stoneground flour is also considered to have a better flavour, owing to the slow grinding of the stones. It is a good alternative to wholemeal flour, as it produces a loaf with a lighter finish but with a denser texture and fuller flavour than white bread. However, because the oily wheat germ is squashed into the flour rather than churned in later, stoneground flour has a higher fat content and may become rancid if stored for too long.

ATTA/CHAPATI FLOUR

This is a fine wholemeal flour, available from Indian grocers, where it is sometimes labelled as *atta*. It is used to make chapatis and other Indian flat breads.

ORGANIC FLOUR

This flour has been milled from organic wheat, which is wheat produced without the use of artificial fertilizers or pesticides.

GRANARY FLOUR

A proprietary name of a blend of brown and rye flours and malted wheat grain is known as Granary (whole-wheat). The tasty malted grain gives this bread its characteristic sweet and slightly sticky flavour and texture. Granary flour is sold in health food stores and supermarkets. It is often mixed with rye, wholemeal and white bread flour in multigrain loaves.

MALTHOUSE FLOUR

A speciality flour available from some large supermarkets and health food stores, malthouse flour is a combination of stoneground brown flour, rye flour, and malted wheat flour with malted wheat flakes. It resembles Granary flour.

GRAHAM FLOUR

This popular American flour is slightly coarser than ordinary wholemeal (wholewheat). It is named after a 19th-century Connecticut cleric, Revd Sylvester Graham, who developed the flour and advocated using the whole grain for bread making because of the beneficial effects of the bran.

BROWN FLOUR

This flour contains about 85 per cent of the original grain, with some of the bran and wheat germ extracted. It produces a lighter loaf than 100 per cent wholemeal flour, while still retaining a high percentage of wheat germ.

WHEAT GERM FLOUR

Available as brown or white, wheat germ flour must contain at least 10 per cent added wheat germ. Wheat germ is highly nutritious, and bread made from it is held to be particularly healthy.

SEMOLINA

This is the wheat kernel or endosperm, once the bran and wheat germ have been removed from the grain by milling, but before it is fully milled into flour. Semolina can be ground either coarsely or finely.

SPELT

Although spelt, a variety of wheat, is no longer widely grown, one or two smaller flour mills still produce a spelt flour, which is available in some health food stores.

OTHER FLOURS

Alternative grains, such as barley, cornmeal and oatmeal, are full of flavour but contain little or no gluten. Breads made solely from them would rise poorly and would be extremely dense. The milled grains are therefore often mixed with strong wheat flour. Rye is rich in gluten, but pure rye doughs are difficult to handle; once again the addition of strong wheat flour can provide a solution.

RYE FLOUR

Apart from wheat, rye is the only other cereal that is widely used to make bread. It has a good gluten content, although rye doughs are notoriously sticky and difficult to handle. For this reason, rye meal is often blended with other flours to create a dough that is more manageable. There are as many different rye meals as there are wheat flours, ranging in colour and type of grind. Pumpernickel and other dense and steamed box-shaped rye breads use a coarsely ground wholemeal rye, while finer flour, which contains neither the bran nor the germ, is used for the popular rustic, crusty black breads.

BARLEY

Low in gluten, barley meal is seldom used for bread making in Britain and western Europe. In Russia and other eastern European countries, however, barley loaves

continue to be produced, the flour mostly blended with some proportion of wheat or rye flour to give the loaf volume. They tend to be rather grey and flat and have an earthy, rather mealy flavour.

Barley meal is the ground whole grain of the barley, while barley flour is ground pearl barley, with the outer skin removed. Either can be added in small quantities to wholemeal or white flour.

BUCKWHEAT FLOUR

This grain is blackish in colour, hence its French name, *blé noir*. It is not strictly a cereal but is the fruit of a plant belonging to the dock family. The three-cornered grains are milled to a flour and used for pancakes, blinis and, in France, for crêpes or galettes. It can also be added to wheat flour and is popular mixed with other grains in multigrain loaves. Buckwheat has a distinctive, earthy flavour.

CORNMEAL

This meal is ground from white or yellow corn and is normally available in coarse, medium or fine grinds. Coarse-ground cornmeal is used for the Italian dish of polenta; for bread making choose one of the finer grinds, available from most health food stores. There are numerous corn breads from the southern states of America, including the famous double corn bread. Corn contains no gluten so will not make a loaf unless it is blended with wheat flour, when the corn adds a pleasant flavour and a delicate, golden colour.

MILLET FLOUR

Although high in protein, millet flour is low in gluten and is not commonly used by itself in bread making. It is pale yellow in colour, with a gritty texture. The addition of wheat flour produces a slightly nutty flavour.

STORAGE

Although most flours keep well, they do not last indefinitely and it is important to pay attention to the "use-by" date on the packet. Old flour will begin to taste stale and will make a disappointing loaf. Keep the flour in its bag and place in a tin or storage jar with a tight-fitting lid, and always store on a cool, dry shelf. Wash and dry the jar thoroughly whenever replacing with new flour, and avoid adding new flour to old. Wholemeal (whole-wheat) flour does not keep as well as white flours.

OATMEAL

Because oatmeal does not contain gluten it is only very rarely used by itself for bread making. The exception is in Scotland where flat, crisply baked oatmeal biscuits have been popular for centuries. These are baked on a griddle and served with butter or marmalade. Oatmeal can also be used in wheat or multigrain loaves. Choose finely ground oatmeal for making oatcakes or for using in loaves.

RICE

When ground very finely, polished rice becomes rice flour. It is useful for people with wheat allergies and is also occasionally used for some Indian breads. Ground rice is more granular, similar to semolina. Either rice flour or ground rice can replace some white bread flour in a recipe, adding a sweet flavour and chewy texture to the bread.

GRAM FLOUR

This is a flour made from ground chickpeas. It is also known as besan. Missi rotis – spicy, unleavened breads from northern India – are made using gram flour.

Yeasts & Other Leavens

Almost all breads today are leavened in one way or another, which means that a substance has been added to the dough to initiate fermentation and make the dough rise. Yeast is the most familiar leavening agent. It is available fresh or dried; dried yeast is more convenient, but bakers would say there's no substitute for fresh yeast. There are also a variety of other ways of aerating the dough.

Without yeast or another leavening agent, the combination of flour and water, once cooked, would be merely a flat and rather unappetizing cake. At some point in history, our ancestors discovered how dough, if left to ferment in the warmth, produced a lighter and airier bread when cooked.

The transformation of dough into bread is caused by yeast or another leavening ingredient producing carbon dioxide. The carbon dioxide expands and the dough stretches. Tiny air pockets are introduced into the dough. When the bread is cooked the process is set, and the air becomes locked in, improving the texture.

The most popular leavening ingredient in bread making is yeast. However, raising agents such as bicarbonate of soda are also used for making certain breads. When using a bread machine, raising agents other than yeast are best used for teabreads and cakes that are mixed in a bowl, and then baked in the bread pan.

Yeast

The most popular choice for bread making, yeast is simple to use, more reliable than a natural leaven and considerably quicker to activate. Conventional dried yeast and easy-blend (rapid-rise) dried yeast, which is also known as fast-action yeast, have been produced for the convenience of those making bread at home. Some bakers prefer fresh yeast, since it is considered to have a superior flavour and to be more manageable and reliable. However, when fresh yeast is not available or convenient, dried yeast becomes a handy substitute.

When making bread in a bread machine, easy-blend dried yeast is almost always used. Fresh yeast can be used with caution when baking in a bread machine, but is best used in the "dough only" cycle. It is hard to give exact quantities for breads, which will be made using a range of machines operating in different temperatures. The difficulty lies in preventing the bread from rising over the top of the bread pan during baking; doughs made from easy-blend dried yeast are easier to control where uniform results are required.

There are several ways of adding yeast to flour. Fresh yeast is usually blended with lukewarm water before being mixed into the flour; conventional dried yeast is first reconstituted in warm water and then left until frothy; easy-blend and fast-action dried yeasts are added directly to the flour.

BREWER'S YEAST

Some old cookery books call for brewer's yeast or ale or beer barm. Until the last century, this was the common and only leavening ingredient. During the 1950s in the USA and Britain it was considered a wonder food owing to its nutritional value. It is not, however, suitable for bread making, being too bitter, and should only be used for making beer.

NATURAL LEAVENS

Long before yeast was sold commercially, sourdough starters were used to make breads. These are natural leavens made by fermenting yeast spores that occur naturally in flour, dairy products, plant matter and spices. Breads are still produced by the same method today. Breads made using natural leavens have different flavours and textures from breads made with commercial yeast.

BICARBONATE OF SODA

Sometimes just called soda, bicarbonate of soda (baking soda), is the leavening ingredient in Irish soda bread. It is an alkaline chemical which, when mixed with an acid in a moisture-rich environment, reacts to produce carbon dioxide. Cream of tartar, an acid that is made from fermented grapes, is commonly used in conjunction with bicarbonate of soda for soda breads, or else the soda is combined with soured milk, which is naturally acidic. Buttermilk can also be used.

BAKING POWDER

This is made up of a mixture of acid and alkaline chemicals, usually bicarbonate of soda and cream of tartar and sometimes bicarbonate of soda and sodium pyrophosphate. When these come into contact with moisture, as in a dough or a

DOUGH CONDITIONERS

These are added to breads to help stabilize the gluten strands and hold the gases formed by the yeast. Chemical conditioners are frequently added to commercially-produced bread, and bread improvers are often listed among the ingredients on fast-action yeast packets.

Two natural dough conditioners that help to ensure a higher rise, lighter texture and stronger dough are lemon juice and malt extract. Gluten strength can vary between bags of flour, so you can add some lemon juice to the dough to help to strengthen it, particularly when making wholegrain breads. Adding 5ml/1 tsp lemon juice with every 225g/8oz/2 cups bread flour will not affect the flavour of the bread.

Malt extract helps to break down the starch in wheat into sugars for the yeast to feed on and so encourages active fermentation. Use up to 5ml/1 tsp malt extract with every 225g/8oz/2 cups bread flour. If you like the flavour of malt extract, increase the amount used.

batter, the reaction of the chemicals produces tiny bubbles of air so the dough rises and becomes spongy, just as it does with yeast. However, it is important to work fast as the carbon dioxide will quickly escape and the loaf will collapse.

LIQUIDS

Although flour and yeast are the most obvious ingredients used in bread making, there are a number of other ingredients that are just as important. For successful bread making liquids need to be measured accurately and used at the correct temperature. Ingredients like honey or eggs add to the liquid component and must be considered as such.

As a general rule, savoury loaves are made using water; teabreads and sweeter breads use milk. Whatever the liquid, it is always heated slightly when making handmade bread. Breads made with milk are softer in both the crumb and the crust than those made using water alone.

WATER

The most frequently used liquid in bread making is water. Bread made with water has a crisper crust than when milk is included. Tap water is chemically treated, and if it has been heavily chlorinated and fluorinated this may well slow down the rising. Hard water can also affect the rise, because it is alkaline, which retards the yeast. If your breads are not rising very well and you have tried other remedies, try using cool boiled water or bottled water.

MILK

As well as helping to enrich the dough, milk produces a creamy-coloured, tender crumb and golden crust. Use full-cream (whole), semi-skimmed (low-fat) or skimmed milk, or replace fresh milk with skimmed milk powder. This can be useful if you are using a bread machine and intend using the timer to delay the starting time for making bread, as, unlike fresh milk, the milk powder will not deteriorate. Sprinkle it on top of the flour in the bread pan to keep it separated from the water until mixing starts.

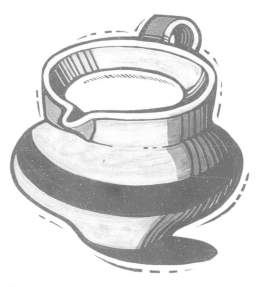

BUTTERMILK

If used instead of regular milk, buttermilk creates a moister bread and produces an almost cake-like texture. Buttermilk is made from skimmed milk which is pasteurized, then cooled. A cultured bacterium is then added which ferments the milk under controlled conditions to produce its slightly tangy, acidic, but pleasant flavour. This flavour is noticeable in the finished loaf.

YOGURT

Another alternative to milk, yogurt also has good tenderizing properties. Use natural (plain) yogurt or try flavoured yogurts, such as lemon or hazelnut, in breads which include these ingredients.

OTHER DAIRY PRODUCTS

Sour cream, cottage cheese and soft cheeses such as ricotta, fromage frais and mascarpone can all be used as part of the liquid content of the bread. They are valued more for their tenderizing properties than for their flavour.

COCONUT MILK

Use equal proportions of coconut milk and water to add a beautifully rich flavour to sweet breads and buns.

FRUIT JUICES

Fresh fruit juices such as orange, peach, apricot, pineapple, mango or cranberry can be added to the dough for fruit-flavoured breads. Try using freshly squeezed juices for the best flavour.

VEGETABLE JUICES AND COOKING LIQUIDS

The liquid left over from cooking vegetables will add flavour and extra nutritional value to breads, and is particularly useful when making savoury breads. Potato water, for example, has many benefits: the extra starch acts as an additional food for the yeast, and produces a greater rise and a softer and longer-lasting loaf.

Vegetables themselves also contain liquid juices and, when added to a recipe made in the bread machine, they will alter the liquid balance.

SOAKING JUICES

When dried vegetables such as mushrooms – especially wild ones – and sun-dried tomatoes are rehydrated in water, a very flavoursome liquid is produced. This is much too good to waste. Rehydrate the vegetables, drain off the liquid, strain it, and then add it as part of the liquid when making a savoury bread.

In sweet breads, the liquid drained from dried fruits that have been plumped up in fruit juices, spirits and liqueurs can be used to make up the liquid content of the recipe to add extra flavour.

BEERS, ALES, CIDERS AND LIQUEURS

All of these can be added to bread recipes. Beers and ales, in particular, have a great affinity with dark, heavy flours. The added sugars stimulate the yeast by providing more food. Dark beers and ales impart a stronger flavour.

EGGS

If a bread recipe includes eggs, these should be considered part of the liquid content. Eggs add colour, improve the structure and give the bread a richer flavour, although breads that have been enriched in this way are inclined to dry out more quickly than plain bread. It is worth adding a little extra fat to compensate for this. All the recipes in this book use medium (US large) eggs unless stated otherwise.

MACHINE BREAD

Some form of liquid is essential when making bread. It rehydrates and activates the yeast, and brings together the flour and any other dry ingredients to make the dough. Whatever the liquid, the temperature is important for successful machine breads. If your machine has a preheating cycle, cold liquids, straight from the refrigerator, can be used. If not, use liquids at room temperature, unless it is a very hot day. Water from the tap, providing it is merely cool, is fine. On a very cold day, measure the water and leave it to stand in the kitchen for a while before you use it so that it acclimatizes.

Fats & Sweeteners

It is important to use the correct quantities of both fats and sweeteners for successful bread making. Although both can enrich and flavour the dough, too much of either can upset the yeast fermentation process, causing the dough to rise too little or too much. This is particularly important to note if you are using a bread machine, as the rising is timed by the machine and cannot be overruled.

Fats

Small amounts of fat enrich doughs and add flavour. Used with eggs, they give a soft, tender texture to the crumb. Fats help to extend the freshness of the loaf, and, in rich doughs, help to cancel out the drying effect that eggs can cause. Although oils and melted butter can be poured into the flour with the yeast and liquid, solid butter or fats are normally kneaded into the flour before the liquid is added.

In small amounts, fat contributes to the elasticity of the gluten, but using too much causes the opposite effect. The fat coats the gluten strands and this forms a barrier between the yeast and flour. This slows down the action of the yeast, and hence increases the rising time. For this reason it is best to limit the amount of fat in a machine-baked bread, or risk a heavy, compact loaf.

When making rich bread in the bread machine, it is best to use it only for making the dough. You may need to use the cycle twice. Then, shape the dough by hand and leave it to rise for as long as required, before baking the bread conventionally.

Solid Fats

Butter, margarine, lard or white cooking fat can all be used in small quantities (of up to 15g/½oz/1 tbsp) without contributing any noticeable flavour to the dough. Where a recipe calls for a larger quantity of fat, use butter, preferably unsalted (sweet). If you are using quite a lot of salted butter, reduce the amount of salt added to the dough. Avoid allowing the butter to come into contact with the yeast as it may inhibit the yeast dissolving.

Where butter is layered in yeast pastry for croissants, it is important to soften it so it has the same consistency as the dough. Don't substitutue low-fat spreads for butter: they contain up to 40 per cent water and do not have the same properties as butter.

Liquid Fats

Sunflower oil is a good alternative to butter if you are concerned about the cholesterol level, while olive oil can be used where the flavour is important. The Italians particularly love adding olive oil to their breads. Use a fruity, full-flavoured extra virgin olive oil from the first pressing of the olives for the finest flavour. Nut oils, such as walnut and hazelnut, have very distinctive flavours, but are wonderful when teamed with similarly flavoured breads.

Fats Versus Oils

Fats and oils are interchangeable in many recipes. If you wish to change a solid fat for a liquid fat or oil, the amount of liquid in the bread dough needs to be adjusted to accommodate the change. This is only necessary for amounts over 15ml/1 tbsp.

Sweeteners

Sugars and liquid sweeteners accelerate the fermentation process by providing the yeast with extra food. Modern types of yeast no longer need sugar; they are able to use the flour efficiently to obtain food. Even so, it is usual to add a small amount of sweetener. This makes the yeast dough more active than if it were left to feed slowly on the natural starches and sugars in the flour. Enriched breads and heavy wholegrain breads need the increased yeast action to help the heavier dough to rise.

Sugar helps delay the staling process in bread because it attracts moisture. It also creates a tender texture. Too much sugar can cause dough to over-rise and collapse. Sweet breads have a moderate sugar level and gain extra sweetness from dried fruits, sweet glazes and icings. Sweeteners contribute to the colour of the bread. A small amount enhances the crust colour, giving a golden finish. Some bread machines over-brown sweet doughs, so select a light crust setting or a sweet bread setting, if available, when making sweet yeast cakes.

Any liquid sweetener can be used instead of sugar, but should be counted as part of the total liquid content of the bread. Adjustments may need to be made. Sugars are normally added with the flour, while liquids, such as treacle (molasses) and honey, are more often stirred into whatever lukewarm liquid you are using, so that they are gently warmed as well.

White Sugars

Granulated or caster (superfine) sugars can be used for bread making. They are almost pure sucrose and add little flavour to the finished bread. Icing (confectioners') sugar is not suitable as the anti-caking agent can affect the flavour. Save icing sugar for glazing and dusting.

Brown Sugars

Use light or dark brown, refined or unrefined brown sugar. The darker unrefined sugars will add more flavour, having a higher molasses content. Brown sugars add a touch of colour and also increase the acidity.

Malt Extract

An extract from malted wheat or barley, this has a strong flavour, so use it sparingly. Malt extract is best used in fruit breads.

Honey and Maple Syrup

Clear honey can be used as a substitute for sugar, but only use two-thirds of the amount suggested for sugar, as it is sweeter. Maple syrup is the reduced sap of the maple tree; use it in bread making in place of honey or sugar. It is slightly sweeter than sugar but not as sweet as honey.

Molasses, Golden Syrup and Treacle

All these sweeteners are by-products of the sugar refining process. Molasses is a thick concentrated syrup with a sweet, slightly bitter flavour. It adds a lovely golden colour to bread. Golden (light corn) syrup is light and sweet, with a slight butterscotch flavour. Corn syrup, which can be light or dark, can be used instead of golden syrup. Treacle (molasses) gives the bread a very dark, rich colour, and an intense flavour. It gives bread a slightly bitter taste.

ADDITIONAL INGREDIENTS

There is a wide variety of ingredients that can be added to sweet and savoury breads to give them flavour and texture. Always use ingredients of the very best quality, as these will give the best results. Fresh herbs, for instance, impart a superb flavour and aroma. Dried herbs can work well, too, but some are better than others and, in general, fresh herbs will produce a better tasting bread.

Many flavouring ingredients, such as chopped meats and dried fruits, are added during kneading, but if you are using a bread machine some ingredients can be added earlier in the process to enable them to be finely chopped and evenly distributed throughout the bread.

SALT

Almost all handmade bread recipes add salt at the beginning, stirring or sifting it into the flour. Salt is one of the few essential ingredients in bread making. It is important for both flavour and the effect it has on the yeast and dough. Essentially, it slows down the yeast's action – which is why it should not be added directly to the yeast. This means that the dough rises in a controlled and even way, giving a well-risen, even loaf. Too little salt means the loaf will stale more quickly; too much salt and the crust will harden.

When adding salt to the bread-machine pan, it is vital to keep it away from the yeast, as concentrated salt will severely impede the activity of the yeast.

Fine table salt and coarse sea salt can both be used in bread. Coarse salt is best used as a topping: it can be sprinkled on top of unbaked breads and rolls to give a crunchy texture and agreeable flavour. Look out for coarse sea salt with added flavourings, such as herbs or flakes of dried citrus peel.

HERBS

Use fresh herbs, if you can, for bread making. They have the most wonderful aroma, matched only by their flavour. Dried herbs that are oily and pungent, such as sage, rosemary and thyme, also work well. Rosemary is especially pungent, so use it sparingly. Dried oregano is a fine substitute for fresh. As dried herbs have a more concentrated flavour, use only a third of the quantity recommended for fresh. Add fresh herbs toward the end of kneading. Dried herbs can be added with the dry ingredients. Avoid using dried parsley; substitute a different herb instead.

SPICES

The fresher the spices are, the more aromatic they will be, as their volatile oils fade with age. Use freshly ground black pepper and grated nutmeg. Cumin, fennel, caraway and cardamom can be bought as whole seeds and ground as needed in a spice mill or a coffee mill kept for this purpose. Use ready-ground spices within six months.

Nuts

The crunchiness and flavour of nuts make a wonderful addition to home-made breads. Nuts combine equally well with the sweet chewiness of dried and semi-dried fruits and with fresh fruits. They also go well with savoury additions, such as cheese, herbs and spices, and they can be used on their own to make rustic-style breads.

Nuts contain natural oils, which turn rancid if stored in too warm conditions or for too long. Buy in small quantities, store in an airtight container in a cool place and use them within a few weeks.

Pecan nuts, almonds, macadamia nuts, pistachio nuts and walnuts give wonderful flavour and texture when added to basic breads towards the end of the kneading process. They can be added to teabreads or used as a decoration on top of sweet breads or yeast cakes. Lightly toast pine nuts, hazelnuts and almonds first to bring out their flavour. Spread the nuts on a baking sheet and place them in an oven preheated to 180°C/350°F/Gas 4 for 5–8 minutes, or grill (broil) until golden. Avoid scorching, and leave the nuts to cool before adding them to the bread.

Hazelnuts, almonds and walnuts can be finely ground and used as a nutritious and flavoursome flour substitute. Replace up to 15 per cent of the flour with the ground nuts. If using hazelnuts, remove the bitter skin first. This will easily rub off if you toast the nuts in the oven.

Use freshly grated coconut or desiccated (dry unsweetened shredded) coconut, either plain or toasted.

If you are planning to add nuts to a bread or teabread, it is important to consider who might be the recipient of a slice. Nut allergies can be extremely serious, so if you use nuts in cooking, make sure everyone knows you've done so.

CHESTNUT BREAD IN THE MACHINE

These quantities are for a medium loaf. Increase all ingredients by 25 per cent if you are using a large machine; decrease by 25 per cent for a small machine.

1 Put 175g/6oz/½ cup unsweetened chestnut purée in a bowl and stir in 250ml/8fl oz/1 cup water. Mix well. Place in the bread pan. Add the dry ingredients first if necessary for your machine.

2 Sprinkle over 450g/1lb/4 cups white bread flour and 50g/2oz/½ cup wholemeal (whole-wheat) flour. Add 30ml/2 tbsp skimmed milk powder, 2.5ml/½ tsp ground cloves and 5ml/1 tsp freshly grated nutmeg. Place 5ml/1 tsp salt, 15ml/1 tbsp light muscovado (brown) sugar and 40g/1½oz/3 tbsp butter in separate corners. Make a shallow indent and add 7.5ml/1½ tsp easy-blend (rapid-rise) dried yeast.

3 Set the machine to the basic/normal setting, with raisin setting (if available), light crust. Press Start. Add 75g/3oz/¾ cup coarsely chopped walnuts at the beep or about 5 minutes before the end of the kneading cycle.

CHEESES

Added to a wide variety of breads, cheese will provide fabulous flavour and can make the bread more moist. Some cheeses have powerful flavours that really impact on the bread, while others are more subtle and are indistinguishable except for the richness they impart. Soft cheeses such as cottage cheese, fromage frais and ricotta are added as part of the liquid content of the recipe. They contribute little to the taste, but create a more tender loaf with a softer crumb.

Grated hard cheeses can be added at the beginning of kneading so that they are incorporated in the dough. Alternatively, they can be added towards the end of kneading to give small amounts scattered through the bread. Cheeses can also be sprinkled over the top, just before baking, to add colour and texture to the crust.

For maximum flavour, use small amounts of strongly flavoured hard cheeses, such as mature Cheddar or Parmesan, or blue cheeses such as Roquefort. If the cheese is salty, reduce the amount of additional salt, or the action of the yeast will be retarded and the bread may taste unacceptably salty.

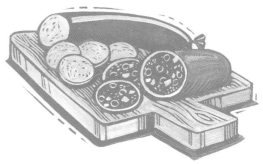

MEATS

A variety of meats can be used to flavour bread recipes. The best results often come from using cured meats, such as ham, bacon or salami, and cooked sausages, such as pepperoni.

When you use a strongly flavoured meat, it is best to chop it finely and add it to the dough during its final kneading. You do not need much: 25–50g/1–2oz will be quite sufficient to add extra flavour without overpowering the bread.

Ham and bacon are best added as small pieces during the final kneading or towards the end of the kneading cycle, if using a bread machine. Dice ham small. Fry or grill (broil) bacon rashers, then crumble them or cut into pieces, or use ready-cut cubes of bacon or pancetta and sauté them first.

Thinly sliced preserved meats, such as prosciutto, pastrami, speck, pepperoni and smoked venison can be added as thin strips during the final kneading or towards the end of the kneading cycle, if you are using a machine. They can also be incorporated into the dough during shaping.

Some meats are best kept whole or coarsely chopped and used as a filling, as when sausage is layered through a brioche dough, or used as a topping on tray-baked breads and pizzas. There are many different types of salami, flavoured with spices such as peppercorns, coriander or paprika, as well as pepperoni and cooked spicy Continental-style sausages.

USING CHEESE IN A BREAD MACHINE

- *Add soft cheeses with the liquids before adding the dry ingredients, unless the instructions for your machine state that you should add dry ingredients first.*
- *Add grated cheese at the beginning of the dough cycle so that it is evenly incorporated through the bread.*
- *Add coarsely chopped cheeses when the machine beeps towards the end of the kneading, so that it retains its form and remains in pockets in the dough.*
- *Machine-made breads incorporating hard cheeses may not rise high.*

VEGETABLES

Raw, canned, dried and freshly cooked vegetables all make perfect additions to savoury breads. Making bread also provides a good opportunity to use up any leftover cooked vegetables. Vegetable breads are richer than basic breads, the vegetables contributing flavour and texture to the finished loaves. Many vegetable breads are subtly coloured or dotted with attractive flecks. Manoucher, "Mediterranean nights" bread, is a rainbow of colours. Based on the Italian focaccia, it contains rosemary, red, green and yellow (bell) peppers, and goat's cheese. The Italians add olives or sun-dried tomatoes to their ciabatta, giving it a full flavour.

Fresh vegetables are relatively high in liquid, so if you add them, calculate that about half of their weight will be water and deduct the equivalent amount of liquid from the recipe.

STARCHY VEGETABLES

Potatoes, sweet potatoes, parsnips, carrots, swede (rutabaga) and other varieties of starchy vegetables sweeten the bread and contribute a soft texture. You can use leftover mashed or even instant mashed potato. Add 115–225g/4–8oz/1⅓–2⅔ cups to a basic bread recipe. If you are using a bread machine, bear its size in mind when adding starchy vegetables and adjust the liquid if necessary.

ONIONS, LEEKS AND CHILLIES

These vegetables are best if you sauté them first in a little butter or oil, which brings out their flavour. Caramelized onions will add richness and a light golden colour to the bread. For speed, you can add dried sliced onions instead of fresh onions, but you may need to add an extra 15ml/1 tbsp or so of liquid to compensate.

SPINACH

Fresh spinach leaves need to be blanched briefly in boiling water before being used. Chop them if making bread by hand, and add them during kneading. If using a machine, add them whole with the liquid ingredients at the beginning of the kneading cycle. They will mix in and become finely chopped as the cycle progresses. Frozen chopped spinach can be substituted for fresh, but thaw it completely first and drain it well. Reduce the liquid in the recipe to allow for the extra water.

TOMATOES

Ripe tomatoes are versatile and give bread a delicious flavour. Tomatoes can be puréed, canned, fresh or sun-dried. When making bread by hand, sun-dried tomatoes should be roughly chopped before being kneaded into the dough after the first rising. When using a bread machine, the stage at which you add the sun-dried tomatoes will determine whether they will remain as pieces – making a bread with interesting flecks of colour – or be fully integrated into the dough to add flavour. For a more intense taste, choose regular sun-dried tomatoes, rather than the ones preserved in oil, reconstitute them in water, then use the soaking water as the liquid in the recipe.

Other tomato products are best added at the beginning, to ensure the loaf is richly coloured, with a distinct tomato taste.

MUSHROOMS

Dried wild mushrooms can be added in the same way as sun-dried tomatoes for a tasty loaf to serve with soups, stews and casseroles. Strain the soaking water, if using it in a recipe, to remove any grit.

OTHER VEGETABLES

Corn kernels, chopped olives or chopped spring onions (scallions) will all impart flavour, colour and texture. Knead them into the dough after the first rising, if making bread by hand, or towards the end of the kneading cycle if using a machine.

Frozen vegetables should be thawed completely before use. You may need to reduce the liquid quantity in the recipe if you use frozen vegetables instead of fresh. Canned vegetables should be well drained.

FRUIT

Whether you use them fresh, dried or as purées or juices, fruits add complementary flavours to breads and teacakes. The natural sugars help to feed the yeast and improve the leavening process, while fruits with natural pectin will improve the keeping quality of baked goods.

FRESH FRUITS

Some fruits, such as berries, are best frozen before they are added to the dough. This helps to keep them intact. Add to the dough in the machine just before the end of the kneading cycle. When adding juicy fruits, toss them with a little extra flour, to keep the consistency of the bread dough correct. Soft fruits can be added to teabread mixtures: fold them in at the end of mixing.

ADDING VEGETABLES AND FRUIT TO BREAD IN A BREAD MACHINE

There are several ways of preparing vegetables and fruit before adding them to the machine.

- *Add grated raw vegetables such as courgettes (zucchini), carrots or beetroot (beet), when you add the water to the pan.*
- *Sweet potatoes, parsnips, potatoes, winter squashes and pumpkin should be cooked first. Drain, reserving the cooking liquid, and mash them. When cool, use the cooking liquid instead of plain water and add the mashed vegetable to the dough and mix well.*
- *If you want vegetables to remain identifiable in the finished bread add them when the machine beeps for adding extra ingredients or 5 minutes before the end of the kneading cycle, so they stay as slices or small pieces.*

- *Add frozen orange concentrate or fruit juice right at the beginning of the mixing process, unless the instructions for your machine state you should add the dry ingredients first.*
- *Add purées, such as apple, pear or mango, after the water in the recipe has been poured into the bread pan. Alternatively, blend the two together first, and then add the mixture to the bread pan.*
- *If you wish to add mashed or grated fruits, such as bananas or pears, put them in after the liquids.*
- *Add fresh or frozen whole fruits, such as berries, when the machine beeps or about 5 minutes before the end of the kneading cycle. Chopped fruits, such as apples and plums, as well as dried fruits, such as raisins and currants, should also be added towards the end of the kneading process.*

DRIED CAKE FRUITS

The familiar dried cake fruits, such as sultanas (golden raisins), currants and raisins, can easily be incorporated in most basic breads, adding their own distinctive textures and flavours.

If making bread by hand, dried fruits can be added during mixing or during the second kneading. If adding at the second kneading, warm the fruit first, so that it does not inhibit the action of the yeast. If you are using an electric mixer or food processor for kneading, note that the blades, particularly on the food processor, will chop the fruit. This spoils both the appearance and the flavour of the loaf, so only knead by mixer or food processor to begin with, and then knead the fruit in by hand after the initial rising.

If using a bread machine, sprinkle the fruit in gradually when the machine beeps or towards the end of the kneading cycle. For added flavour, plump the fruit up by soaking it beforehand in fruit juice or a liqueur. If baking by machine you can add up to 50g/2oz/⅓ cup of dried fruit for a small machine; 115g/4oz/⅔ cup for a large one. If you soak the dried fruit first, use the excess juice or liqueur as part of the measured liquid quantity. You may need to add a spoonful or so of extra liquid to a basic bread recipe if you do not soak the dried fruit first.

PINEAPPLE AND BANANA BREAD IN THE MACHINE

The quantities given here are for a medium bread machine. Increase by 25 per cent for a large machine; decrease by 25 per cent for a small one.

1 Pour 60ml/4 tbsp pineapple juice and 200ml/7fl oz/scant 1 cup buttermilk into the bread pan. Mash 1 large banana (about 185g/6½oz) and add. Add the dry ingredients first if your machine specifies this method.

2 Sprinkle in 450g/1lb/4 cups unbleached white bread flour and 50g/2oz/½ cup wholemeal (whole-wheat) flour, covering the liquid. Place 5ml/1 tsp salt, 45ml/ 3 tbsp caster (super-fine) sugar and 40g/ 1½oz/3 tbsp butter in separate corners. Make an indent in the flour; add 5ml/ 1 tsp easy-blend (rapid-rise) dried yeast.

3 Set to the basic/normal setting, with raisin setting (if available), light crust. Press Start. Add 75g/3oz/½ cup chopped canned pineapple chunks at the beep or towards the end of the cycle. Remove from the pan and turn out on to a wire rack.

DRIED, SEMI-DRIED AND READY-TO-EAT DRIED FRUITS

These are perfect for breads, because their flavours are so concentrated, and there is a vast range to choose from. Use mixtures of exotic dried fruits, such as mango, papaya, melon and figs. Small dried fruits such as cranberries and cherries can be added whole, while the larger exotic fruits need to be chopped coarsely, as do apricots, pears, prunes, dates and peaches. Dried fruits, such as stoned prunes, can be soaked in sherry or a liqueur, as for cake fruits. Add them as described for cake fruits.

Glazes

Both machine-baked breads and hand-shaped loaves benefit from a glaze to give that final finishing touch. Glazing has two important functions: it gives an attractive finish to the loaf and it introduces moisture during cooking. All sorts of ingredients can be used for glazing, from a simple milk or egg wash to melted jam or marmalade.

The moisture in a glaze that is applied before baking produces steam, which helps to expand the gases in the loaf and ensures it cooks through. Glazes also change the consistency and taste of the crust.

Bread can be glazed before, during or just after baking; sometimes recipes will suggest all three. If you glaze before and during baking by hand, take care not to brush sticky glazes up to the sides of the pan or let the glaze drip on to the baking sheet, thereby gluing the bread to its container. This will cause the loaf to crack and rise unevenly, spoiling its appearance.

Although glazes are generally used for hand-shaped breads, good glazing results may also be obtained with machine-baked loaves. Glazes can also be applied after baking to give flavour and a glossy finish. Another important role for glazes is to act as an adhesive: to help any topping applied to the loaf stick to the surface of the dough.

For machine-baked breads, the glaze should either be brushed on to the loaf just before the baking cycle commences, or within 10 minutes of the start of the baking cycle. Apply the glaze quickly.

Glazes using egg, milk and salted water can also be brushed over freshly cooked loaves. If using a bread machine, brush over the glaze as soon as the baking cycle finishes, then leave the bread inside the machine for 3–4 minutes, to allow the glaze to dry to a shine.

Glazes Used Before or During Baking

For a crust with an attractive glossy shine, apply a glaze before or during baking.

Milk

Before baking brush on loaves where a softer golden crust is desired. Milk is also used for bridge rolls, buns (such as teacakes) and flatbreads where a soft crust is wanted.

Olive Oil

This is mainly used with Continental-style breads, such as focaccia and fougasse. It adds flavour and a shiny finish. The darker the oil the fuller the flavour. Apply before and/or after baking.

Butter

Rolls are brushed with melted butter before baking to add colour and to keep the dough soft. Glazing with butter adds a rich flavour.

Salted Water

Mix 10ml/2 tsp salt with 30ml/2 tbsp water and brush over the dough immediately before baking. This gives a crisp, baked crust with a slight sheen.

EGG WHITE

Use 1 egg white mixed with 15ml/1 tbsp water for a lighter golden, slightly shiny crust. This is often a better alternative to egg yolk for savoury breads. Brush the glaze on before baking.

EGG YOLK

Mix 1 egg yolk with 15ml/1 tbsp milk or water to make this classic glaze, also known as egg wash. It is used to give a very golden, shiny crust. For sweet breads add 15ml/ 1 tbsp caster (superfine) sugar, for extra colour and flavour.

GLAZES ADDED AFTER BAKING

Some glazes are used after baking, often on sweet breads. These glazes generally give a glossy and/or sticky finish, and also help to keep the bread fresh. They are suited to both machine and hand-shaped breads.

BUTTER

Breads such as Italian Panettone and German Stollen are brushed with melted butter after baking to soften the crust. Clarified butter is sometimes used as a glaze to soften flatbreads such as naan.

SUGAR GLAZE

Dissolve 30–45ml/2–3 tbsp granulated sugar in the same amount of milk or water. Bring to the boil, then simmer for 1–2 minutes, until syrupy. Brush over fruit loaves or buns for a glossy sheen. For extra flavour, use rose water.

ICING SUGAR GLAZE

In a bowl, mix 30–45ml/2–3 tbsp icing (confectioners') sugar with 15ml/1 tbsp fruit juice, milk, single (light) cream (flavoured with vanilla essence or extract, if you like) or water and drizzle or brush over warm sweet breads. You can also add a pinch of spice to the icing sugar to bring out the flavour of the loaf. Maple syrup can be mixed with icing sugar for glazing nut-flavoured breads.

HONEY, MALT, MOLASSES AND GOLDEN SYRUP

Liquid sweeteners can be warmed and brushed over breads, rolls and teabreads to give a soft, sweet and sticky crust. Honey is a traditional glaze and provides a lovely flavour. Both malt and molasses have quite strong flavours, so use these sparingly, matching them to compatible breads such as fruit loaves. Or you could mix them with a milder-flavoured liquid sweetener, such as golden (light corn) syrup, to soften their impact.

PRESERVES

Jam or marmalade can be melted with a little liquid. Choose water, liqueur, spirits (such as rum or brandy) or fruit juice, to complement the bread to be glazed. The liquid thins the preserve and adds flavour. It can be brushed over freshly baked warm teabreads and sweet breads to give a glossy, sticky finish. Dried fruit and nuts can then be sprinkled on top.

SYRUPS

A sugar syrup, flavoured with liqueur, spirits or lemon juice, can be drizzled over a sweet bread. The syrup moistens the bread, while adding a decorative topping.

TOPPINGS

There are as many toppings for bread as there are glazes, all of which add to the appearance, taste and texture of your bread. The dough can be rolled in a topping before the second rising, or it can be glazed and sprinkled with the topping just before baking. Good toppings to try include seeds, grated cheese, cracked wheat, oats, sea salt, herbs, cornmeal or wheat flakes.

For basic breads and rolls, toppings are simply a matter of preference – for dinner parties offer guests a selection of white and wholemeal (whole-wheat) rolls, each one sprinkled with a different topping. Some breads traditionally have their own topping. Challah, for example, is usually sprinkled with poppy seeds. Many British and American breads have no toppings as such, but a dusting of flour gives an attractive finish to the loaf.

Grated cheese and fried onion rings make more substantial as well as tasty and attractive toppings. Many of the Italian breads excel themselves in the use of a rich variety of ingredients – whole olives, sun-dried tomatoes and strips of roasted (bell) pepper are frequently added to ciabattas and focaccias.

Toppings can also be added during and sometimes after cooking. Small breads, such as Vienna rolls, are baked until just golden, brushed with milk and then strewn with sea salt, cumin or caraway seeds. They are then returned to the oven for a few more moments until cooked.

MACHINE-BAKED BREADS

A topping can be added at various stages: at the beginning of the baking cycle, about 10 minutes after baking begins, or immediately after baking, while the bread is still hot. If you add the topping at the beginning of baking, open the lid for only the shortest possible time, to minimize heat loss. Before you add a topping, brush the bread with a glaze. This will ensure that the topping sticks to the loaf. Most machine breads are brushed with an egg, milk or water glaze.

If applying a topping to bread after baking, remove the bread pan carefully from the machine and close the lid to retain the heat. Using oven gloves, quickly loosen the bread from the pan, then put it back in the pan again. Brush the loaf with the glaze and sprinkle over the chosen topping. Return the bread in the pan to the bread machine for 3–4 minutes to allow the glaze to bake on and secure the topping. The chosen topping will not cook and brown in the same way it would if it were added at the beginning of baking.

FLOUR

To create a farmhouse-style finish, brush the loaf with water or milk glaze just before baking – or within 10 minutes of the start of baking – and dust lightly with flour. Use white flour, or wholemeal (whole-wheat) or Granary for a more rustic finish.

CORNMEAL OR POLENTA

Use cornmeal, polenta, semolina or other speciality flours as a finish for Mixed Grain Onion Rolls or similar small breads.

ROLLED OATS

These are sliced oat kernels, steamed and rolled. They make a decorative finish for white breads and other breads flavoured with oatmeal. They are best added just before or at the very beginning of baking.

SMALL SEEDS

Seeds can be used to add flavour and texture in addition to a decorative finish. Try sesame, poppy, aniseed, caraway or cumin seeds. If adding sesame seeds immediately after baking, lightly toast until golden before adding.

LARGE SEEDS

Gently press pumpkin or sunflower seeds on to the top of a freshly glazed loaf to give an attractive finish and a bonus crunch.

WHEAT AND OAT BRAN FLAKES

These add both texture and fibre to bread as well as visual appeal. Sprinkle them over the top of the loaf after glazing at the beginning of baking.

PEPPER AND PAPRIKA

Freshly ground black pepper and paprika both add spiciness to savoury breads. These tasty toppings can be added before, during or after baking.

SALT

Brush the top of a white loaf with water or egg glaze and sprinkle with a little coarse sea salt, to give an attractive and crunchy topping. Sea salt is best applied at the beginning of baking or 10 minutes into the baking cycle.

ICING SUGAR

Dust cooked sweet breads or teabreads with icing (confectioners') sugar after baking, for a neat, finished look. Add 2.5ml/½ tsp spice before sprinkling, for added flavour, if you like.

HAND-SHAPED BREAD

All of the toppings used on machine-baked breads can also be added to breads that are hand-shaped and baked in an oven. There are several simple methods that can be used.

SPRINKLING WITH FLOUR

If you are using flour, this should be sprinkled over the dough immediately after shaping and again before slashing and baking, to give a rustic finish. Match the flour to the type of bread being made. Unbleached white bread flour is ideal for giving soft rolls and breads a fine finish. Use cornmeal, ground rice or rice flour for crumpets and muffins, and brown, wholemeal and Granary (whole-wheat) flours on wholegrain breads.

MATCHING FLAVOURS

When using grain as a topping, the general rule is to match it to the grain or flour used in the bread itself; for example, a bread containing millet flakes or millet seeds is often sprinkled with millet flour.

If a flavouring has been incorporated into the dough, you may be able to top the loaf with the same ingredient, to provide a hint of what is inside. Try sprinkling a little grated Parmesan on to a cheese loaf about 10 minutes after baking begins, or, for a loaf flavoured with herbs, add an appropriate dried herb as a topping after baking.

GROUND RICE OR RICE FLOUR
Muffins are enhanced with a ground rice or rice flour topping.

WHOLEMEAL FLOUR
Complement wholegrain dough, whether made into loaves or rolls, with wholemeal (whole-wheat) flour toppings.

ROLLING DOUGH IN SEEDS
Sprinkle seeds, salt or any other fine topping on a work surface, then roll the shaped but unproved dough in the chosen topping until it is evenly coated. This is ideal for coating wholegrain breads with pumpkin seeds or wheat flakes.

SESAME SEEDS
Dough sticks can be rolled in small seeds for a delicious crunchy topping.

ADDING A TOPPING AFTER A GLAZE
Some toppings are sprinkled over the bread after glazing and immediately before the loaf is baked. In addition to toppings suggested for machine-baked breads, these toppings can be used:

CANDIED FRUITS
Whole or chopped candied fruits make an attractive topping for festive breads. Add the fruits after an egg glaze. Candied fruits can also be used after baking, with a jam or icing (confectioners') sugar glaze to stick the fruits to the bread.

NUTS
Just before baking, brush sweet or savoury breads and rolls with glaze and sprinkle with chopped or flaked (sliced) almonds, chopped cashews, chopped or whole walnuts or pecan nuts.

VEGETABLES
Brush savoury breads and rolls with an egg glaze or olive oil and then sprinkle with finely chopped raw onion, raw (bell) peppers, sun-dried tomatoes or olives for an extremely tasty crust.

CHEESE
Grated cheeses, such as Parmesan, Cheddar or Pecorino, are best for sprinkling on to dough just before baking, resulting in a chewy, flavoursome crust.

FRESH HERBS
Use fresh herbs, such as rosemary, thyme, sage or basil for Italian-style flatbreads. Chopped herbs also make a good topping for individual bread rolls.

SUGAR
Sugar is available in many forms, so choose one appropriate for your topping. Before baking, brush buns and cakes with butter or milk, then sprinkle with demerara (raw) sugar for a sweet, crunchy finish. Yeast doughs that are deep-fried can be sprinkled or tossed in a sugar coating.

Breads such as Panettone and Kugelhopf benefit from a very light dusting of icing (confectioner's) sugar. Use a fine sieve to do this. Dust with icing sugar when ready to serve the bread to avoid the topping soaking into the crust.

USING YEASTS

There are several different forms of yeast, some easier to use than others, but none of them particularly tricky if you follow a few simple rules. Whichever yeast you use, if must be in good condition – neither too old nor stale – and must not be subjected to too much heat.

USING FRESH YEAST FOR HANDMADE BREADS

Fresh yeast is available from baker's, healthfood stores and most supermarkets with an in-store bakery. It is pale beige in colour, has a sweet, fruity smell and should crumble easily. It can be stored in the refrigerator, wrapped in clear film (plastic wrap), for up to 2 weeks or can be frozen for up to 3 months. A quantity of 15g/½oz fresh yeast should be sufficient for 675–900g/1½–2lb/6–8 cups flour.

1 Put the yeast in a small bowl. Using a spoon, mash or "cream" it with a little of the measured water until smooth.

2 Pour in the remaining liquid, which may be water, milk or a mixture of the two. Mix well. Use as directed in the recipe.

USING DRIED YEAST FOR HANDMADE BREADS

Dried yeast is the dehydrated equivalent of fresh yeast, but it needs to be blended with liquid before use. Store dried yeast in a cool dry place and check the "use-by" date on the tin or packet. You will need about 15g/½oz (7.5ml/1½ tsp) dried yeast for 675g/1½lb/6 cups flour. Some bakers add sugar or honey to the mixing liquid, but this is not necessary – the granules will contain enough nourishment to enable the yeast to work.

1 Pour the measured lukewarm liquid into a small bowl and sprinkle the dried yeast evenly over the surface.

2 Cover with clear film and leave in a warm room for 10–15 minutes, or until frothy. Stir well and use as directed.

USING EASY-BLEND AND FAST-ACTION DRIED YEASTS

These are the most convenient of the dried yeasts as they can be stirred directly into the flour. Fast-action yeasts and some easy-blends (rapid-rises) contain a bread improver, which eliminates the need for two kneadings and risings. Most of these yeasts come in 7g/¼oz sachets, which are sufficient for 675g/1½lb/6 cups flour.

For handmade breads, sift together the flour and salt into a medium bowl and rub in the fat, if using. Stir in the easy-blend or fast-action dried yeast, and then add warm water or milk, plus any other ingredients.

For machine-made breads, follow your machine manual. Usually the liquid ingredients are added to the bread pan first, followed by other dry ingredients, then the butter or oil and finally the yeast.

WATER TEMPERATURE

When making bread by hand, use lukewarm water for fresh and regular dried yeast. For easy-blend (fast-action) yeast the water can be a little hotter, as the yeast is mixed with flour before the liquid is added.

SOURDOUGHS

Breads based on a natural leaven are known as sourdoughs. An authentic sourdough relies entirely on the wild yeasts that exist in the air. Given the right conditions, any dough of flour and water or batter of vegetable origin will start to ferment spontaneously and will continue to do so if starch or sugar is added to feed it. Recipes for some of the traditional American and German breads use a variety of rather surprising starters for their sourdoughs, including potatoes, beer, ginger beer, hops and treacle. In Britain sourdoughs are sometimes called acids or acid breads. There are many types of sourdough. In France the sourdough method is known as the *chef* or *levain*, and is used for *pain de campagne* as well as their delicious sourdough baguettes.

In spite of their many variations, sourdoughs do have some elements in common. Each begins with a "starter", which can take anything up to a week to ferment and become established. This "starter" or leaven is used, daily by bakers or less frequently by home bread makers, for the day's bread. A small amount of the dough is then kept back and used for the next batch of bread. Alternatively, a slightly more liquid starter can be made and kept in the refrigerator until it is ready for use. Each time part of the starter is used, the remaining starter is refreshed with equal amounts of flour and water.

MAKING A FRENCH SOURDOUGH STARTER

It is not difficult to make a sourdough starter. The starter can be kept in the refrigerator for up to 10 days, but for longer than that it should be frozen. Bring the starter to room temperature before adding to the next batch of bread.

1 Place 115g/4oz/1 cup flour in a large bowl and add 75ml/5 tbsp water. Mix together, and then knead for 3–4 minutes to form a dough. Cover the bowl with clear film (plastic wrap) and set aside at room temperature for 2–3 days. The type of flour will depend on the type of bread; it can be wholemeal (whole-wheat), white or rye, or a combination of two or three.

2 After 2–3 days, the mixture will rise and aerate slightly and turn a light greyish colour. A soft crust may form on top of the starter and it should develop a slightly sweet-sour smell.

3 Remove any crust that has formed on top of the starter and discard it. Stir in 120ml/4fl oz/½ cup lukewarm water to make a paste and then add 175g/6oz/1½ cups flour. The flour can be wholemeal or a mixture of wholemeal and white. Mix together to make a dough, then transfer to a work surface and knead lightly until the dough becomes firm.

4 Place the ball of dough in a bowl, cover again with clear film and leave for 1–2 days at room temperature.

5 Remove and discard any crust that forms. What remains – the *chef* – can now be used to make a sourdough bread, such as Pain de Campagne rustique. To keep the chef going, save about 225g/8oz of the dough each time you make sourdough.

6 Place the dough starter in a crock or bowl, cover and keep in the refrigerator for up to 10 days. Freeze the dough if you do not plan to use it within this time.

Yeast Know-how

- Check "use-by" dates on dried and fast-action yeasts. If a product is past its "use-by" date, replace it. If it is marginal and you cannot immediately replace it, you can find out if it is still active. Take a measuring jug (cup) and pour in 120ml/4fl oz/½ cup warm water (43–46°C/110–115°F). Add 5ml/ 1 tsp sugar, stir to dissolve and then sprinkle over 10ml/2 tsp dried yeast. Stir and leave for 10 minutes. The yeast should begin to rise to the surface after the first 5 minutes, and after 10 minutes a rounded crown of foam should have developed that reaches to the 250ml/8fl oz/1 cup level of the measuring jug. If this happens the yeast is active; if not, the yeast has lost its potency and should be discarded.
- Fresh yeast can be stored in the refrigerator, wrapped in clear film, for up to 2 weeks, or it can be frozen for up to 3 months.

- Yeast needs warmth to activate it, but must not be subjected to too hot a temperature or it will die. The optimum heat is 38°C/100°F. If you do not have a thermometer, mix 300ml/ ½ pint/1¼ cups boiling water with 600ml/1 pint/2½ cups cold water, and then measure the required amount of water from the mixture.
- If you are using easy-blend or fast-action dried yeast you can afford to have the water slightly hotter, since the yeast is mixed with the flour, and the heat of the water will rapidly dissipate.
- The amount of yeast you require should not increase proportionally as the amount of flour increases, so take care if you decide to double the quantities in a recipe. You will not need to double the amount of yeast. Similarly, if you halve a recipe, you are likely to need proportionally more yeast, or be prepared to wait a bit longer for the bread to rise.

THE SPONGE METHOD

Some yeasted breads are made by the sponge method, in which the yeast is dissolved in more lukewarm water than usual, and then mixed with some of the flour to make a batter. The batter is left for at least 20 minutes and often much longer. The advantage of this method is that it enables the yeast to start working without being inhibited by ingredients like eggs, fat and sugar, which slow down its action.

Many French breads are also sponged. A slightly different technique is used and the batter is left to ferment for 2–12 hours. The slow fermentation makes for wonderfully flavoured bread with very little acidity, yet with a fragile and crunchy crust.

MAKING A YEAST DOUGH BY THE SPONGE METHOD

1 Mix 7g/¼oz fresh yeast with 250ml/ 8fl oz/1 cup lukewarm water in a large bowl. Stir in 115g/4oz/1 cup unbleached plain (all-purpose) flour, using a wooden spoon, then use your fingers to draw the mixture together until you have a smooth liquid with the consistency of a thick batter. (Do not add salt; this inhibits the yeast.)

2 Cover with a damp dishtowel and leave in a warm place. The sponge will double or triple in bulk and then fall back after 5–6 hours, which indicates that it is ready to use.

3 Mix the sponge starter to a dough with the remaining flour and other ingredients as directed in the recipe.

MAKING AN ITALIAN STARTER

Italian bakers employ a similar sponging process called a *biga*. This uses less liquid than that required for the classic sponge method, and the sponge takes about 12–15 hours to mature. The reason the dough takes so long to rise is because the concentration of yeast cells is lower than would be present in fresh yeast or a packet of dried yeast. However, there are benefits in being able to leave the dough to rise slowly – you can make it early in the day for baking that evening, for instance. The lengthy rising period also means that the dough develops a very good flavour. It is important not to leave it for much longer than the recommended time, or it may develop an unacceptably sour taste. If you wish to make an Italian *biga* for Pane Toscano or a similar Italian country bread, use 175g/6oz/1½ cups unbleached plain flour instead.

1 Cream the yeast with 90ml/6 tbsp lukewarm water, then pour it into a well in the centre of the flour. Gradually mix in the surrounding flour to form a firm dough.

2 The dough should be kneaded for a few minutes and then left, covered with lightly oiled clear film (plastic wrap) for 12–15 hours in a cool room.

THE OLD DOUGH METHOD IN A BREAD MACHINE

A small piece of dough is removed from a batch of risen dough and set aside for adding to the dough for the next loaf of bread. This is a quick and easy alternative to making a starter, and will add texture and improve the taste of the bread to which it is added. The following recipe is suitable for a medium or large machine. If you have a smaller machine reduce the quantities by a quarter.

1 Tear about 115g/4oz dough off bread that is ready for shaping. Place in a bowl and cover with clear film (plastic wrap). Set aside at room temperature or, if not using within 4 hours, in the refrigerator. Return to room temperature before use.

2 Pour 300ml/½ pint/1¼ cups water into the bread machine pan. Add the old dough that has been reserved. However, if the instructions for your machine specify that the dry ingredients are to be placed in the bread pan first, reverse the order in which you add the dry ingredients and the water and reserved dough.

3 Gently sprinkle over 450g/1lb/4 cups unbleached strong white bread flour. Add 7.5ml/1½ tsp salt, 15ml/1 tbsp granulated sugar and 25g/1 oz butter, placing these ingredients in separate corners of the bread pan.

4 Make a small indent in the centre of the flour and spoon in 5ml/1 tsp easy-blend (rapid-rise) dried yeast.

5 Set the bread machine to the basic/ normal setting, medium crust. Press Start. At the end of the baking cycle, remove the bread from the pan and turn out on to a wire rack to cool.

Mixing, Kneading & Rising Handmade Breads

The sequence and method of adding ingredients to make your dough are surprisingly important. For some breads, fresh or dried yeast is dissolved in lukewarm water and then stirred into the flour; if easy-blend dried yeast or fast-action dried yeast is used, this is added directly to the flour.

Making bread is easy, but yeast can be temperamental, so it is worth giving a little thought to the preparation environment before you start. Choose a draught-free area of the kitchen, and warm your mixing bowls if they are slightly chilly.

Read your recipe carefully before you begin, and wash and dry your hands and wrists, since they will be doing all the work, unless you are using an electric mixer or food processor for kneading.

Mixing

The easiest way to mix the dough is with your hand but, if you prefer, start mixing with a spoon until the mixture is too stiff to stir, and then mix by hand.

1 If using fresh or regular dried yeast, mix it with lukewarm water or milk as described in the recipe. Sift the flour, salt and any other dry ingredients (including easy-blend or fast-action dried yeast, if using) into a large, warm mixing bowl.

2 If using butter, lard or white vegetable fat, rub it in. Make a well in the centre of the flour mixture and pour in the yeast mixture with the remaining lukewarm water. If oil is being used, add it now.

3 Mix the liquid into the flour, stirring in a wide motion so that the dry ingredients are evenly incorporated and the mixture forms a dough. Knead lightly in the bowl.

Kneading

You just cannot avoid kneading when making bread by hand. If you do not have strong wrists, or simply do not enjoy it, you will have to resort to using the food processor, which takes all the effort – and much of the time – out of kneading. Better still though, learn to love the craft.

Kneading dough, whether by hand or machine, is the only way of warming and stretching the gluten in the flour. As the strands of gluten warm and become more elastic, so the dough becomes more springy. It is the elasticity of the dough combined with the action of the yeast that gives bread its characteristic light and springy texture. Insufficient kneading means that the dough cannot hold the little pockets of air, and the bread will collapse in the oven to leave a heavy and dense loaf.

Adding Extra Ingredients
Ingredients, such as olives, can be added after kneading, or they can be kneaded in after the first rising.

A Few Simple Rules

The following will ensure success.

- *Warm bowls and other equipment before use.*
- *Use the correct amount of yeast: too much will speed up the rising process but will spoil the flavour and will mean the loaf stales more quickly.*
- *If you have a thermometer, check the temperature of the lukewarm liquid, at least until you can gauge it yourself. It should be between 37–43°C/98–110°F. Mixing two parts cold water with one part boiling water gives you water at roughly the right temperature.*
- *The amount of liquid required for a dough depends on several factors: type of flour; other ingredients; even the room temperature. Recipes therefore often give approximate quantities of liquid. You will soon learn to judge the ideal consistency of a dough.*
- *Do not skimp on kneading. It is essential for stretching the gluten to give a well-risen, light-textured loaf.*
- *Avoid leaving dough to rise in a draught and make sure the ambient temperature is not too high, or the dough will begin to cook.*
- *Always cover the bowl during rising, as a crust will form on top if the air gets to it. Clear film (plastic wrap) can be pressed on to the dough itself or stretched over the bowl. Either way, oil the film first or the dough will stick to it as it rises.*

Kneading by Hand

You can be as heavy-handed as you like with dough – this will ensure a good result.

1 Place the mixed dough on a floured surface and flour your hands generously.

2 Press the heel of your hand firmly into the centre of the dough, then curl your fingers around the edge of the dough.

3 Pull and stretch the dough towards you and press down again, giving the dough a quarter turn as you do so.

4 Continue pressing and stretching the dough in this way. After about 10 minutes the dough should be supple and elastic. However, some breads need more kneading, so do check the recipe.

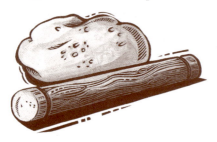

Kneading in a Food Processor

Unless you have an industrial-size machine, it is likely that your food processor will only be able to knead moderate amounts of dough at a time. Do not attempt to knead more dough than is recommended by the manufacturer as it may damage the motor. If necessary, knead the dough in small batches and then knead the batches together by hand.

Fit the dough blade into the processor and then blend together all the dry ingredients. Add the yeast mixture, and extra lukewarm liquid and butter or oil, if required; process until the mixture comes together. Knead for 60 seconds, or for the time suggested in your handbook, and then knead by hand on a floured board for 1–2 minutes.

Depending on the size of your machine, you may find that it is just as quick to knead all the dough by hand in one go as it is to process it in separate batches.

KNEADING IN A FOOD MIXER

Check the manufacturer's instructions to make sure bread dough can be kneaded in your machine.

1 Mix the dry ingredients together. Add the yeast, liquid and oil or butter, if using, and mix slowly, using the dough hook. The dough will tumble and fall to begin with, and then it will slowly come together.

2 Continue kneading the dough vigorously for about 3 minutes, or according to the instructions for the food mixer.

RISING

This is the easy part of bread making – all you need is to give the dough the right conditions, and nature and chemistry will do the rest. While kneading stretches and conditions the gluten in the flour, during rising the yeast does the real work. The fermentation process creates carbon dioxide, which is trapped within the dough by the elastic gluten. This process also has the effect of conditioning the flour, improving the flavour and texture of the eventual loaf.

The number of times you leave your bread to rise will depend on the yeast you are using and the recipe. An easy-blend or fast-action yeast needs no first rising, but dough using fresh yeast and other dried yeasts normally requires two risings, with some recipes calling for even more.

TEMPERATURE AND TIME

For most recipes, dough is left to rise at a temperature of about 24–27°C/75–80°F, the equivalent of an airing cupboard or near a warm oven. At a cooler temperature the bread rises more slowly. The quantity of yeast used will also determine the time required for rising. More yeast means quicker rising.

1 Place the kneaded dough in a bowl that has been lightly greased with oil. This will prevent the dough from sticking. Cover the bowl with a damp dishtowel or a piece of oiled clear film (plastic wrap), to prevent a skin from forming on top of the dough.

2 Leave to rise until the dough has doubled in bulk. At room temperature, this should take 1½–2 hours – less if the ambient temperature is warmer and more if the room is cool. The dough can even be left to rise in the refrigerator for about 8 hours or overnight.

KNOCKING BACK & SHAPING

After the dough has risen it must be knocked back (punched down) before it is shaped. It will then be left for its final rising before it is cooked. This applies to both handmade bread and bread dough that has been made in a bread machine, ready for shaping by hand and baking in the oven. Bread that is cooked in a bread machine does not need to be manually knocked back.

KNOCKING BACK

It seems a shame to knock back (punch down) the dough back after its initial rising. However, this process not only redistributes the gases in the dough that were created by the fermentation process, but it also reinvigorates the yeast, making sure that it is evenly distributed and that the bread has an even texture throughout. It should take only a few minutes to knock back the dough. It will then be ready for shaping.

KNOCKING BACK HANDMADE DOUGH

The dough is fully risen when it has doubled in bulk. If you are not sure that it is ready, test by gently inserting a finger into the centre of the dough. The dough should not immediately spring back. If it does, leave for a little longer.

1 Knock back (punch down) the risen dough using your knuckles.

2 Having knocked back the dough, place it on a floured work surface and knead lightly for 1–2 minutes.

DOUGH SETTING FOR MACHINE-MADE BREAD

The dough setting on a bread machine allows it to automatically mix the ingredients for the dough, and then knead and rest the dough before providing the ideal conditions for it to rise for the first time. The whole cycle, from mixing through to rising, takes around 1¾ hours, but will vary slightly between machines.

Although most bread machines are only suitable for making relatively small quantities of dough, it is ideal for items like rolls and pizzas.

KNOCKING BACK MACHINE-MADE DOUGH

It is necessary to knock back machine-made dough when the first rising cycle is complete:

1 At the end of the cycle, the dough will have almost doubled in bulk and will be ready for shaping. Remove the bread pan from the machine.

2 Lightly flour a work surface. Gently remove the dough from the bread pan and place it on the floured surface. Knock back or deflate the dough.

3 Knead the dough lightly for about 1–2 minutes. At this stage, a recipe may suggest you cover the dough with oiled clear film (plastic wrap) or an upturned bowl and leave it to rest for a few minutes. This allows the gluten to relax so that the dough will be easier to handle.

- *Always knock back the dough after the first rising and knead lightly to redistribute the yeast and the gases formed by fermentation, otherwise you may end up with large holes in the loaf or the crust may lift up and become detached from the crumb.*

- *Rising the dough in a warm place is not always necessary – it is simply a method of speeding up the process. Dough will rise (albeit very slowly) even in the refrigerator. However, wherever you decide to rise your dough the temperature must be constant. Avoid draughts or hot spots, as both will spoil the bread and may cause it to bake unevenly.*

- *Some breads may need slashing, either before final rising or during this period (see next section).*

- *Selecting the right size of loaf pan can be a tricky business. If it is too small the dough will spill over the top. If it is too large, the final loaf will be badly shaped and uneven. As a general rule the pan should be about twice the size of the dough. Professional bakers use black pans, which are considered to be better than shiny metal ones as they absorb the heat better, giving a crisper crust. Always warm a pan or baking sheet before using, and then grease it with melted lard or white vegetable fat, vegetable oil or unsalted (sweet) butter.*

SHAPING

Handmade and machine-made doughs can be hand-shaped into a great variety of breads, from cobs and baguettes to braids and twists.

The following examples describe how to form the most popular basic bread, roll and yeast pastry shapes.

TIN LOAF

There are several ways of shaping the bread dough to fit a tin loaf pan.

- The easiest way is to shape the dough roughly into an oval and place it in the pan, with the smooth side on top.

- Alternatively, roll out the dough into a rectangle, a little longer than the loaf pan. Roll up the dough like a Swiss (jelly) roll, tuck in the ends and place the roll in the pan, with the seam side down.

- Another alternative is to roll out the dough into a rectangle and fold it in half lengthways, pinching the edges together on the sides and flattening the dough out slightly with the heel of your hand. Fold the dough over once more to make a double thickness, and pinch the edges together again. Now gently roll the dough backwards and forwards on the work surface until it has a well-rounded shape. Fold in the two short ends of the dough, and place it in the prepared pan with the seam along the bottom.

COB LOAF

1 Shape the dough into a round and then press along the centre with your hand. Turn the dough over, so that the smooth side is uppermost.

2 Shape the dough into a round or oval and place it on a baking sheet. Cover with an inverted bowl and leave in a warm place to finish rising.

BAGUETTE

1 Divide the dough into equal pieces. Shape each piece into a ball and then into a rectangle measuring 15 × 7.5cm/6 × 3in. Fold the bottom third up and the top third down lengthways. Press the edges together to seal them. Repeat twice, then stretch each piece to a 33–35cm/13–14in loaf.

2 Place within the folds of a pleated, floured dishtowel or in a banneton, or proving (rising) basket, for the final rising.

BRAID

1 Divide the dough into three equal pieces. Roll each piece into a 25cm/10in sausage about 4cm/1½in thick.

2 Place the three "sausages" on a greased baking sheet. Either start the braid in the centre, braiding to each end in turn, or pinch the pieces firmly together at one end, and then braid.

3 When you have finished, pinch the ends together, and turn them under. Cover and leave in a warm place for the final rising.

BLOOMER

1 Roll the dough out to a rectangle 2.5cm/1in thick. Roll up from one long side and place it, seam side up, on a floured baking sheet. Cover the dough with lightly oiled cling film (plastic wrap) and leave to rest for 15 minutes.

2 Turn the loaf over and place on another floured baking sheet. Use your fingertips to tuck the sides and ends of the dough under. Cover and leave for the final rising.

COTTAGE LOAF

1 To shape a cottage loaf, divide the dough into two pieces, approximately one-third and two-thirds in size. Shape each piece of dough into a plump round ball and place on lightly floured baking sheets. Cover with inverted bowls and leave to rise for about 30 minutes, or until each piece of dough is 50 per cent larger.

2 Flatten the top of the large loaf. Using a sharp knife cut a cross about 4cm/1½in across in the centre. Brush the area lightly with water; place the small round on top.

3 Using the floured handle of a wooden spoon, press a hole in the centre of the top round, penetrating right down into the middle of the larger round beneath.

PROVING BASKETS

Professional bakers use proving (rising) baskets called bannetons for baguettes, and circular couronnes for round loaves. The baskets give extra support to the bread during its final rising. Some proving baskets are lined with linen, while others are lined with canvas. Proving baskets for home use are available from good kitchenware stores. A lightly floured dishtowel can often be used as an alternative, depending on the recipe.

TWIST

1 To shape bread for a twist, divide the dough into two equal pieces. Using the palms of your hands, roll each piece of dough on a lightly floured surface into a long rope, about 4–5cm/1½–2in thick. Make both ropes the same length.

2 Place the two ropes side by side. Starting from the centre, twist one rope over the other. Continue in the same way until you reach the end, then pinch the ends together and tuck the join underneath. Turn the dough around and repeat the process with the other end, twisting the dough in the same direction as the first.

BREADSTICK

1 To shape a breadstick, roll the dough to a rectangle about 1cm/½in thick, and cut out strips that are about 7.5cm/3in long and 2cm/¾in wide. Using the palm of your hand, roll each strip into a long thin rope.

2 It may help to lift each rope and pull it very gently to stretch it. If it is still difficult to stretch the dough, leave it to rest for a few minutes, then try again.

COURONNE

1 Shape the dough into a ball. Using the heel of your hand, make a hole in the centre. Gradually enlarge the hole until it measures 13cm/5in across.

2 Place the dough ring on a lightly oiled baking sheet with a small, lightly oiled bowl in the centre to prevent it from filling in during rising. Cover and leave to rise.

CROISSANT

1 Roll out the dough on a lightly floured surface and cut it into strips that are about 15cm/6in wide.

2 Cut each strip along its length into triangles with about 15cm/6in bases and 18cm/7in sides.

3 Place a triangle with the pointed end towards you. Gently pull each corner of the base to stretch it slightly.

4 Roll up the dough with one hand from the base, finishing with the dough point underneath. Finally, curve the corners around in the direction of the pointed end to make the curved croissant shape.

FILLED BRAID

1 Place the dough on a lightly floured surface. Roll out and shape into a rectangle. Make diagonal cuts down each of the long sides of the dough, about 2cm/⅔in apart. Place the filling over the uncut strip.

2 Fold over alternate strips of dough to form a braid over the filling. Tuck in the ends to seal the braid.

PREPARING TO BAKE

The actual baking is perhaps the simplest part of the bread-making process, yet even here the yeast still has a part to play and it is important that you play your part too, by making sure conditions are as ideal as possible. It can be helpful to slash the top of the dough before you put it in the oven, so that the crust expands without tearing as it cooks. When the loaf goes into the oven the heat kills the yeast, but for the first few minutes of baking, there is a final burst of life and the bread will rise even further before the air is finally locked in.

FINAL RISING

After shaping the dough and placing it on the baking sheet or in the pan, there is usually a final rising before baking. This is sometimes referred to as proving the dough. Depending on the warmth of the room, this can take ¾–1½ hours, although in a very cool room it may take up to 4 hours. Cover the dough so that the surface does not crust over. Oiled clear film (plastic wrap) placed over the pan or directly on the bread is the best method. The timing is important as over-rising means the loaf may collapse in the oven or when it is slashed before baking, while too little will mean the loaf will be heavy and flat. To test if the dough is ready, press it lightly with your fingertip; it should feel springy. The indentation made by your finger should slowly fill and spring back.

PREHEATING THE OVEN

While the shaped dough is having its final rise, you will need to preheat the oven to the required temperature. It is important that the oven is at the right temperature when the bread goes in – almost always a hot oven, between 220–230°C/425–450°F/Gas 7–8. Sweet loaves or those containing a lot of butter cook at a lower temperature. Many recipes recommend that the oven temperature is reduced either immediately after putting the bread in the oven or some time during cooking. This means the bread gets a good blast of heat to start with, and then cooks more gradually. This mimics the original bread ovens, which would have cooled down slowly after all the embers had been removed.

SLASHING

The tops of traditional loaf shapes such as bloomers and French sticks are attractively slashed. However, slashing bread dough before baking serves a useful purpose as well as adding a decorative finish. When the dough goes into the oven it has one final rise, known as "oven spring", so the cuts or slashes allow the bread to expand without tearing or cracking the sides. Slashing provides escape routes for the air and gives direction to the spring, so that the loaf will open out around the slashes and retain an even shape.

The earlier you slash the dough the wider the splits will be. Depth is important, too: the deeper the slashes the more the bread will open during baking. Loaves that have not been allowed enough time to rise will tend to have more spring, and it is therefore important to slash these fairly deeply.

You will find that some recipes suggest slashing either before the final rising or some time during it. This will depend on how much you want your loaf to "open up". The earlier it is slashed the more the split will develop. However, unless the recipe specifies otherwise, the general rule is to slash the loaf just before you glaze it and put it in the oven.

If you think a bread has slightly over-risen, keep the slashes fairly shallow and gentle to minimize the possibility of the dough collapsing. Use a sharp knife or scalpel blade to make a clean cut. Used with care, a scalpel is perfectly safe and has the advantage that the blades can be changed to ensure you always have a sharp edge. Move smoothly and swiftly to avoid tearing the dough. Scissors can also be used to make an easy decorative finish to rolls or breads.

SLASHING A SPLIT TIN OR FARMHOUSE LOAF

A long slash, about 1cm/½in deep, can be made along the top of the dough just before the loaf is baked in the oven. You can use this slashing procedure for both machine- and hand-shaped loaves. Using a very sharp knife, plunge into one end of the dough and pull the blade smoothly along the entire length. Take care not to drag the dough as you pull the blade. If you wish to flour the top of the loaf, sprinkle over the flour before slashing.

SLASHING A BAGUETTE

To slash a baguette, cut long slashes across the bread, keeping the slashes of equal length and depth. Make four or five slashes along the length of the baguette.

SLASHING A COB OR COBURG

Just before baking, slash a deep cross across the top of the loaf.

PORCUPINE

Slashing in a porcupine pattern not only looks attractive, but also gives a wonderful crunchy crust to bread. Make five or six cuts across the bread in one direction, and then slice the dough again at right angles, chequerboard fashion.

USING SCISSORS TO SLASH ROLLS

Rolls can be given quick and interesting finishes using a pair of sharp-pointed scissors. You could experiment with all sorts of ideas. Try the following:
- Just before baking cut across the top of the dough first in one direction, then the other to make a cross.
- Make six horizontal or vertical cuts equally spaced around the sides of the rolls. Leave for 5 minutes before baking.
- Cut through the rolls in four or five places, from the edge almost to the centre, just before baking.

GLAZES AND TOPPINGS

Remember to add any glazes or toppings that need to be applied prior to baking before you put the bread into the oven, for example chopped nuts over an egg glaze, or freshly grated Parmesan or Pecorino cheese. Apply flour toppings before slashing the tops of traditional loaf shapes.

Baking Times & Tips

Once the bread has had its final rising and any glazing or topping has been applied, handmade bread and machine-made bread that has been hand shaped are ready to be baked in the oven. Preheat the oven for at least 15 minutes to ensure it has reached the temperature noted in the recipe. This is important as the initial blast of heat completes the rising process.

The time hand-shaped bread will take to cook will depend on the recipe, the size of the loaf and the heat of the oven. As a general rule, rolls take about 20 minutes, round country breads 40–50 minutes and tin loaves a little longer, 45–60 minutes.

Very little preparation is involved when using a machine to bake bread. The cooking times will be set by the integral timer so, if you have followed the recipe instructions and read the information in this section, you should have delicious bread with the minimum of effort.

Approximate Baking Times for Hand-shaped Bread
Bagels: 20–25 minutes
Baguettes: 20–25 minutes
Bloomer (large): 45 minutes
Braided fruit bread: 40–45 minutes
Ciabatta: 25–30 minutes
Cob (large): 35 minutes
Corn bread (large): 20–25 minutes
Spiral herb loaf: 40–50 minutes
Cottage loaf (large): 35–40 minutes
Croissants: 15–20 minutes
Focaccia: 25–30 minutes
Grissini: 15–20 minutes
Large shaped loaves: 30–45 minutes
Pitta bread: 4–6 minutes
Rich fruit loaf (large): 30 minutes
Shaped dinner rolls: 15–18 minutes
French dimpled rolls: 15–18 minutes
Soda bread: 35–45 minutes

Glazed Loaves
Glazed fruit loaves, such as Bara Brith, can sometimes over-brown before they are sufficiently cooked. If this begins to happen, cover the bread loosely with foil for the last 10 minutes of cooking.

Griddle-cooked Loaves
Loaves that are cooked on a griddle, such as Barley Bannock, need careful cooking over a gentle heat. Do not cook too quickly or the outside will burn before the centre is fully cooked.

Pitta Bread
It is essential that the oven has reached the recommended temperature, 230°C/450°F/ Gas 8, before pitta breads are put into it. Otherwise they will not puff up sufficiently.

Testing
For most breads, there is a simple method to check if the bread is cooked through: remove it from the oven and tap firmly on the base of the loaf with your knuckles. It should have a hollow sound. If not and it feels soft, bake the loaf for a little longer.

Rolls
Check rolls by turning one over in a clean dishtowel. The underside should be firm and golden, with no trace of moisture.

Cooling & Storing

As soon as bread is cooked it needs to be allowed to cool quickly so that it will have a good crust. If it is left in the pan, moisture will be trapped and this will affect the consistency of the crust. To serve bread warm, wrap it in foil and place in an oven preheated to 180°C/350°F/Gas 4 for 10–15 minutes, to heat through. This method can also be used to freshen bread.

Cooling Handmade Bread

As soon as the bread has been taken out of the oven, remove it from the pan or baking sheet and place on to a cooling rack to cool for at least 30 minutes before slicing.

Removing Machine-made Bread from the Pan

Once the bread is baked it is best removed from the bread pan immediately. Turn the bread pan upside down, holding it with oven gloves – it will be very hot – and shake it several times to release the bread.

If removing the bread is difficult, rap the corner of the bread pan on a wooden board several times or try turning the base of the shaft underneath the base of the bread pan. Do not try to free the bread by using a knife or similar metal object, or you will scratch the non-stick coating.

If the kneading blade remains inside the loaf, you should use a heat-resistant plastic or wooden implement to prise it out. The metal blade and the bread will be too hot to hold with your fingers.

Place the bread on a wire rack to allow the steam to escape and leave it for at least 30 minutes before slicing.

Slicing

Always slice bread using a serrated knife to avoid damaging the crumb structure. A wooden breadboard will make slicing easier and will not damage the knife.

Freezing Bread Doughs

Bread dough can be frozen in a freezer-proof bag for up to 1 month. When you are ready to use it, thaw the dough overnight in the refrigerator or at room temperature for 2–3 hours. Once the dough has thawed, place it in a warm place to rise, but bear in mind that it will take longer than freshly made dough.

Storing

Cool the bread, then wrap it in foil or place it in a plastic bag and seal it, to preserve the freshness. If your bread has a crisp crust, this will soften on storage, so until it is sliced it is best left uncovered. After cutting, put the loaf in a large paper bag, but try to use it fairly quickly, as bread starts to dry out as soon as it is cut. Breads containing eggs tend to dry out even more quickly, while those made with honey or added fats stay moist for longer. Ideally, freshly baked bread should be consumed within 2–3 days. Avoid storing bread in the refrigerator as this causes it to go stale more quickly.

Freeze cooked breads if you need to keep them for longer in a freezer bag. Seal and freeze for up to 3 months. If you intend to use the bread for toast or sandwiches, slice it before freezing, so you can remove only the number of slices you need. Thaw the bread at room temperature.

Using Your Bread Machine

The instructions that follow will help you to achieve a perfect loaf the first time you use your bread machine. The guidelines are general, that is they are applicable to any bread machine and should be read in conjunction with the handbook provided for your specific machine. The more you use your bread machine, the more proficient you will become.

Basic Controls

It will take you some practice to become familiar with and confident about using your new bread machine. Most manufacturers now produce excellent manuals, which are supplied with their machines. The manual is a good place to start, and should also help you if you come up against a problem. It is important to understand the function of each control on your bread machine before starting to make a loaf of bread. Features may vary slightly between different machines, but they all work in a basically similar manner.

Start and Stop Buttons

The Start button initiates the whole process. Press it only after you have placed all the ingredients in the bread pan and selected all the settings.

The Stop button may actually be the same control or a separate one. Press it to stop the programme, either during the programme, if you need to override it, or at the end to turn off the machine. This cancels the "keep warm" cycle at the end of baking.

Time Display and Status Indicator

A window displays the time remaining until the end of the programme selected. In some machines the selected programme is also shown. Some models use this same window or a separate set of lights to indicate what stage the bread making process has reached.

Programme Indicators or Menu

Each bread machine has a number of programmes for different types of bread. Some models have more than others. This function allows you to choose the correct programme for your recipe, as the kneading, rising and baking times of breads do vary. Always read the manufacturer's instructions for your bread machine and check the instructions in your recipes.

Delay Timer

This button allows you to pre-set the bread machine to switch on automatically at a specified time. So, for example, you can have freshly baked bread for breakfast or when you return from work. The timer should not be used for dough that contains perishable ingredients such as fresh dairy products or meats, which deteriorate in a warm environment.

Pre-heat cycle

Some machines start all programmes with a warming phase, either prior to mixing or during the kneading phase. This feature can prove useful on colder days or when you are using larger quantities of ingredients, such as milk, straight from the refrigerator, as you do not have to wait for them to come to room temperature before making the bread.

CRUST COLOUR CONTROL

The majority of bread machines have a default medium-crust setting. If, however, you prefer a paler crust or the appearance of a high-bake loaf, most machines will give you the option of a lighter or darker crust. Breads high in sugar, or that contain eggs or cheese, may colour too much on a medium setting, so choose the lighter crust for these loaves.

WARMING INDICATOR

When the bread has finished baking, it is best to remove it from the machine immediately. If for any reason this is not possible, the warming facility will switch on as soon as the bread is baked, to help prevent the steam from condensing, which otherwise would result in a soggy loaf. Most machines continue in this mode for an hour, some giving an audible reminder every few minutes in case you forget to remove the bread.

REMINDER LIGHTS

A few models are fitted with a set of lights which change colour after being activated, to serve as a reminder that certain essential steps have been followed. This helps to ensure that the kneading blade is fitted and that basic ingredients such as liquid, flour and yeast have been put in the bread pan.

LOAF SIZE

On larger bread machines you may have the option of making up to three different sizes of loaf. The actual sizes vary between individual machines, but approximate to small, medium and large bread loaves of about 450g/1lb, 675g/1½lb and 900g/2lb respectively. However, this control in some machines is for visual indication only and does not alter the baking time or cycle. Check the manufacturer's instructions.

BAKING PROGRAMMES

All machines have a selection of programmes to help ensure you produce the perfect loaf of bread. The lengths of kneading, rising and baking times are varied to suit the different flours and to determine the texture of the finished loaf.

BASIC OR NORMAL

This mode is the most commonly used programme, ideal for white and mixed-grain loaves, where white bread flour is the main ingredient.

RAPID

This cycle reduces the time to make a standard loaf of bread by about 1 hour and is handy when speed is the main criterion. The finished loaf may not rise as much as one made on the basic programme and may therefore be a little denser.

WHOLEMEAL

This is a longer cycle, to allow time for the slower rising action of dough containing a high percentage of strong wholemeal (whole-wheat) flour. Some machines also have a multigrain mode for breads made with cereals and grains, such as Granary and rye, although it is possible to make breads using the basic mode, depending on the percentages of the flours.

FRENCH

This programme is best suited for low-fat and low-sugar breads, and it produces loaves with an open texture and crispier crust. More time within the cycle is devoted to rising, and in some machines the loaf is baked at a higher temperature.

SWEET BREAD

A few bread machines offer this feature in addition to crust colour control. It is useful if you intend to bake breads with a high fat or sugar content, which darken readily.

CAKE

Again, this is a feature offered on a few machines. Some will mix a quick, non-yeast teabread-type cake and then bake it; others will mix yeast-raised cakes. If you do not have this facility, non-yeast cakes can easily be mixed in a bowl and cooked in the bread pan on a "bake only" cycle.

BAKE

This setting allows you to use the bread machine as an oven, either to bake cakes and ready-prepared dough from the supermarket, or to extend the standard baking time if you prefer your bread to be particularly well done.

RAISIN BEEP

Additional ingredients can be added mid-cycle on most programmes. The machine gives an audible signal – usually a beep – and some machines pause late in the kneading phase so that ingredients such as fruit and nuts can be added. This late addition reduces the risk of them being crushed during the kneading phase. If your machine does not have this facility, you can set a kitchen timer to ring 5 minutes before the end of the kneading cycle and add the extra ingredients then.

SPECIAL FEATURES

Extra programmes can be found on more expensive machines. These may include cooking jam or rice and making pasta dough. For instance, jam-making could not be easier: you simply add equal quantities of fresh fruit and sugar to the bread machine pan, set the programme and, when the cycle ends, you will have jam ready to pour into sterilized jars.

DOUGH PROGRAMMES

Most machines include a dough programme; some models have dough programmes with extra features.

DOUGH

This programme allows you to make dough without baking it in the machine, which is essential for all hand-shaped breads. The machine mixes, kneads and rises the dough, ready for shaping, final rising and baking in a conventional oven.

OTHER DOUGH PROGRAMMES

Some machines include cycles for making different types of dough, such as a rapid dough mode for pizzas and focaccia or a longer mode for wholemeal dough and bagel dough. Some "dough only" cycles also include the raisin beep facility.

Getting Started – Step-by-step

Always use fresh, top quality ingredients. You cannot expect good results with out-of-date flour or yeast.

1 Stand the bread machine on a level, heat-resistant surface. Position in a draught-free area away from any heat source, as these factors can affect the temperature inside the machine. Do not plug the bread machine into the power socket at this stage. Open the lid. Remove the bread pan.

2 Make sure the kneading blade and shaft are free from any breadcrumbs left behind when the machine was last used. Fit the blade on the shaft in the base of the pan.

3 Pour the water, milk and/or other liquids into the bread pan, unless the instructions for your particular machine require you to add the dry ingredients first.

4 Sprinkle over the flour, ensuring that it covers the liquid completely. Add any other dry ingredients specified in the recipe, such as dried milk powder. Add the salt, sugar or honey and butter or oil, placing them in separate corners so they do not come into contact with each other.

5 Make a small indent in the centre of the flour (but not down as far as the liquid) with the tip of your finger, and add the yeast. Wipe away any spillages from the outside of the bread pan.

6 Place the pan inside the machine, fitting it firmly in place. Depending on the model, the pan may have a designated front and back, or clips on the outer edge that need to engage in the machine to hold the bread pan in position. Fold the handle down and close the lid. Plug into the socket and switch on.

7 Select the programme you require, including crust colour and loaf size, if available. Press Start. The kneading process will begin, unless your machine has a "rest" period to settle the temperature first.

8 Towards the end of the kneading process the machine will beep to alert you to add any additional ingredients, such as dried fruit. Leaving the machine switched on, open the lid, add the extra ingredients and close it again.

9 At the end of the cycle, the machine will beep once more to let you know that the dough is ready or the bread is cooked. Press Stop. Open the lid of the machine. If you are removing baked bread, remember to use oven gloves to lift out the bread pan, as it will be extremely hot.

10 Still using oven gloves, turn the pan upside down and shake it several times to release the bread. If necessary, tap the base of the pan on a heatproof board.

11 If the kneading blade is not of the fixed type, and comes out inside the bread, use a heat-resistant utensil to remove it, such as a wooden spatula.

12 Place the bread on a wire rack to cool. Unplug the bread machine and leave to cool before using it again. A machine that is too hot will not make a successful loaf. Refer to the manufacturer's manual for guidance. Wash the pan and kneading blade and wipe down the machine. All parts must be cool and thoroughly dry before the bread machine is stored.

Easy Measuring

If you have a set of electronic scales with an add-and-weigh facility, then accurate measuring of ingredients is very easy indeed. Stand the bread pan securely on the scales, pour in the liquid and then set the display to zero. Add the dry ingredients directly to the pan, each time zeroing the display. Finally, add the fat, salt, sweetener and yeast before placing the bread pan in your machine.

GETTING THE BEST FROM YOUR BREAD MACHINE

Even a comprehensive bread machine manual cannot cover all the hints and tips you will need. As you gain experience you will be able to solve more of the little problems that may crop up, but here are a few pointers to start off with.

TEMPERATURE AND HUMIDITY

The bread machine is not a totally sealed environment, and external temperatures and humidity levels can affect how the machine-baked bread turns out.

The temperature of the ingredients used to make the bread is a very important factor in determining the success of machine-baked bread. Some machines specify that all ingredients should be at room temperature, while others state that ingredients can be added straight from the refrigerator. Some bread machines have preheating cycles which will bring any ingredients taken straight from the refrigerator to an optimum temperature of around 20–25°C/68–77°F before the mixing process starts. Generally, it is recommended that you use ingredients at room temperature, although water can be used straight from the cold tap lukewarm water may be beneficial for the rapid bake cycle on particularly cold days.

In hot weather the dough will rise faster, so on very hot days start with chilled ingredients, using milk or eggs straight from the refrigerator. Conversely, icy winter weather and cold draughts will inhibit the action of the yeast, so either move your machine to a warmer spot or warm liquids before adding them to the bread pan. On very cold days let the water stand at room temperature for about half an hour before adding the other ingredients, or add a little warm water to bring it to around 20°C/68°F.

QUALITY PRODUCE

Use only fresh, good quality ingredients. The bread machine cannot improve poor quality produce. Make sure the yeast is within its use-by date.

MEASURING INGREDIENTS

Always measure the liquids and dry ingredients carefully. Most problems occur when the ingredients have been inaccurately measured, when one ingredient is forgotten or when the same ingredient is added twice. Do not use a mixture of imperial and metric measures, as they are not interchangeable. Stick to one set for the whole recipe.

Do not exceed the quantities of flour and liquid recommended for your machine. Mixing the extra ingredients may overload the motor, and if you have too much dough it is likely to rise over the top of the pan.

FOLLOW THE INSTRUCTIONS

Always add the ingredients in the order suggested by the manufacturer. Whatever the order, keep the yeast dry and separate from any liquids added to the bread pan.

ADDING INGREDIENTS

Cut butter into pieces, especially if it is fairly firm, and/or when larger amounts than usual are required in the recipe. If a recipe calls for ingredients such as cooked vegetables or fruit or toasted nuts to be added, leave them to cool to room temperature before adding them.

USING THE DELAY TIMER

The facility to set the bread machine to mix, knead and bake the loaf at a time convenient to the cook is a great asset. Only use the delay timer for bread doughs that contain non-perishable ingredients. Do not add dairy produce, meat, fruit or vegetables to the dough.

CLEANING YOUR MACHINE

Unplug the machine before starting to clean it. Wipe down the outside regularly using a mild washing-up liquid and a damp, soft cloth. Avoid all abrasive cleaners and materials, even those that are designated for use on non-stick items, and do not use alcohol-based cleaners.

BREAD PAN AND KNEADING BLADE

Clean the bread pan and blade after each use. These parts should not be washed in the dishwasher as this might affect the non-stick surface and damage the packing around the shaft. Avoid immersing the bread pan in water. If you have difficulty extracting the blade from the pan, fill the base of the pan with lukewarm water and leave it to soak for a few minutes. Remove the blade and wipe it with a damp cloth. Wash the bread pan with mild washing-up liquid then rinse thoroughly. Always store the bread machine with the kneading blade removed from the shaft. The bread machine and components must be completely dry before they are put away.

WATCHING THE DOUGH

Keep a flexible rubber spatula next to the machine and, if necessary, scrape down the sides of the pan after 5–10 minutes of the initial mixing cycle; the kneading blade sometimes fails to pick up thick or sticky dough from the corners of the pan.

SPECIAL CONSIDERATIONS

- *Breads made with whole grains and heavier flours, such as wholemeal (whole-wheat), oatmeal or rye flour or with added ingredients, such as dried fruits and nuts, are likely to rise more slowly than basic white loaves, and will be less tall.*
- *Breads made with a lot of fat or egg will also rise more slowly than standard white loaves and may not be as large.*
- *Breads that include cheese, eggs or a high proportion of fats and/or sugar are more susceptible to burning. To avoid overcooked crusts, select a light-bake crust setting for these.*

CHECKING THE DOUGH

When you make bread by hand you can feel whether it is too wet or dry, simply by kneading it. However, when you use a bread machine, you need to adopt a different strategy to determine if your bread has the right moistness and, if not, how you can adjust it to produce a perfect loaf. When you first use your new machine get to know what a good dough should look like. After the machine has been mixing for a few minutes, take a quick look at the dough – it should be pliable and soft. When the machine stops kneading, the dough should start to relax back into the shape of the bread machine pan. The dough should be slightly tacky to the touch. If it is very soft add a little more flour; if the dough feels very firm and dry add a little more liquid.

It is also worth checking the dough towards the end of the rising period. On particularly warm days your bread may rise too high. If this happens it may rise over the bread pan and begin to travel down the outside during the first few minutes of baking. If your bread looks ready for baking before the baking cycle is due to begin, you have two options. You can either override and cancel the programme, then reprogramme using a "bake only" cycle, or you can try pricking the top of the loaf with a cocktail stick to deflate it slightly and let the programme continue.

BAKING BREAD WITH A CRISP CRUST

For a crisper crust on hand-shaped breads, it is necessary to introduce steam into the oven. The moisture initially softens the dough so that it can rise, resulting in a crispier crust. Moisture also improves the crust colour by encouraging caramelization of the natural sugars in the dough. Standing the loaf on a baking stone or unglazed terracotta tiles also helps to produce a crisp crust, the effect being similar to when breads are cooked in a clay or brick oven. The porous tiles or stone hold heat and draw moisture from the bread base while it is baking.

1 About 30 minutes before you intend to bake, place the baking stone on the bottom shelf of the oven, and then preheat the oven.

2 Using a water spray bottle, mist the oven walls two or three times during the first 5–10 minutes of baking. Open the oven door as little as possible, spray, then quickly close the door to avoid unnecessary heat loss. Avoid the electric oven light, fan or heating elements.

BROWNING

Different bread-making machines will give different browning levels using the same recipe. Check the browning level of the baked bread when you try a new recipe and make a note to select a lighter or darker setting next time, if necessary.

COOLING THE BREAD

It is always best to remove the loaf from the bread pan as soon as the baking cycle has finished, or it may become slightly damp, even if your machine features a "stay warm" programme.

Adapting Recipes for Use in a Bread Machine

After you have cooked a number of the recipes from this book you may wish to branch out and adapt some of your own favourites. A sample recipe is used to explain some of the factors you will need to take into consideration.

Useful Guidelines

Here are a few guidelines that are worth following when adapting your own recipes.

Quantities

Make sure the quantities will work in your machine. If you have a small bread machine it may be necessary to reduce them. Use the flour and water quantities in recipes in the book as a guide, or refer back to your manufacturer's handbook.

It is important that you keep the flour and the liquid in the correct proportions, even if reducing the quantities means that you end up with some odd amounts. You can be more flexible with spices and flavourings such as fruit and nuts, as exact quantities are not so crucial.

Checking the Dough

Check the consistency of the dough when the machine starts mixing. You may need to add one or two extra spoonfuls of water, as breads baked in a machine require a slightly softer dough which is wet enough to relax back into the shape of the bread pan.

Dough Cycle

If a dough mixes perfectly in your machine but then fails to bake properly, or if you want bread of a special shape, use the dough cycle on your machine, then shape by hand before baking in a conventional oven.

Comparing Recipes

Look through bread-machine recipes and locate something that is similar. This will give you some idea as to quantities and which programme you should use. Be prepared to make more adjustments after testing your recipe for the first time.

Monitor the recipe closely the first time you make it and jot down any ideas you have for improvements next time.

Using Bread Mixes

First check that your machine can handle the amount of dough the bread mix makes. If the packet quantity is only marginally more than you usually make, use the dough cycle and then bake the bread conventionally.

- *Select an appropriate setting; for example, use the normal or rapid setting for white bread.*
- *Place the recommended amount of water in the bread pan. Spoon over the bread mix and place the pan in the machine.*
- *Select the programme required and press Start. Check the dough after 5 minutes; add a little more water if it seems too dry.*
- *At the end of the baking cycle, remove the cooked bread from the bread pan and turn out on to a wire rack to cool.*

INGREDIENTS

When adapting this recipe for a handmade Malted Fruit Loaf so you can use it for a bread machine (see box), begin by reading the list of ingredients carefully before you start, and adjust the quantities if necessary.

BUTTER

High fat levels mean that the bread will take longer to rise and will turn out smaller. Reduce by 50g/2oz/½ cup per 450g/1lb/4 cups flour. You may need to add an extra 30ml/2 tbsp liquid to compensate.

MALT EXTRACT AND GOLDEN SYRUP

High sugar levels and/or the inclusion of a lot of dried fruit in a recipe may cause the bread to over-brown. Reduce the malt extract and golden (light corn) syrup quantities by one-third and increase other liquids to compensate. For machine breads it is necessary to add sugar. Allow 5–10ml/1–2 tsp sugar per 225g/8oz/2 cups flour.

FLOUR

This recipe uses white flour, but you could use wholemeal (whole-wheat) flour if you prefer. However it is useful to remember that a wholemeal loaf works better if you replace half the wholemeal flour with strong white bread flour.

YEAST

Replace fresh yeast with easy-blend (rapid-rise) dried yeast. In wholemeal bread, for example, start by using 5ml/1 tsp for up to 375g/13oz/3¼ cups flour or 7.5ml/1½ tsp for up to 675g/1½lb/6 cups flour.

MILK

Use skimmed milk at room temperature where possible. However, if you wish to use the time delay cycle replace the fresh milk with milk powder, or the milk may curdle.

DRIED FRUIT

Additions that enrich the dough, such as dried fruits, nuts, seeds and whole grains, make the dough heavier and the bread will not rise as well. Limit them to about a quarter of the total flour quantity and add them when prompted by the raisin beep.

METHOD

Use a similar bread machine recipe as a guide for adapting a conventional recipe. Consult your instruction book.

STEP 1

Obviously, you can only make one machine-baked loaf at a time. Make 1 large loaf or reduce the quantity of ingredients if your machine is small.

STEP 2

There is no need to melt the ingredients before you add them, but remember to chop the butter into fairly small pieces.

STEP 3

When adding ingredients to the bread pan, pour in the liquid first then sprinkle over the flour, followed by the mixed spice. (Check your handbook. Some machines require you to place the dry ingredients in the bread pan before the liquids are added.) Add easy-blend dried yeast to a small indent in the flour, but make sure it does not touch the liquid underneath.

Place salt and butter in separate corners of the pan. If your recipe calls for egg, add this with the water or other liquid.

Steps 4–8

Ignore these steps, apart from step 6. The bread machine will automatically mix, rise and cook the dough. Use a light setting for the crust due to the sugar, fat and fruit content of the Malted Fruit Loaf. Ordinary breads, such as a plain white loaf, need a medium setting, while loaves containing any wholemeal flour should be baked on the wholemeal setting.

If you are adding extra ingredients, such as dried fruit, set the bread machine to raisin setting and add the ingredients when it beeps. If you do not have this facility, add them approximately 5 minutes before the end of the kneading cycle.

Step 9

Make the glaze as usual and brush over the loaf at the end of the baking cycle.

MALTED FRUIT LOAF (HANDMADE)

Makes 2 loaves

50g/2oz/scant ¼ cup malt extract
30ml/2 tbsp golden (light corn) syrup
*75g/3oz/6 tbsp butter, plus extra
    for greasing*
*450g/1lb/4 cups unbleached strong white
    bread flour*
5ml/1 tsp mixed spice
20g/¾oz fresh yeast
150ml/¼ pint/⅔ cup lukewarm milk
50g/2oz/¼ cup currants
50g/2oz/⅓ cup sultanas (golden raisins)
*50g/2oz/¼ cup ready-to-eat dried
    apricots, chopped*
25g/1oz/2 tbsp mixed chopped peel

For the glaze
30ml/2 tbsp milk
30ml/2 tbsp caster (superfine) sugar

1 Grease two 450g/1lb loaf pans.

2 Melt the malt extract, syrup and butter in a pan. Leave to cool.

3 Sift the flour and spice into a large bowl; make a central well. Cream the yeast with a little of the milk and blend in the rest.

Add the yeast mixture with the malt extract to the flour and mix to a dough.

4 Knead on a floured surface until smooth and elastic, about 10 minutes. Place in an oiled bowl and cover with oiled clear film (plastic wrap). Leave to rise in a warm place for 1½–2 hours, or until doubled in bulk.

5 Turn the dough out on to a lightly floured surface and knock back (punch down).

6 Gently knead in the dried fruits.

7 Divide the dough in half and shape into two loaves. Place in the pans and cover with oiled clear film. Leave to rise for 1–1½ hours, or until the dough reaches the top of the pans.

8 Meanwhile, preheat the oven to 200°C/400°F/Gas 6. Bake the loaves for 35–40 minutes, or until golden. When cooked, transfer to a wire rack to cool.

9 Meanwhile, heat the milk and sugar for the glaze in a pan and immediately brush the warm loaves with the glaze.

TROUBLESHOOTING HANDMADE BREAD

If you follow the recipes and read the methods contained in previous sections you should produce good bread. However, if problems arise when you are making bread by hand, you should try to pinpoint the cause and apply a solution.

DOUGH WILL NOT RISE
- You may have forgotten to add the yeast.
- The yeast may be past its "use-by" date and is inactive.

Remedies
- To save the dough, make up another batch, making certain the yeast is active. This dough can then be kneaded into the original dough.
- Alternatively, dissolve the new yeast in warm water and work it into the dough. Next time, check that any yeast that has just passed or is close to its "use-by" date is active before adding to flour.

SIDES AND BOTTOM OF BREAD ARE TOO PALE
- The oven temperature was too low.
- The bread pan did not allow sufficient heat to penetrate the crust.

Remedy
- Turn the loaf out of its tin and return it to the oven, placing it upside-down on a shelf, for 5–10 minutes.

CRUST IS TOO SOFT
- There was insufficient steam in the oven.

Remedies
- You could glaze the crust before baking next time, and spray the inside of the oven with water.
- Alternatively, place a little hot water in an ovenproof dish in the bottom of the oven during baking.

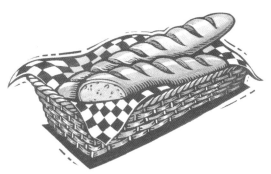

CRUST IS TOO HARD
- Using too much glaze or having too much steam in the oven can harden the crust.

Remedy
- Use less glaze next time. To soften a crusty loaf, leave it overnight in a plastic bag.

CRUST SEPARATES FROM THE BREAD
- The dough has dried out during the rising.
- The oven temperature was too low and the dough has expanded unevenly.
- Sometimes the crust of a loaf separates from the crumb as a result of freezing.

Remedies
- Cover the dough with clear film (plastic wrap) or waxed paper to prevent any moisture loss while rising.
- Ensure that the oven is preheated to the correct temperature so that heat penetrates throughout the loaf.
- Some breads simply don't freeze well. The crustiest loaves are usually most at risk, so avoid freezing French Couronnes or similar breads.

Soft Pale Crust

- This could be because the bread was not baked for long enough.
- The oven temperature was too low.

Remedy

- When you think the bread is ready, tap it firmly underneath; it should sound hollow. If it does not, return the bread to the oven, only this time placing it directly on the oven shelf. Leave it for a few minutes, then test again.

Loaf is Crumbly and Dry

- The bread was baked for too long or the oven was too hot.
- You used too much flour.

Remedy

- Next time, check the quantities in the recipe.
- Reduce the temperature and check the loaf when the crust looks golden brown next time.

Large Holes in the Loaf

- The dough was not knocked back (punched down) properly before shaping.
- The dough was not kneaded enough originally.

Remedy

- Dough should be kneaded firmly for at least 10 minutes.

Bread has a Yeasty Flavour

- Too much yeast was used.

Remedy

- If doubling recipe quantities, do not double the amount of yeast but use one-and-a-half times the amount in the original recipe. Do not over-compensate for a cool room by adding extra yeast. Wait a little longer instead – the bread will rise in the end.

Loaf Collapses in the Oven

- The wrong flour was used.
- The dough was left too long for the second rising and has over-risen.

Remedy

- Check the flour before using.
- As a rule, only allow the dough to double in bulk.

Loaf is Dense and Flat

- Too much liquid was used and the dough has become too soft.
- The dough was not kneaded enough.

Remedies

- Always check the recipe for quantities of any liquid needed until you are confident about judging the consistency of the dough.
- Dough should be kneaded firmly for at least 10 minutes.

TROUBLESHOOTING MACHINE-MADE BREAD

Bread machines are incredibly easy to use and, once you have become familiar with yours, you will wonder how you ever did without it. However, things can go wrong, and it always helps to understand why.

BREAD RISES TOO MUCH

- Usually caused by too much yeast.
- Too much sugar used, which promotes yeast action.
- Salt was left out. If so, the yeast would have been uncontrolled and a tall loaf would have been the likely result.
- Too much liquid can sometimes cause a loaf to over-rise.
- Other possibilities are too much dough or too hot a day.

Remedies

- Reduce the yeast by 25 per cent.
- Try reducing the quantity of sugar.
- Try reducing the liquid by 15–30ml/ 1–2 tbsp next time.

BREAD DOES NOT RISE ENOUGH

- Insufficient yeast or yeast that is past its expiry date.
- A rapid cycle was chosen, giving the bread less time to rise.
- The yeast and salt came into contact with each other before mixing. Make sure they are placed in separate areas when added to the bread pan.
- Too much salt inhibits the action of the yeast. You may have added salt twice, or added other salty ingredients, such as ready-salted nuts or feta cheese.
- Wholegrain and wholemeal (whole-wheat) breads tend not to rise as high as white-flour breads. These flours contain bran and wheat germ, which makes them heavier.

- You may have used plain white flour instead of a strong bread flour, which has a higher gluten content.
- The ingredients were not at the correct temperature. If they were too hot, they may have killed the yeast; if they were too cold, they may have retarded the action of the yeast.
- Insufficient liquid. In order for dough to rise adequately, it needs to be soft and pliable. If the dough was dry and stiff, add more liquid next time.
- The lid of the bread machine was open during the rising stage for long enough to let warm air escape.
- No sugar was added. Yeast works better where there is at least 5ml/1 tsp sugar to feed it. Note, however, that high sugar levels may retard yeast action.

BREAD DOES NOT RISE AT ALL

- No yeast was added or it was past its expiry date.
- The yeast was not handled correctly and was probably killed by adding ingredients that were too hot.

The Dough is Very Sticky and Does Not Form a Ball

- The dough is too wet.

Remedy

- Try adding a little extra flour, a spoonful at a time, waiting for it to be absorbed before adding more. You must do this while the machine is still mixing and kneading the bread dough.

The Dough is Crumbly and Does Not Form a Ball

- The dough is too dry.

Remedy

- Add extra liquid until the ingredients combine to form a pliable dough.

Bread Mixed But Not Baked

- A dough cycle was selected.

Remedy

- Remove the dough, shape it and bake it in a conventional oven or bake it in the machine on the "bake only" cycle.

Bread Collapsed after Rising or During Baking

- Too much liquid was added.
- The bread rose too much.
- Insufficient salt. Salt helps to prevent the dough from over-rising.
- The machine may have been placed in a draught or may have been jolted while the bread was rising.
- High humidity and warm weather may have caused the dough to rise too fast.
- Too much yeast may have been added.
- The dough may have contained a high proportion of cheese.

Remedies

- Reduce the amount of liquid by 15–30ml/1–2 tbsp next time, or add a little extra flour.
- Reduce the amount of yeast slightly in the future, or use a quicker cycle.

There are Deposits of Flour on the Sides of the Loaf

- The dry ingredients stuck to the sides of the pan and then adhered to the dough.

Remedy

- Next time, use a flexible rubber spatula to scrape down the sides of the pan after 5–10 minutes of the initial mixing cycle.

Crust too Chewy and Tough

Remedy

- Increase the butter or oil and milk.

Crust is Shrivelled or Wrinkled

- Moisture condensed on top of the loaf while it was cooling.

Remedy

- Remove from the bread machine as soon as it is cooled next time.

Crumbly, Coarse Texture

- The bread rose too much.
- The dough did not have enough liquid. or too many whole grains were added, which soaked up the liquid.

Remedy

- Reduce the quantity of yeast next time.
- Next time, either soak the whole grains in water first or increase the liquid content.

Burnt Crust

- There was too much sugar in the dough.

Remedies

- Choose the sweet-bread setting if the machine has this option.
- Use less or try a light-crust setting for sweet breads.

Pale Loaf

Remedies

- Add milk, either dried or fresh, to the dough. This encourages browning.
- Set the crust colour to dark.
- Increase the sugar slightly.

Bread Not Baked in the Centre or on Top

- Too much liquid was added.
- The quantities were too large and your machine could not cope with the dough.
- The dough was too rich: it contained too much fat, sugar, eggs, nuts or grains.
- The bread machine lid was not closed properly, or the machine was used in too cold a location.
- The flour may have been too heavy. This can occur when you use rye, bran and wholemeal (whole-wheat) flours.

Remedies
- Next time, reduce the liquid by 15ml/ 1 tbsp or add a little extra flour.
- Replace some of the heavy flour with white bread flour next time.

Crust too Soft or Crisp

Remedies
- For a softer crust, increase the fat and use milk instead of water. For a crisper crust, do the opposite.
- Try using the French bread setting for a crisper crust.

Air Bubble Under the Crust

- The dough was not mixed well or did not deflate properly during the knock-back (punch-down) cycle between risings.

Remedy
- This is likely to be a one-off problem, but if it persists, try adding an extra spoonful of water.

Added Ingredients Were Chopped Up Instead of Remaining Whole

- They were added too soon and were chopped by the kneading blade.

Remedy
- Add ingredients on the machine's audible signal, or about 5 minutes before the kneading cycle finishes.

Added Ingredients Not Mixed In

- They were probably added too late in the kneading cycle.

Remedy
- Next time, add the ingredients a couple of minutes sooner.

The Bread is Dry

- The bread was left uncovered to cool too long and dried out.
- Breads low in fat dry out rapidly.
- The bread was stored in the refrigerator.

Remedies
- Increase the fat or oil in the recipe.
- Next time place the bread in a plastic bag when cool and store in a bread bin.

Bread has a Holey Texture

- The dough was too wet.
- Salt was omitted.
- Warm weather and/or high humidity caused the dough to rise too quickly.

Remedy
- Use less liquid next time.

A Sticky Layered Unrisen Mess

- You forgot to put the kneading blade in the pan before adding the ingredients.
- The kneading blade was not correctly inserted on the shaft.
- The bread pan was incorrectly fitted.

SAFETY & GOOD SENSE

Whether you are baking bread by hand or in a bread machine, good kitchen practice is essential. Make sure your kitchen is a hygienic working environment, and observe common-sense safety rules. That way, nothing will mar your enjoyment of your daily bread.

In a bread machine, mixing, rising and baking is done in an enclosed space, so the risk of food contamination is minimal. However, it is important to make sure that the baking pan and kneading blade are scrupulously clean.

Take especial care when making breads that contain perishable ingredients such as eggs, fresh milk, cheese, fruit and vegetables. If you are baking by machine, never use the delay timer, as ingredients such as these may deteriorate, especially in warm conditions, and could present a health risk.

Making bread in the conventional way is much more "hands on" than machine bread making, so it follows that not only must bowls and kneading surfaces be perfectly clean, but so too must your hands. Wash hands and wrists well, and scrub your nails if necessary.

During rising, covering the dough with a freshly laundered dishtowel or clear film (plastic wrap) has two benefits. It prevents a dry crust from forming on the dough, and also keeps flies and other insects away.

Homemade bread does not contain any preservatives, so it will not keep quite as long as the commercial product. The shelf life can be prolonged if the bread is wrapped in foil or placed in a sealed plastic bag shortly after it has cooled. Homemade bread will also freeze well, but the loaves must be completely cold before being bagged and frozen.

SAFETY REMINDERS

- *Read the manufacturer's instructions before operating your machine. The instruction manual for your machine should be kept handy for reference.*
- *If you touch the machine while it is in operation, be careful. The outside walls become hot when it is in baking mode.*
- *Position the machine on a firm, level, heat-resistant surface, away from any other heat source.*
- *Do not stand the bread machine in sunlight and allow at least 5–7.5cm/ 2–3in clearance on all sides when in use.*
- *Do not place anything on top of the machine lid.*
- *Do not use the machine outdoors.*
- *Do not immerse the machine, cable or plug in water, and avoid using it near a source of water.*
- *Be careful to keep your fingers away from the blade while the machine is kneading the dough, and never reach inside the bread machine during the baking cycle.*
- *Keep the machine out of the reach of small children, and make sure there is no trailing cable.*
- *Unplug the machine before cleaning or moving it and when it is not in use. Allow the bread machine to cool completely before cleaning it and putting it away.*

HANDMADE BREADS

There's something enormously satisfying about making bread by hand. As you stand there, feeling the dough between your fingers, then heeling it down with the palm of your hand, stress starts to ebb away. Any residual irritation can safely be taken out on the dough, for the good news is that a good pummelling is precisely what it needs to develop the gluten and ensure a good rise.

The best breadmakers begin by getting their hands dirty. They may well go on to use a bread machine for speed and convenience, but it is only by manually working the dough that you get to know what it should look and feel like if success is to be assured.

The recipes in this part of the book provide the perfect introduction to breadmaking, whether you are a beginner or – quite literally – an old hand. From basic white bread to fancy rolls, muffins, flatbreads and elaborately shaped braids, there's something here for every taste, sweet or savoury. All you have to do is choose your loaf!

BASIC BREADS

In many parts of the world, daily bread is just that – a vital staple that is enjoyed at almost every meal, from breakfast through to late night snacks – and the everyday loaves that enjoy the greatest popularity are the ones you'll find right here. There are British favourites, like the Granary Cob and Poppy Seed Bloomer; American specialities like the easy-to-make Grant Loaves and Anadama Bread; and from France, baguettes and a wonderfully rustic country bread made using a chef starter. Finally – just for fun – there are two loaves cooked in novel containers: Welsh Claypot Loaves and Boston Brown Bread, the latter providing a novel alternative use for a cafetière or press pot.

PLAIN WHITE LOAF

This may be described as plain, but the taste is anything but. Simple white bread, spread with farm butter or served with a chunk of good cheese, is an everyday treat.

MAKES 2 LOAVES

INGREDIENTS
50ml/2fl oz/¼ cup lukewarm water
30ml/2 tbsp sugar
7.5ml/1½ tsp active dry yeast
475ml/16fl oz/2 cups lukewarm milk
30ml/2 tbsp butter or margarine, at room temperature
10ml/2 tsp salt
675g/1½lb/6 cups white bread flour

1 Grease two 23 × 13cm/9 × 5in loaf pans. Combine the water and 15ml/1 tbsp sugar in a bowl. Sprinkle the yeast over and leave to stand 15 minutes until frothy.

2 Pour the milk into a large bowl. Add the remaining sugar, the butter or margarine and salt. Stir in the yeast mixture, then add the flour, 115g/4oz/1 cup at a time, until a stiff dough is obtained.

3 Transfer the dough to a floured surface. Knead for about 10 minutes, until the dough is smooth and elastic. Place in a large greased bowl, cover with lightly oiled clear film (plastic wrap) and leave to rise in a warm place for 2–3 hours, until the dough has doubled in bulk.

4 Knock back (punch down) the risen dough and divide in half. Form into loaf shapes and place in the pans, seam-side down. Cover and leave to rise in a warm place for about 45 minutes, until almost doubled in bulk.

5 Preheat the oven to 190°C/375°F/Gas 5. Bake the bread for 45–50 minutes, until the top of each loaf is firm and brown, and the base sounds hollow when tapped. Cool on a rack.

BROWN BREAD

Honey and wheatgerm enrich the flavour of this delicious loaf, which is very good for sandwiches, toast, or just enjoying with your favourite spread.

MAKES 1 LOAF

INGREDIENTS
400g/14oz/4½ cups wholemeal (whole-wheat) flour
10ml/2 tsp salt
20ml/4 tsp active dry yeast
400ml/14fl oz/1⅔ cups lukewarm water
30ml/2 tbsp clear honey
45ml/3 tbsp oil
25g/1oz/½ cup wheat germ
milk, for glazing

1 Grease a 23 × 13cm/9 × 5in loaf pan. Combine the flour and salt in a large mixing bowl and place in a low oven (about 110°C/225°F/Gas 4) for about 8–10 minutes, until warmed through. Meanwhile, sprinkle the active dry yeast over 175ml/6fl oz/¾ cup of the lukewarm water in a small bowl and leave to stand until frothy.

2 Make a well in the centre of the flour. Pour in the yeast mixture, the remaining water, honey and oil. Add the wheat germ. With a wooden spoon, stir from the centre until smooth. Transfer the dough to a lightly floured surface and knead just enough to shape into a loaf.

3 Place the dough in the pan and cover with oiled clear film (plastic wrap). Leave to rise in a warm place for about 1 hour until the dough is about 2.5cm/1in above the rim of the pan.

4 Preheat the oven to 200°C/400°F/Gas 6. Bake the dough for 35–40 minutes until the top of the loaf is browned and the base sounds hollow when tapped. Cool on a rack.

GRANARY COB

Cob is an old word meaning "head". If you make a slash across the top of the dough, the finished loaf, known as a Danish cob, will look like a large roll.

MAKES 1 ROUND LOAF

INGREDIENTS
450g/1lb/4 cups Granary (whole-wheat) or malthouse flour
10ml/2 tsp salt
15g/½oz fresh yeast
300ml/½ pint/1¼ cups lukewarm water or milk and water mixed

FOR THE TOPPING
30ml/2 tbsp water
2.5ml/½ tsp salt
cracked wheat

1 Lightly flour a baking sheet. Sift the flour and salt into a large bowl and make a well in the centre. Place in a very low oven for 5 minutes to warm.

2 Mix the yeast with a little of the water or milk mixture then blend in the rest. Add the yeast mixture to the centre of the flour and mix to a dough.

3 Knead on a lightly floured surface for about 10 minutes until smooth and elastic. Place in a lightly oiled bowl, cover with lightly oiled clear film (plastic wrap) and leave to rise in a warm place for 1¼ hours, or until doubled in bulk.

4 Knead the dough on a lightly floured surface for 2–3 minutes, then roll into a ball, making sure the dough looks like a plump round cushion. Place in the centre of the prepared baking sheet. Cover with an inverted bowl and leave to rise in a warm place, for 30–45 minutes.

5 Preheat the oven to 230°C/450°F/Gas 8. Mix the water and salt and brush over the bread. Sprinkle with cracked wheat. Bake for 15 minutes, then reduce the oven temperature to 200°C/400°F/Gas 6 and bake for a further 20 minutes, or until the loaf sounds hollow when tapped on the base. Cool on a rack.

COTTAGE LOAF

Snipping the top and bottom sections of the dough at 5cm/2in intervals not only looks good but also helps the loaf to expand in the oven.

MAKES 1 LARGE ROUND LOAF

INGREDIENTS
675g/1½lb/6 cups unbleached white bread flour
10ml/2 tsp salt
20g/¾oz fresh yeast
400ml/14fl oz/1⅔ cups lukewarm water

1 Lightly grease 2 baking sheets. Sift the flour and salt together into a large bowl and make a well in the centre. Mix the yeast with 150ml/¼ pint/⅔ cup of the water until dissolved. Pour into the centre of the flour with the remaining water and mix to a firm dough.

2 Knead on a lightly floured surface for 10 minutes until smooth and elastic. Place in a lightly oiled bowl, cover with lightly oiled clear film (plastic wrap) and leave to rise in a warm place, for about 1 hour, or until doubled in bulk.

3 Turn out on to a lightly floured surface and knock back (punch down). Knead for 2–3 minutes then divide the dough into two-thirds and one-third; shape each to a ball. Place the balls of dough on the prepared baking sheets. Cover with inverted bowls and leave to rise, in a warm place, for about 30 minutes.

4 Gently flatten the top of the larger round of dough. With a sharp knife, cut a cross in the centre, about 4cm/1½in across. Brush with a little water and place the smaller round on top.

5 Carefully press a hole through the middle of the top ball, down into the lower part, using your thumb and first two fingers of one hand. Cover with lightly oiled clear film and leave to rest in a warm place for about 10 minutes. Preheat the oven to 220°C/425°F/Gas 7 and place the bread on the lower shelf. It will finish expanding as the oven heats up. Bake for 35–40 minutes, or until golden brown and sounding hollow when tapped. Cool on a wire rack.

POPPY SEED BLOOMER

This satisfying white bread, which is the British version of the chunky baton loaf found throughout Europe, is made by a slower rising method and with less yeast than usual. It produces a longer-keeping loaf with a fuller flavour. The dough takes about 8 hours to rise, so you'll need to start this bread early in the morning.

MAKES 1 LARGE LOAF

INGREDIENTS
675g/1½lb/6 cups unbleached white bread flour
10ml/2 tsp salt
15g/½oz fresh yeast
430ml/15fl oz/1⅞ cups water

FOR THE TOPPING
2.5ml/½ tsp salt
30ml/2 tbsp water
poppy seeds, for sprinkling

> ### COOK'S TIP
> *The traditional cracked, crusty appearance of this loaf is difficult to achieve in a domestic oven. However, you can get a similar result by spraying the oven with water before baking. If the underneath of the loaf is not very crusty at the end of baking, turn the loaf over on the baking sheet, switch off the heat and leave in the oven for a further 5–10 minutes.*

1 Lightly grease a baking sheet. Sift the flour and salt together into a large bowl and make a well in the centre.

2 Mix the yeast and 150ml/¼ pint/⅔ cup of the water in a bowl. Stir in the remaining water. Add to the centre of the flour. Mix, gradually incorporating the surrounding flour, until the mixture forms a firm dough.

3 Turn out on to a lightly floured surface and knead the dough very well, for at least 10 minutes, until smooth and elastic. Place the dough in a lightly oiled bowl, cover with lightly oiled clear film (plastic wrap) and leave to rise at a cool room temperature, about 15–18°C/60–65°F, for 5–6 hours, or until the dough has doubled in bulk.

4 Knock back (punch down) the dough, turn out on to a lightly floured surface and knead thoroughly for about 5 minutes. Return the dough to the bowl, and re-cover. Leave to rise, at cool room temperature, for a further 2 hours.

5 Knock back again and repeat the thorough kneading. Leave the dough to rest for 5 minutes, then roll out on a lightly floured surface into a rectangle 2.5cm/ 1in thick. Roll the dough up from one long side and shape it into a square-ended thick baton shape about 33 × 13cm/13 × 5in.

6 Place it seam side up on a lightly floured baking sheet, cover and leave to rest for 15 minutes. Turn the loaf over and place on the greased baking sheet. Plump up by tucking the dough under the sides and ends. Using a sharp knife, cut 6 diagonal slashes on the top.

7 Leave to rest, covered, in a warm place, for 10 minutes. Meanwhile preheat the oven to 230°C/450°F/Gas 8.

8 Mix the salt and water together and brush this glaze over the bread. Sprinkle with poppy seeds.

9 Spray the oven with water, bake the bread immediately for 20 minutes, then reduce the oven temperature to 200°C/400°F/Gas 6 and bake for 25 minutes more, or until golden. Transfer to a wire rack to cool.

VARIATION
For a more rustic loaf, replace up to half the flour with wholemeal (whole-wheat) bread flour.

SPLIT TIN

This loaf gets its name from the centre split. Some bakers mould the dough in two loaves – they join together while proving but retain the crack.

MAKES 1 LOAF

INGREDIENTS
500g/1¼lb/5 cups unbleached white bread flour, plus extra for dusting
10ml/2 tsp salt
15g/½oz fresh yeast
300ml/½ pint/1¼ cups lukewarm water
60ml/4 tbsp lukewarm milk

1 Lightly grease an 18.5 × 11.5cm/7¼ × 4½in loaf pan. Sift the flour and salt together into a large bowl and make a well in the centre. Mix the yeast with half the lukewarm water in a bowl. Stir in the remaining water.

2 Pour the yeast mixture into the centre of the flour and using your fingers, mix in a little flour. Gradually mix in more flour to form a thick, smooth batter.

3 Sprinkle a little more flour from around the edge over the batter and leave in a warm place to "sponge". Bubbles will appear in the batter after about 20 minutes. Add the milk and remaining flour; mix to a firm dough.

4 Knead on a lightly floured surface for 10 minutes until smooth and elastic. Place in a lightly oiled bowl, cover with lightly oiled clear film (plastic wrap) and leave to rise, in a warm place, for 1–1¼ hours, or until nearly doubled in bulk.

5 Knock back (punch down) the dough and turn out on to a lightly floured surface. Shape it into a rectangle, the length of the tin. Roll up lengthways, tuck the ends under and place seam-side down in the prepared tin. Cover and leave to rise, in a warm place, for about 20–30 minutes, or until nearly doubled in bulk.

6 Using a sharp knife, make one deep central slash the length of the bread; dust with flour. Leave for 10–15 minutes. Preheat the oven to 230°C/450°F/Gas 8. Bake for 15 minutes, then reduce the oven temperature to 200°C/400°F/Gas 6. Bake for 20–25 minutes more, or until the bread is golden and sounds hollow when tapped on the base. Cool on a wire rack.

GRANT LOAVES

This quick and easy recipe was created in the 1940s by Doris Grant. The dough requires no kneading and takes only a minute to mix.

MAKES 3 LOAVES

INGREDIENTS
1.4kg/3lb/12 cups wholemeal (whole-wheat) bread flour
15ml/1 tbsp salt
15ml/1 tbsp easy-blend (rapid-rise) dried yeast
1.2 litres/2 pints/5 cups warm water (35–38°C/95–100°F)
15ml/1 tbsp muscovado (molasses) sugar

1 Thoroughly grease 3 loaf pans, each about 21 × 11 × 6cm/8½ × 4½ × 2½in and set aside in a warm place. Sift the flour and salt together in a large mixing bowl, and warm slightly to take off the chill.

2 Sprinkle the dried yeast over 150ml/¼ pint/⅔ cup of the water. After a couple of minutes stir in the sugar. Leave for 10 minutes.

3 Make a well in the centre of the flour and stir in the yeast mixture and remaining water. The dough should be slippery. Mix for about 1 minute, working the sides into the middle.

4 Divide among the prepared pans, cover with oiled clear film (plastic wrap) and leave to rise, in a warm place, for 30 minutes, or until the dough has risen by about a third to within 1cm/½in of the top of the pans.

5 Meanwhile, preheat the oven to 200°C/400°F/Gas 6. Bake the dough for 40 minutes, or until the loaves are crisp and sound hollow when tapped on the base. Cool on a wire rack.

COOK'S TIP
Muscovado sugar gives this bread a rich flavour. An unrefined cane sugar, it is dark and moist.

WELSH CLAYPOT LOAVES

Clay flower pots make the prettiest little loaves and are a great talking point. These breads are flavoured with chives, sage, parsley and garlic. For even more flavour, try adding a little grated raw onion and grated cheese to the dough.

MAKES 2 LOAVES

INGREDIENTS
115g/4oz/1 cup wholemeal (whole-wheat) bread flour
350g/12oz/3 cups unbleached white bread flour
7.5ml/1½ tsp salt
15g/½oz fresh yeast
150ml/¼ pint/⅔ cup lukewarm milk
120ml/4fl oz/½ cup lukewarm water
50g/2oz/4 tbsp butter, melted
15ml/1 tbsp chopped fresh chives
15ml/1 tbsp chopped fresh parsley
5ml/1 tsp chopped fresh sage
1 garlic clove, crushed
beaten egg, for glazing
fennel seeds, for sprinkling (optional)

> ### COOK'S TIP
> To prepare and seal new clay flower pots, clean them thoroughly, oil them inside and outside and bake them three or four times. Preheat the oven to about 200°C/400°F/Gas 6 and bake the pots for 30–40 minutes. To save energy, do this while you are baking other foods.

1 Lightly grease two clean 14cm/5½in diameter, 11cm/4½in high clay flower pots. Sift the flours and salt into a large bowl and make a well in the centre.

2 Blend the yeast with a little of the milk until smooth, then stir in the remaining milk. Pour the yeast liquid into the well in the centre of the flour and sprinkle over a little of the flour from around the edge. Cover the bowl with clear film (plastic wrap) and leave in a warm place for 15 minutes.

3 Add the lukewarm water, melted butter, chives, parsley and sage to the flour mixture. Stir in the garlic and mix together to form a dough. Turn out on to a lightly floured surface and knead for about 10 minutes, until the dough is smooth and elastic.

4 Place in a lightly oiled bowl, cover with lightly oiled clear film and leave to rise, in a warm place, for 1¼–1½ hours, or until doubled in bulk.

5 Turn the dough out on to a lightly floured surface and knock back (punch down). Divide in two. Shape and fit into the prepared flower pots. The dough should about half fill the pots. Cover with oiled clear film and leave to rise for 30–45 minutes, in a warm place, or until the dough is 2.5cm/1in from the top of the pots.

6 Meanwhile, preheat the oven to 200°C/400°F/Gas 6. Brush the top of each loaf with beaten egg and sprinkle with fennel seeds, if using. Bake for 35–40 minutes or until golden. Turn out on to a wire rack to cool.

Irish Soda Bread

Soda bread can be prepared in minutes and is excellent served warm, fresh from the oven. For a finer texture, use all plain white flour.

MAKES 1 ROUND LOAF

INGREDIENTS
225g/8oz/2 cups unbleached plain (all-purpose) flour
225g/8oz/2 cups wholemeal (whole-wheat) flour, plus extra for dusting
5ml/1 tsp salt
10ml/2 tsp bicarbonate of soda (baking soda)
10ml/2 tsp cream of tartar
40g/1½oz/3 tbsp butter or lard (shortening)
5ml/1 tsp caster (superfine) sugar
350–375ml/12–13fl oz/1½–1⅔ cups buttermilk

1 Preheat the oven to 190°C/375°F/Gas 5. Lightly grease a baking sheet. Sift the flour and salt into a large mixing bowl.

2 Add the bicarbonate of soda and cream of tartar, then rub in the butter or lard. Stir in the sugar.

3 Pour in sufficient buttermilk to mix to a soft dough. Do not over-mix or the bread will be heavy and tough. Shape into a round on a lightly floured surface.

4 Place on the prepared baking sheet and mark a cross using a sharp knife, cutting deep into the dough.

5 Dust lightly with wholemeal flour and bake for 35–45 minutes or until well risen and the bread sounds hollow when tapped on the base. Serve warm.

VARIATION
Shape the dough into two small loaves and bake for 25–30 minutes.

BOSTON BROWN BREAD

Rich, moist and dark, this steamed bread is flavoured with molasses and can include raisins. In Boston it is often served with savoury baked beans.

MAKES 1 OR 2 LOAVES

INGREDIENTS
90g/3½oz/scant 1 cup cornmeal
90g/3½oz/scant 1 cup unbleached plain (all-purpose) white flour or wholemeal (whole-wheat) flour
90g/3½oz/scant 1 cup rye flour
5ml/1 tsp bicarbonate of soda (baking soda)
2.5ml/½ tsp salt
90g/3½oz/generous ½ cup seedless raisins
120ml/4fl oz/½ cup milk
120ml/4fl oz/½ cup water
120ml/4fl oz/½ cup molasses or black treacle

1 Line the base of a 1.2 litre/2 pint/5 cup cylindrical metal or glass container, such as the heatproof glass jug (pitcher) from a cafetière or press pot, with greased greaseproof (waxed) paper. Alternatively, remove the lids from two 450g/1lb coffee cans, wash and dry the cans, then line with greased greaseproof paper.

2 Mix the cornmeal, plain or wholemeal flour, rye flour, bicarbonate of soda, salt and raisins in a large bowl. Warm the milk and water in a small pan and stir in the molasses or black treacle.

3 Add the molasses mixture to the dry ingredients and stir the mixture until it forms a moist dough. Do not overmix. Fill the jug or cans with the dough; they should be about two-thirds full. Cover neatly with foil or greased greaseproof paper and tie securely.

4 Bring water to a depth of 5cm/2in to the boil in a deep, heavy pan large enough to accommodate the jug or cans. Place a trivet in the pan, stand the jug or cans on top, cover the pan and steam for 1½ hours, adding more boiling water to maintain the required level as necessary. Cool the loaves for a few minutes in the jug or cans, then turn them on their sides and the loaves should slip out. Serve warm.

ANADAMA BREAD

A traditional bread from Massachusetts, made with molasses, cornmeal, wholemeal and unbleached white flour. According to legend, it was created by the husband of a woman called Anna, who had left a cornmeal mush and some molasses in the kitchen. On finding only these ingredients for supper her husband mixed them with some flour, water and yeast to make this bread, while muttering, "Anna, damn her"!

MAKES 2 LOAVES

INGREDIENTS
40g/1½oz/3 tbsp butter
120ml/4fl oz/½ cup molasses
560ml/scant 1 pint/scant 2½ cups water
50g/2oz/½ cup cornmeal
10ml/2 tsp salt
25g/1oz fresh yeast
30ml/2 tbsp lukewarm water
275g/10oz/2½ cups wholemeal (whole-wheat) flour
450g/1lb/4 cups unbleached white bread flour

VARIATION
Use a 7g/¼oz sachet easy-blend (rapid-rise) dried yeast instead of fresh. Mix it with the wholemeal flour. Add to the cornmeal mixture, then add the lukewarm water, which would conventionally be blended with the fresh yeast.

1 Grease two 1.5 litre/2½ pint/6 cup loaf pans. Heat the butter, molasses and measured water in a pan until the butter has melted. Stir in the cornmeal and salt and stir over a low heat until boiling. Cool until lukewarm.

2 In a small bowl, cream the yeast with the lukewarm water, then set aside for 5 minutes until the mixture is frothy.

3 Mix the cornmeal mixture and yeast mixture together in a large bowl. Fold in the wholemeal flour and then the unbleached white bread flour to form a sticky dough. Knead on a lightly floured surface until smooth and elastic.

4 Place in a lightly oiled bowl, cover with lightly oiled clear film (plastic wrap) and leave to rise, in a warm place, for about 1 hour, or until doubled in bulk.

5 Knead the dough lightly on a well floured surface, shape into two loaves. Place in the prepared pans. Cover with lightly oiled clear film and leave to rise, in a warm place, for about 35–45 minutes, or until doubled in size and the dough reaches the top of the tins.

6 Meanwhile, preheat the oven to 200°C/400°F/Gas 6. Using a sharp knife, slash the tops of the loaves three or four times. Bake for 15 minutes, then reduce the oven temperature to 180°C/350°F/Gas 4 and bake for a further 35–40 minutes, or until each loaf sounds hollow when tapped on the base. Turn out on to a wire rack to cool slightly. Serve warm.

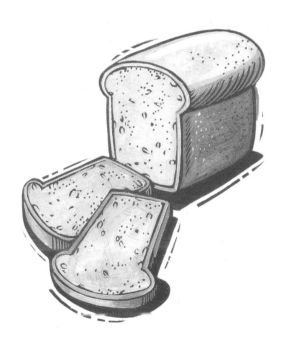

PANE TOSCANO

This bread from Tuscany is made without salt and probably originates from the days when salt was heavily taxed. To compensate for the lack of salt, this bread is usually served with salty foods, such as anchovies and olives.

MAKES 1 LOAF

INGREDIENTS
550g/1¼lb/5 cups unbleached white bread flour
350ml/12fl oz/1½ cups boiling water
15g/½oz fresh yeast
60ml/4 tbsp lukewarm water

1 First make the starter. Sift 175g/6oz/1½ cups of the flour into a large bowl. Pour over the boiling water, leave for a couple of minutes, then mix well. Cover the bowl with a damp dishtowel and leave for 10 hours.

2 Lightly flour a baking sheet. Cream the yeast with the lukewarm water. Stir into the starter. Gradually add the remaining flour and mix to form a dough. Turn out on to a lightly floured surface, and knead for 5–8 minutes until smooth and elastic.

3 Place in a lightly oiled bowl, cover with lightly oiled clear film (plastic wrap) and leave to rise, in a warm place, for 1–1½ hours, or until doubled in bulk.

4 Turn out the dough on to a lightly floured surface, knock back (punch down), and shape into a round. Fold the sides of the round into the centre and seal. Place seam side up on the prepared baking sheet. Cover with lightly oiled clear film and leave to rise, in a warm place, for 30–45 minutes, or until doubled in size.

5 Flatten the loaf to about half its risen height and flip over. Cover with a large upturned bowl and leave to rise, in a warm place, for 30 minutes.

6 Meanwhile, preheat the oven to 220°C/425°F/Gas 7. If wished, slash the top of the loaf, using a sharp knife. Bake for 30–35 minutes, or until golden brown. Transfer to a wire rack to cool.

KOLACH

This simple Bulgarian bread gets its name from its circular shape – kolo means circle in Bulgarian. It has a golden crust sprinkled with poppy seeds and a moist crumb, which makes this loaf a very good keeper.

MAKES 1 LOAF

INGREDIENTS
675g/1½lb/6 cups unbleached white bread flour
10ml/2 tsp salt
25g/1oz fresh yeast
120ml/4fl oz/½ cup lukewarm milk
5ml/1 tsp clear honey
2 eggs, beaten
150ml/¼ pint/⅔ cup natural (plain) yogurt
50g/2oz/¼ cup butter, melted
beaten egg, for glazing
poppy seeds, for sprinkling

1 Grease a large baking sheet. Sift the flour and salt together into a large bowl and make a well in the centre. Cream the yeast with the milk and honey. Add to the centre of the flour with the eggs, yogurt and melted butter. Gradually mix in the flour to form a firm dough.

2 Knead on a lightly floured surface for 8–10 minutes until smooth and elastic. Place in a lightly oiled bowl, cover with lightly oiled clear film (plastic wrap) and leave to rise, in a warm place, for 1½ hours, or until doubled in bulk.

3 Knock back (punch down) the dough and place on a lightly floured surface. Knead lightly and shape into a ball. Place seam side down and make a hole in the centre with your fingers. Gradually enlarge this, turning the dough to make a 25cm/10in circle. Transfer to the baking sheet, cover with oiled clear film and leave to rise, in a warm place, for 30-45 minutes, or until doubled in size.

4 Preheat the oven to 200°C/400°F/Gas 6. Brush the loaf with beaten egg and sprinkle with poppy seeds. Bake for 35 minutes, or until golden. Cool on a rack.

French Baguettes

Baguettes are difficult to reproduce at home as they require a very hot oven and steam. However, by using less yeast and a triple fermentation you can produce a bread with a superior taste and far better texture than mass-produced baguettes. These are best eaten on the day of baking.

Makes 3 loaves

Ingredients
500g/1¼lb/5 cups unbleached white bread flour
115g/4oz/1 cup fine French plain (all-purpose) flour
10ml/2 tsp salt
15g/½oz fresh yeast
525ml/18fl oz/2¼ cups lukewarm water

Cook's Tip
Salt controls the action of yeast in bread so the leavening action is more noticeable. Don't let unsalted bread over-rise or it may collapse.

1 Sift the flours and salt together into a large bowl. Add the yeast to the water in another large bowl and stir to dissolve. Gradually beat in half the flour mixture to form a batter. Cover with clear film (plastic wrap) and leave at room temperature for about 3 hours, or until nearly trebled in size and starting to collapse.

2 Add the remaining flour a little at a time, beating with your hand. Turn out on to a lightly floured surface and knead for 8–10 minutes to form a moist dough. Place in a lightly oiled bowl, cover with lightly oiled clear film, and leave to rise, in a warm place, for about 1 hour.

3 When the dough has almost doubled in bulk, knock it back (punch it down), turn out on to a lightly floured surface and divide into three equal pieces. Shape each into a ball, then into a rectangle measuring about 15 × 7.5cm/6 × 3in.

4 Fold the bottom third up lengthways and the top third down and press down to make sure the pieces of dough are in contact. Seal the edges. Repeat two or three more times until each loaf is an oblong. Leave to rest in between folding for a few minutes, if necessary, to avoid tearing the dough.

5 Gently stretch each piece of dough lengthways into a 33–35cm/13–14in long loaf. Pleat a floured dishtowel on a baking sheet to make 3 moulds for the loaves. Place the breads between the pleats of the towel, to help hold their shape while rising. Cover with lightly oiled clear film and leave to rise, in a warm place, for about 45–60 minutes.

6 Meanwhile, preheat the oven to maximum, at least 230°C/450°F/Gas 8. Roll the loaves on to a baking sheet, spaced well apart. Using a sharp knife, slash the top of each loaf several times with long diagonal slits. Place at the top of the oven, spray the inside of the oven with water and bake the dough for 20–25 minutes, or until golden. Spray the oven twice more during the first 5 minutes of baking. Transfer the baguettes to a wire rack to cool.

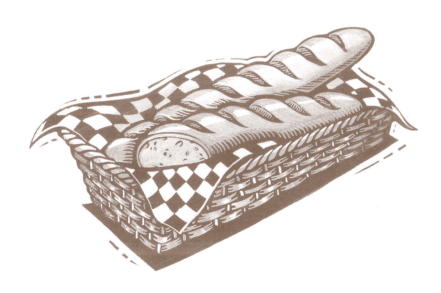

PAIN DE CAMPAGNE RUSTIQUE

This superb country bread is made using a natural French chef starter to produce a rustic flavour and texture. Making it is time-consuming but well worth the effort.

MAKES 1 LOAF

INGREDIENTS

FOR THE CHEF
50g/2oz/½ cup wholemeal (whole-wheat) bread flour
45ml/3 tbsp warm water

FOR THE 1ST REFRESHMENT
60ml/4 tbsp warm water
75g/3oz/¾ cup wholemeal (whole-wheat) bread flour

FOR THE 2ND REFRESHMENT
120ml/4fl oz/½ cup lukewarm water
115g/4oz/1 cup unbleached white bread flour
25g/1oz/¼ cup wholemeal (whole-wheat) bread flour

FOR THE DOUGH
150–175ml/5–6fl oz/⅔–¾ cup lukewarm water
350g/12oz/3 cups unbleached white bread flour
10ml/2 tsp salt

> ### COOK'S TIP
> *You will need to start making this bread about four days before you'd like to eat it.*

1 To make the chef, place the flour in a small bowl, add the water and knead for 3–4 minutes to form a dough. Cover with clear film (plastic wrap) and leave the chef in a warm place for 2 days.

2 Pull off the hardened crust and discard, then remove 30ml/2 tbsp of the moist centre. Place in a large bowl and gradually mix in the water for the first refreshment. Gradually mix in the flour and knead for 3–4 minutes to form a dough or *levain*, then cover with clear film and leave in a warm place for 1 day.

3 Discard the crust from the levain and gradually mix in the water for the second refreshment. Mix in the flours a little at a time, mixing well after each addition to form a firm dough. Cover with lightly oiled clear film and leave to rise, in a warm place, for about 10 hours, or until doubled in bulk.

4 For the final stage in the preparation of the dough, gradually mix the water into the *levain* in the bowl, then gradually mix in the flour, then the salt. Knead the dough on a lightly floured surface for about 5 minutes until smooth and elastic.

5 Place the dough in a large lightly oiled mixing bowl, cover with oiled clear film and leave to rise, in a warm place, for 1½–2 hours, or until the dough has almost doubled in bulk.

6 Knock back (punch down) the dough and cut off 115g/4oz/½ cup. Set aside for making the next loaf. Shape the remaining dough into a ball – you should have about 350g/12oz/1½ cups.

7 Line a 10cm/4in high, 23cm/9in round basket or large bowl with a dish towel and dust with flour. Place the dough ball seam side up in the prepared basket or bowl. Cover with lightly oiled clear film and leave to rise, in a warm place, for 2–3 hours, or until almost doubled in bulk.

8 Preheat the oven to 230°C/450°F/Gas 8. Invert the loaf on to a lightly floured baking sheet and sprinkle with flour. Slash the top of the loaf, using a sharp knife, four times at right angles to each other, to form a square pattern. Sprinkle with a little more flour, if you like, then bake for 30–35 minutes, or until the loaf has browned and sounds hollow when tapped on the base. Transfer to a wire rack to cool. Note: the reserved piece of dough becomes the starter for your next loaf. Use it for the second refreshment in place of the *levain* in step 3.

SAVOURY BREADS

For many years the bit players on the culinary stage, breads now often play a leading role. When a simple salad is served with a delicious savoury loaf, the bread gets at least as much attention as the tossed leaves, and adds substance, a variation in texture and extra flavour to what is essentially a light meal. Ciabatta and Focaccia are as popular at home as they are in the restaurants that have promoted them to their current status. Neither loaf is difficult to make, once you've mastered the basic techniques explained in detail at the start of this book. Taking the time and trouble to make Cheese and Onion Loaf or Corn Bread for your guests is a real compliment, and the wonderful aroma as the bread bakes is a great way of stimulating their appetite.

PROSCIUTTO LOAF

This savoury Italian bread from Parma is spiked with the local dried ham.
Just a small amount fills the loaf with marvellous flavour.

MAKES 1 LOAF

INGREDIENTS
350g/12oz/3 cups unbleached white bread flour
7.5ml/1½ tsp salt
15g/½oz fresh yeast
250ml/8fl oz/1 cup lukewarm water
40g/1½oz prosciutto, torn into small pieces
5ml/1 tsp freshly ground black pepper

VARIATIONS
• *To make pesto bread, spread 45ml/3 tbsp pesto over the flattened dough in step 6, then continue as above.*
• *For sweet pepper bread, add 45ml/3 tbsp finely chopped roasted yellow and red (bell) peppers instead of the ham in step 4.*

1 Lightly grease a baking sheet. Sift the flour and salt together into a large bowl and make a well in the centre. Cream the yeast with 30ml/2 tbsp of the water, then gradually mix in the rest. Pour into the centre of the flour.

2 Gradually beat in most of the flour with a wooden spoon to make a batter. Beat gently to begin with and then more vigorously as the batter thickens. After most of the flour has been incorporated, beat in the remainder with your hand to form a moist dough.

3 Knead on a lightly floured surface for 5 minutes until smooth and elastic. Place in a lightly oiled bowl, cover with lightly oiled clear film (plastic wrap), and leave to rise, in a warm place, for 1½ hours, or until doubled in bulk.

4 Turn out the dough on to a lightly floured surface, knock back (punch down) and then knead for 1 minute. Flatten to a round, then sprinkle with half the prosciutto and pepper. Fold the dough in half and repeat with the remaining ham and pepper. Roll up, tucking in the sides.

5 Place on the prepared baking sheet, cover with lightly oiled clear film, and leave to rise, in a warm place, for about 30 minutes. On a lightly floured surface, roll into an oval, fold in half and seal the edges. Flatten and fold again. Seal and fold again to make a long loaf.

6 Roll into a stubby long loaf. Draw out the edges by rolling the dough under the palms of your hands. Place on the baking sheet, cover with lightly oiled clear film and leave to rise, in a warm place, for 45 minutes, or until the loaf has doubled in size. Meanwhile, preheat the oven to 200°C/400°F/Gas 6.

7 Slash the top of the loaf diagonally three or four times, using a sharp knife, and bake for 30 minutes, or until golden. Cool on a wire rack.

Cheese & Onion Loaf

Almost a meal in itself, this hearty bread tastes delicious as an accompaniment to salads and cold meats, or eat it with soup.

Makes 1 large loaf

Ingredients

45g/1¾oz/3½ tbsp butter
1 onion, finely chopped
450g/1lb/4 cups unbleached white bread flour
7g/¼oz sachet easy-blend (rapid-rise) dried yeast
5ml/1 tsp mustard powder
175g/6oz/1½ cups grated mature Cheddar cheese
150ml/¼ pint/⅔ cup lukewarm milk
150ml/¼ pint/⅔ cup lukewarm water
salt and ground black pepper

1 Lightly grease a 25 × 10cm/10 × 4in loaf pan. Melt 25g/1oz/2 tbsp of the butter in a frying pan and sauté the onion until it is soft. Set aside to cool.

2 Sift the flour into a large bowl and stir in the yeast, mustard, salt and pepper. Stir in three-quarters of the grated cheese and the onion. Make a well in the centre. Add the milk and water; blend to a soft dough.

3 Turn out on to a lightly floured surface and knead for 10 minutes until smooth and elastic. Place the dough in a lightly oiled bowl, cover with lightly oiled clear film (plastic wrap) and leave to rise, in a warm place, for 45–60 minutes, or until doubled in bulk.

4 Turn the dough out on to a lightly floured surface, knock back (punch down), and knead gently. Divide into 20 equal pieces and shape into small rounds. Place half in the prepared tin and brush with some melted butter. Top with the remaining rounds of dough and brush with the remaining butter.

5 Cover with oiled clear film and leave to rise for 45 minutes, until the dough reaches the top of the tin. Meanwhile, preheat the oven to 190°C/375°F/Gas 5. Sprinkle the remaining cheese over the top. Bake for 40–45 minutes or until risen and golden brown. Cool on a wire rack.

Russian Potato Bread

In Russia, potatoes are often used to replace some of the flour in bread recipes.
They endow the bread with excellent keeping qualities.

Makes 1 loaf

Ingredients
225g/8oz potatoes, peeled and diced
7g/¼oz sachet easy-blend (rapid-rise) dried yeast
350g/12oz/3 cups unbleached white bread flour
115g/4oz/1 cup wholemeal (whole-wheat) bread flour, plus extra for sprinkling
2.5ml/½ tsp caraway seeds, crushed
10ml/2 tsp salt
25g/1oz/2 tbsp butter

1 Lightly grease a baking sheet. Add the potatoes to a pan of boiling water and cook until tender. Drain and reserve 150ml/¼ pint/⅔ cup of the cooking water. Mash and sieve the potatoes and leave to cool.

2 Mix the yeast, bread flours, caraway seeds and salt together in a large bowl. Add the butter and rub in. Mix the reserved potato water and sieved potatoes together. Gradually work this mixture into the flour mixture to form a soft dough.

3 Knead on a lightly floured surface for 8–10 minutes until smooth and elastic. Place in a lightly oiled bowl, cover with lightly oiled clear film (plastic wrap), and leave to rise, in a warm place, for 1 hour, or until doubled in bulk.

4 Turn out on to a lightly floured surface, knock back (punch down) and knead gently. Shape into a plump oval loaf, about 18cm/7in long. Place on the prepared baking sheet and sprinkle with a little wholemeal bread flour.

5 Cover the dough with lightly oiled clear film and leave to rise, in a warm place, for 30 minutes, or until doubled in size. Meanwhile, preheat the oven to 200°C/400°F/Gas 6.

6 Using a sharp knife, slash the top with 3–4 diagonal cuts to make a criss-cross effect. Bake for 30–35 minutes, or until golden and sounding hollow when tapped on the base. Transfer to a wire rack to cool.

CIABATTA

This irregular-shaped Italian bread is so called because it looks like an old shoe or slipper. It is made with a very wet dough flavoured with olive oil; cooking produces a bread with holes and a wonderfully chewy crust.

MAKES 3 LOAVES

INGREDIENTS

FOR THE *BIGA* STARTER
7g/¼oz fresh yeast
175–200ml/6–7fl oz/¾–scant 1 cup lukewarm water
350g/12oz/3 cups unbleached plain (all-purpose) flour, plus extra for dusting

FOR THE DOUGH
15g/½oz fresh yeast
400ml/14fl oz/1⅔ cups lukewarm water
60ml/4 tbsp lukewarm milk
500g/1¼lb/5 cups unbleached white bread flour
10ml/2 tsp salt
45ml/3 tbsp extra virgin olive oil

> ### VARIATION
> To make tomato-flavoured ciabatta, add 115g/4oz/ 1 cup chopped, drained sun-dried tomatoes in olive oil. Add with the olive oil in step 5.

1 Cream the yeast for the *biga* starter with a little of the water. Sift the flour into a large bowl. Gradually mix in the yeast mixture and sufficient of the remaining water to form a firm dough.

2 Turn out the *biga* starter dough on to a lightly floured surface and knead for about 5 minutes until smooth and elastic. Return the dough to the bowl, cover with lightly oiled clear film (plastic wrap), and leave in a warm place for 12–15 hours, or until the dough has risen and is starting to collapse.

3 Sprinkle three baking sheets with flour. Mix the yeast for the dough with a little of the water until creamy, then mix in the remainder. Add the yeast mixture to the *biga* and gradually mix in.

4 Mix in the milk, beating thoroughly with a wooden spoon. Using your hand, gradually beat in the flour, lifting the dough as you mix. Mixing the dough will take 15 minutes or more. The mixture that forms will be very wet, impossible to knead on a work surface.

5 Beat in the salt and olive oil. Cover with lightly oiled clear film and leave to rise, in a warm place, for 1½–2 hours, or until doubled in bulk.

6 Using a spoon, carefully tip one-third of the dough at a time on to the prepared baking sheets, trying to avoid knocking back (punching down) the dough.

7 Using floured hands, shape into rough oblong loaf shapes, about 2.5cm/1in thick. Flatten slightly with splayed fingers. Sprinkle with flour and leave to rise in a warm place for 30 minutes.

8 Meanwhile, preheat the oven to 220°C/425°F/Gas 7. Bake for 25–30 minutes, or until golden brown and sounding hollow when tapped on the base. Transfer the cooked loaves to a wire rack to cool.

FOCACCIA

This simple dimple-topped Italian flat bread is punctuated with olive oil and the aromatic flavours of sage and garlic to produce a truly succulent loaf.

MAKES 2 ROUND LOAVES

INGREDIENTS
20g/¾oz fresh yeast
325–350ml/11–12fl oz/1⅓–1½ cups lukewarm water
45ml/3 tbsp extra virgin olive oil
500g/1¼lb/5 cups unbleached white bread flour
10ml/2 tsp salt
15ml/1 tbsp chopped fresh sage

FOR THE TOPPING
60ml/4 tbsp extra virgin olive oil
4 garlic cloves, chopped
12 fresh sage leaves

> ### VARIATION
> *Flavour the bread with other fresh herbs, such as oregano, basil, thyme or rosemary and top with chopped black olives.*

1 Lightly oil 2 × 25cm/10in shallow round cake pans or pizza pans. Cream the yeast with 60ml/4 tbsp of the water, then stir in the remaining water. Stir in the extra virgin olive oil.

2 Sift the flour and salt together into a large bowl and make a well in the centre. Pour the yeast mixture into the well in the centre of the flour and mix well, gradually incorporating the surrounding flour to make a soft dough.

3 Turn out the dough on to a lightly floured surface and knead for 8–10 minutes until smooth and elastic. Place in a lightly oiled bowl, cover with lightly oiled clear film (plastic wrap), and leave to rise, in a warm place, for about 1–1½ hours, or until the dough has doubled in bulk.

4 Knock back (punch down) the dough and turn out on to a lightly floured surface. Gently knead in the chopped sage. Divide the dough into two equal pieces. Shape each into a ball, roll out into 25cm/10in circles and place in the prepared pans. Cover with lightly oiled clear film and leave to rise in a warm place for about 30 minutes.

5 Remove the clear film from both focaccia and, using your fingertips, poke the dough to make deep dimples over the entire surface. Replace the clear film cover and leave to rise until doubled in bulk.

6 Meanwhile, preheat the oven to 200°C/400°F/Gas 6. Drizzle over the olive oil for the topping and sprinkle each focaccia evenly with chopped garlic. Dot the sage leaves over the surface. Bake for 25–30 minutes, or until both loaves are golden. Immediately remove the focaccia from the pans and transfer them to a wire rack to cool slightly. These loaves are best served warm.

SUN-DRIED TOMATO BRAID

Parmesan cheese, pesto and sun-dried tomatoes give this attractive loaf an excellent flavour.

MAKES 1 LOAF

INGREDIENTS
225g/8oz/2 cups wholemeal (whole-wheat) flour
225g/8oz/2 cups strong white flour
5ml/1 tsp salt
1.5ml/¼ tsp ground black pepper
10ml/2 tsp easy-blend (rapid-rise) dried yeast
25g/1oz/⅓ cup grated Parmesan cheese
30ml/2 tbsp red pesto
115g/4oz/⅔ cup drained sun-dried tomatoes in oil, chopped, plus 15ml/1 tbsp oil
  from the jar
300ml/½ pint/1¼ cups hand-hot water
5ml/1 tsp coarse sea salt, for sprinkling

1 Sift the wholemeal and the strong white flour into a mixing bowl, then tip in any bran remaining in the sieve. Stir in the salt, pepper and easy-blend dried yeast. Make a well in the centre and add the grated Parmesan, red pesto and chopped sun-dried tomatoes (with the oil). Stir in enough of the hand-hot water to make a soft dough.

2 Knead the dough on a lightly floured surface for 10 minutes, until smooth and elastic. Divide into 3 equal pieces and roll each to a 33cm/13in long "sausage". Dampen the ends of the "sausages". Press them together at one end, braid them loosely, then press them together at the other end to give a neat finish. Lightly grease a large baking sheet.

3 Place the loaf on the baking sheet, cover with lightly oiled clear film (plastic wrap) and leave to rise in a warm place for 1 hour, or until doubled in bulk. Preheat the oven to 220°C/425°F/Gas 7.

4 Sprinkle the braid with the coarse sea salt. Bake for 10 minutes, then lower the oven temperature to 200°C/400°F/Gas 6. Bake for 15–20 minutes more, or until the loaf sounds hollow when rapped underneath. Cool on a wire rack.

PORTUGUESE CORN BREAD

This tempting bread has a hard crust with a moist, mouthwatering crumb. It slices beautifully, and tastes wonderful served simply with cheese.

MAKES 1 LARGE LOAF

INGREDIENTS
20g/¾oz fresh yeast
250ml/8fl oz/1 cup lukewarm water
225g/8oz/2 cups maize flour (corn meal)
450g/1lb/4 cups unbleached white bread flour
150ml/¼ pint/⅔ cup lukewarm milk
30ml/2 tbsp olive oil
7.5ml/1½ tsp salt
polenta, for dusting

1 Dust a baking sheet with a little maize flour. Put the yeast in a large bowl and gradually mix in the lukewarm water until smooth. Stir in half the maize flour and 50g/2oz/½ cup of the white flour and mix to a batter. Cover the bowl with lightly oiled clear film (plastic wrap) and leave the batter in a warm place for 30 minutes, or until bubbles appear on the surface.

2 Stir in the milk, then the olive oil. Gradually mix in the remaining maize flour, flour and salt to form a pliable dough. Knead on a lightly floured surface for about 10 minutes until smooth and elastic.

3 Place in a lightly oiled bowl, cover with lightly oiled clear film and leave to rise, in a warm place, for 1½–2 hours, or until doubled in bulk.

4 Turn out the dough on to a lightly floured surface and knock back (punch down). Shape into a ball, flatten slightly and place on the baking sheet. Dust with polenta, cover with a large upturned bowl and leave to rise for 1 hour, or until doubled in size. Preheat the oven to 230°C/450°F/Gas 8.

5 Bake for 10 minutes, spraying the inside of the oven with water 2–3 times. Reduce the oven temperature to 190°C/375°F/Gas 5 and bake for a further 20–25 minutes, or until golden and sounding hollow when tapped on the base. Transfer to a wire rack to cool.

POLENTA BREAD

Polenta is widely used in Italian cooking. Here it is combined with pine nuts to make a truly Italian bread with a fantastic flavour.

MAKES 1 LOAF

INGREDIENTS
50g/2oz/½ cup polenta
300ml/½ pint/1¼ cups lukewarm water
15g/½oz fresh yeast
2.5ml/½ tsp clear honey
225g/8oz/2 cups unbleached white bread flour
25g/1oz/2 tbsp butter
45ml/3 tbsp pine nuts
7.5ml/1½ tsp salt

FOR THE TOPPING
1 egg yolk
15ml/1 tbsp water
pine nuts, for sprinkling

1 Lightly grease a baking sheet. Mix the polenta and 250ml/8fl oz/1 cup of the water together in a pan and slowly bring to the boil, stirring continuously with a large wooden spoon. Reduce the heat and simmer for 2–3 minutes, stirring occasionally. Set aside to cool for 10 minutes, or until just warm.

2 In a small bowl, mix the yeast with the remaining water and honey until creamy. Sift 115g/4oz/1 cup of the flour into a large bowl. Gradually beat in the yeast mixture, then gradually stir in the polenta mixture to combine. Turn out on to a lightly floured surface and knead for 5 minutes until smooth and elastic.

3 Cover the bowl with lightly oiled clear film (plastic wrap) or a lightly oiled polythene bag. Leave the dough to rise, in a warm place, for about 2 hours, or until it has doubled in bulk.

4 Meanwhile, melt the butter in a small pan, add the pine nuts and cook over a medium heat, stirring, until pale golden. Set aside to cool.

5 Add the remaining flour and the salt to the polenta dough and mix to a soft dough. Knead in the pine nuts. Turn out on to a lightly floured surface and knead for 5 minutes until smooth and elastic.

6 Place in a lightly oiled bowl, cover with lightly oiled clear film and leave to rise, in a warm place, for 1 hour, or until doubled in bulk.

7 Knock back (punch down) the dough and turn it out on to a lightly floured surface. Cut the dough into 2 equal pieces and roll each piece into a "sausage" about 38cm/15in long. Plait (braid) together and place on the prepared baking sheet. Cover with lightly oiled clear film and leave to rise, in a warm place, for 45 minutes. Meanwhile, preheat the oven to 200°C/400°F/Gas 6.

8 Mix the egg yolk and water and brush over the loaf. Sprinkle with pine nuts and bake for 30 minutes, or until golden and sounding hollow when tapped on the base. Cool on a wire rack.

OLIVE BREAD

Black and green olives and good-quality fruity olive oil combine to make this strongly flavoured and irresistible Italian bread.

MAKES 1 LOAF

INGREDIENTS
275g/10oz/2½ cups unbleached white bread flour
50g/2oz/½ cup wholemeal (whole-wheat) bread flour
7g/¼oz sachet easy-blend (rapid-rise) dried yeast
2.5ml/½ tsp salt
210ml/7½ fl oz/scant 1 cup lukewarm water
15ml/1 tbsp extra virgin olive oil, plus extra, for brushing
115g/4oz/1 cup pitted black and green olives, coarsely chopped

1 Lightly grease a baking sheet. Mix the unbleached white bread and wholemeal flours, easy-blend yeast and the salt together in a large bowl and make a well in the centre.

2 Add the water and oil to the centre of the flour and mix to a soft dough. Knead the dough on a lightly floured surface for 8–10 minutes until smooth and elastic. Place in a lightly oiled bowl, cover with lightly oiled clear film (plastic wrap). Leave to rise, in a warm place, for 1 hour, or until doubled in bulk.

3 Turn out on to a lightly floured surface and knock back (punch down). Flatten out and sprinkle over the olives. Fold up and knead to distribute the olives. Leave to rest for 5 minutes, then shape into an oval loaf. Place on the prepared baking sheet.

4 Make six deep cuts in the top of the loaf, and gently push the sections over. Cover with lightly oiled clear film and leave the loaf to rise, in a warm place, for 30–45 minutes, or until doubled in size.

5 Meanwhile, preheat the oven to 200°C/400°F/Gas 6. Brush the bread with olive oil and bake for 35 minutes. Transfer to a wire rack to cool.

SYRIAN ONION BREAD

The basic Arab breads of the Levant and Gulf have traditionally been made with
a finely ground wholemeal flour, but now are being made with white flour as well.

MAKES 8 BREADS

INGREDIENTS
450g/1lb/4 cups unbleached white bread flour
5ml/1 tsp salt
20g/¾oz fresh yeast
280ml/9fl oz/scant 1¼ cups lukewarm water

FOR THE TOPPING
60ml/4 tbsp finely chopped onion
5ml/1 tsp ground cumin
10ml/2 tsp ground coriander
10ml/2 tsp chopped fresh mint
30ml/2 tbsp olive oil

1 Lightly flour two baking sheets. Sift the flour and salt together into a large bowl and make a well in the centre. Cream the yeast with a little of the water, then mix in the remainder.

2 Add the yeast mixture to the centre of the flour and mix to a firm dough. Turn out on to a lightly floured surface and knead for 8–10 minutes until smooth and elastic. Place in a lightly oiled bowl, cover with lightly oiled clear film (plastic wrap), and leave to rise, in a warm place, for about 1 hour, or until doubled in bulk.

3 Knock back (punch down) the dough and turn out on to a lightly floured surface. Divide into eight equal pieces; roll into 13–15cm/5–6in rounds. Make them slightly concave. Prick all over and space well apart on the baking sheets. Cover with lightly oiled clear film and leave to rise for 15–20 minutes.

4 Meanwhile, preheat the oven to 200°C/400°F/Gas 6. Mix the chopped onion, ground cumin, ground coriander and chopped mint in a bowl. Brush the breads with the olive oil for the topping, sprinkle them evenly with the spicy onion mixture and bake for 15–20 minutes. Serve the onion breads warm.

FOUGASSE

A fougasse is a lattice-shaped, flattish loaf from the South of France. It can be cooked as a plain bread or flavoured with cheese, anchovies, herbs, nuts or olives. On Christmas Eve in Provence a sweet fougasse, flavoured with orange flower water, is part of a table centrepiece of thirteen desserts, symbolizing Christ and the Twelve Apostles and served to celebrate the Nativity.

MAKES 2 LOAVES

INGREDIENTS
450g/1lb/4 cups unbleached white bread flour
5ml/1 tsp salt
20g/³⁄₄oz fresh yeast
280ml/9fl oz/generous 1 cup lukewarm water
15ml/1 tbsp extra virgin olive oil

FOR THE FILLING
50g/2oz/¹⁄₃ cup Roquefort cheese, crumbled
40g/1¹⁄₂oz/¹⁄₃ cup walnut pieces, chopped
25g/1oz/2 tbsp drained, canned anchovy fillets, soaked in milk and drained again, chopped
olive oil, for brushing

VARIATIONS
- *Replace the cheese with 15ml/1 tbsp chopped fresh sage or thyme or 40g/1¹⁄₂oz/¹⁄₃ cup chopped pitted olives.*
- *To make a sweet fougasse, replace 15ml/1 tbsp of the water with orange flower water. Include 50g/2oz/¹⁄₃ cup chopped candied orange peel and 25g/1oz/2 tbsp sugar.*

1 Lightly grease 2 baking sheets. Sift the flour and salt together into a large bowl and make a well in the centre. In a measuring jug (cup), cream the yeast with 60ml/4 tbsp of the water. Pour the yeast mixture into the centre of the flour with the remaining water and the olive oil and mix to a soft dough.

2 Turn out on to a lightly floured surface. Knead the dough for 8–10 minutes until smooth and elastic. Place the dough in a lightly oiled bowl, cover with lightly oiled clear film (plastic wrap) and leave to rise, in a warm place, for about 1 hour, or until it has doubled in bulk.

3 Turn out on to a lightly floured surface and knock back (punch down) the dough. Divide into two equal pieces; flatten one piece of dough. Sprinkle over the cheese and walnuts and fold the dough over on itself 2–3 times to incorporate. Repeat with the remaining piece of dough, this time incorporating the anchovies. Shape each piece of flavoured dough into a ball.

4 Flatten each ball of dough and fold the bottom third up and the top third down, to make an oblong. Roll the cheese dough into a rectangle measuring about 28 × 15cm/11 × 6in. Using a sharp knife, make four diagonal cuts almost to the edge. Pull and stretch the dough evenly, so that it resembles a ladder.

5 Shape the anchovy dough into an oval with a flat base, about 25cm/10in long. Using a sharp knife, make three diagonal slits on each side towards the base, and pull to open the cuts. Transfer to the prepared baking sheets, cover with lightly oiled clear film and leave to rise, in a warm place, for about 30–45 minutes, or until nearly doubled in bulk.

6 Meanwhile, preheat the oven to 220°C/425°F/Gas 7. Brush both loaves with a little olive oil and bake for 25 minutes, or until golden. Place on a rack to cool.

FLATBREADS

Some of the world's most interesting breads are from India, and have come to the attention of the West largely as a result of the enormous popularity of Indian restaurants. The majority of these breads, as the chapter title suggests, are unleavened, but yeast is used in some cases to give a minor or major lift to items like Lavash, Naan and Indian Bhaturas. These breads, like Scottish bannocks and Italian piadine, are ideal for dipping or mopping up savoury sauces. They are also very sociable foods, since it is usual for guests to share one or two loaves, tearing off portions as they are needed. Some flatbreads – notably pitta and tortillas – are also used as wrappers for all sorts of savoury fillings, making eating easy as well as immensely pleasurable.

TANDOORI ROTIS

There are numerous varieties of bread in India, most of them unleavened. This one, as its name suggests, would normally be baked in a tandoor – a clay oven which is heated with charcoal or wood. The oven becomes extremely hot, cooking the bread in minutes. A conventional oven also gives good results.

MAKES 6 ROTIS

INGREDIENTS
350g/12oz/3 cups atta or fine wholemeal (whole-wheat) flour
5ml/1 tsp salt
250ml/8fl oz/1 cup water
30–45ml/2–3 tbsp melted ghee or butter, for brushing

1 Sift the flour and salt into a large bowl. Add the water and mix to a soft dough. Knead on a lightly floured surface for 3–4 minutes until smooth. Place in a lightly oiled bowl, cover with lightly oiled clear film (plastic wrap) and leave to rest for 1 hour.

2 Turn out on to a lightly floured surface. Divide the dough into six pieces and shape each piece into a ball. Press each out into a larger round with the palm of your hand, cover with lightly oiled clear film and leave to rest for 10 minutes.

3 Preheat the oven to 230°C/ 450°F/Gas 8. Place three baking sheets in the oven to heat. Roll the rotis into 15cm/6in rounds, place two on each baking sheet and bake for 8–10 minutes. The rotis are ready when light brown bubbles appear on the surface. Brush with ghee or butter and serve warm.

RED LENTIL DOSAS

Dosas and idlis are the breads of southern India. They are very different from traditional north Indian breads as they are made from lentils or beans and rice rather than flour. Dosas are more like pancakes; they are eaten freshly cooked, often at breakfast time, with a spicy fruit chutney.

MAKES 6 DOSAS

INGREDIENTS
150g/5oz/³⁄₄ cup long grain rice
50g/2oz/¹⁄₄ cup red lentils
250ml/8fl oz/1 cup warm water
5ml/1 tsp salt
2.5ml/¹⁄₂ tsp ground turmeric
2.5ml/¹⁄₂ tsp freshly ground black pepper
30ml/2 tbsp chopped fresh coriander (cilantro)
oil, for frying and drizzling

1 Place the rice and lentils in a bowl, pour over the water, cover and leave in a cool place to soak for 8 hours.

2 Drain off the water and reserve. Place the rice and lentils in a food processor and blend until smooth. Blend in the reserved water. Scrape into a bowl, cover with clear film (plastic wrap) and leave in a warm place to ferment for about 24 hours.

3 Stir in the salt, turmeric, pepper and coriander. Heat a heavy frying pan over a medium heat for a few minutes until hot. Smear with oil and add about 30–45ml/2–3 tbsp batter.

4 Using the rounded bottom of a soup spoon, gently spread the batter out, using a circular motion, to make a 15cm/6in diameter dosa.

5 Cook for 1½–2 minutes, or until set. Drizzle a little oil over the dosa and around the edges. Turn over and cook for about 1 minute, or until golden. Keep warm in a low oven in a dish set in a pan of simmering water while cooking the remaining dosas. Serve the dosas warm.

INDIAN BHATURAS

These light, fluffy leavened breads, made with semolina and flour and flavoured with butter and yogurt, taste delicious served warm.

MAKES 10 BHATURAS

INGREDIENTS
15g/½oz fresh yeast
5ml/1 tsp sugar
120ml/4fl oz/½ cup lukewarm water
200g/7oz/1¾ cups plain (all-purpose) flour
50g/2oz/½ cup semolina
2.5ml/½ tsp salt
15g/½oz/1 tbsp butter or ghee
30ml/2 tbsp natural (plain) yogurt
oil, for frying

1 Mix the yeast with the sugar and water in a jug (pitcher). Sift the flour into a large bowl and stir in the semolina and salt. Rub in the butter or ghee. Add the yeast mixture and yogurt and mix to a dough. Turn out on to a lightly floured surface and knead for 10 minutes until smooth and elastic.

2 Place in a lightly oiled bowl, cover with lightly oiled clear film (plastic wrap) and leave to rise, in a warm place, for about 1 hour, or until doubled in bulk. Turn out on to a lightly floured surface and knock back (punch down). Divide into 10 equal pieces and shape each one into a ball. Flatten into discs with the palm of your hand. Roll out on a lightly floured surface into 13cm/5in rounds.

3 Heat oil to a depth of 1cm/½in in a deep frying pan and slide one bhatura into the oil. Fry for about 1 minute, turning over after 30 seconds, then drain on kitchen paper. Keep warm while frying the remaining bhaturas. Serve warm.

COOK'S TIP
Ghee is easy to make at home. Melt unsalted (sweet) butter in a heavy pan over a low heat. Simmer very gently until the residue changes to a light golden colour, then cool. Strain through muslin before using.

CHAPATIS

These chewy, unleavened breads are eaten throughout Northern India. They are usually served as an accompaniment to spicy dishes.

MAKES 6 CHAPATIS

INGREDIENTS
175g/6oz/1½ cups atta or wholemeal (whole-wheat) flour
2.5ml/½ tsp salt
100–120ml/scant 4fl oz/scant ½ cup water
5ml/1 tsp vegetable oil
melted ghee or butter, for brushing (optional)

1 Sift the flour and salt into a bowl. Add the water and mix to a soft dough. Knead in the oil, then turn out on to a lightly floured surface.

2 Knead for 5–6 minutes until smooth. Place in a lightly oiled bowl, cover with a damp dishtowel and leave to rest for 30 minutes. Turn out on to a floured surface. Divide the dough into 6 equal pieces. Shape each piece into a ball.

3 Press the dough into a larger round with the palm of your hand, then roll into a 13cm/5in round. Layer between clear film (plastic wrap), to keep moist.

4 Heat a griddle or heavy frying pan over a medium heat for a few minutes until hot. Take one chapati, brush off any excess flour, and place on the griddle. Cook for 30–60 seconds, or until the top begins to bubble and white specks appear on the underside.

5 Turn the chapati over using a metal spatula and cook for a further 30 seconds. Remove from the pan and keep warm, layered between a folded dishtowel, while cooking the remaining chapatis. If you like, the chapatis can be brushed lightly with melted ghee or butter immediately after cooking. Serve warm.

COOK'S TIP
Atta or ata is a very fine wholemeal flour, which is only found in Indian stores and supermarkets. It is sometimes simply labelled chapati flour.

Naan

Leavened breads such as naan are served from the Caucasus through the Punjab region of northwest India and beyond. Traditionally cooked in a very hot clay oven known as a tandoor, naan are usually eaten with dry meat or vegetable dishes, such as tandoori. There are many different variations.

MAKES 3 NAAN

INGREDIENTS
225g/8oz/2 cups unbleached white bread flour
2.5ml/½ tsp salt
15g/½oz fresh yeast
60ml/4 tbsp lukewarm milk
15ml/1 tbsp vegetable oil
30ml/2 tbsp natural (plain) yogurt
1 egg
30–45ml/2–3 tbsp melted ghee or butter, for brushing

COOK'S TIP
To help the naan dough to puff up and brown, place the baking sheets in an oven preheated to the maximum temperature for at least 10 minutes before baking to ensure that they are hot. Preheat the grill while the naan are baking, and have ready a clean dishtowel for wrapping the naan.

1 Sift the flour and salt together into a large bowl. In a smaller bowl, cream the yeast with the milk. Set aside for 15 minutes, then add the yeast mixture, oil, yogurt and egg to the flour and mix to a soft dough.

2 Turn out the dough on to a lightly floured surface and knead it for about 10 minutes until smooth and elastic. Place in a lightly oiled bowl, cover with lightly oiled clear film (plastic wrap) and leave to rise, in a warm place, for 45 minutes, or until doubled in bulk.

3 Preheat the oven to its highest setting, at least 230°C/450°F/Gas 8. Place three heavy baking sheets in the oven to heat.

4 Turn the dough out on to a lightly floured surface and knock back (punch down). Divide into 3 equal pieces and shape into balls.

5 Cover two of the balls of dough with oiled clear film and roll out the third into a teardrop shape about 25cm/10in long, 13cm/5in wide and with a thickness of about 5–8mm/¼–⅓in.

6 Preheat the grill (broiler) to its highest setting. Meanwhile, place the naan on the hot baking sheets and bake for 3–4 minutes, or until puffed up.

7 Remove the naan from the oven and place under the hot grill for a few seconds, or until the top of the naan browns slightly. Wrap the cooked naan in a dishtowel to keep warm while rolling out and cooking the remaining naan. Brush with melted ghee or butter and serve warm.

VARIATIONS
You can flavour naan in numerous different ways:
- *To make spicy naan, add 5ml/1 tsp each ground coriander and ground cumin to the flour in step 1. If you would like the naan to be extra fiery, add 2.5–5ml/½–1 tsp hot chilli powder.*
- *To make cardamom-flavoured naan, lightly crush the seeds from 4–5 green cardamom pods and add to the flour in step 1.*
- *To make poppy seed naan, brush the rolled-out naan with a little ghee and sprinkle with poppy seeds. Press lightly to make sure that they stick.*
- *To make onion-flavoured naan, add 114g/4oz/ ½ cup finely chopped or coarsely grated onion to the dough in step 1. You may need to reduce the amount of egg if the onion is very moist to avoid making the dough too soft.*

LAVASH

Thin and crispy, this flat bread is universally eaten throughout the Middle East. It is ideal for serving with soups and starters, and can be made in any size and broken into pieces as desired.

MAKES 10 LAVASH

INGREDIENTS
275g/10oz/2½ cups unbleached white bread flour
175g/6oz/1½ cups wholemeal (whole-wheat) flour
5ml/1 tsp salt
15g/½oz fresh yeast
250ml/8fl oz/1 cup lukewarm water
60ml/4 tbsp natural (plain) yogurt or milk

1 Sift the white and wholemeal flours and salt together into a large bowl and make a well in the centre. Mix the yeast with half the lukewarm water until creamy, then stir in the remaining water.

2 Add the yeast mixture and yogurt or milk to the centre of the flour and mix to a soft dough. Turn out on to a lightly floured surface and knead for about 8–10 minutes until smooth and elastic. Place in a lightly oiled bowl, cover with lightly oiled clear film (plastic wrap), and leave to rise, in a warm place, for about 1 hour, or until doubled in bulk. Knock back (punch down) the dough, re-cover with lightly oiled cling film and leave to rise for 30 minutes.

3 Return the dough to a lightly floured surface. Knock back gently and divide into 10 equal pieces. Shape into balls, then flatten into discs with the palm of your hand. Cover and leave to rest for 5 minutes. Meanwhile, preheat the oven to the maximum temperature – at least 230°C/450°F/Gas 8. Place three or four baking sheets in the oven to heat.

4 Roll the dough as thinly as possible, then lift it over the backs of your hands and gently stretch and turn the dough. Let rest in between rolling for a few minutes if necessary to avoid tearing. When they are ready, place four lavash on the baking sheets and bake for 6–8 minutes, or until starting to brown. (Layer the remaining uncooked lavash, between clear film, and cover, to keep moist.) Transfer to a wire rack to cool and cook the remaining lavash.

Wheat Tortillas

Tortillas are the staple flatbread in Mexico, where they are often made from masa harina, a flour milled from corn. These soft wheat tortillas are also popular in the south-western states of the United States.

Makes 12 tortillas

Ingredients
225g/8oz/2 cups unbleached plain (all-purpose) flour
5ml/1 tsp salt
4ml/¾ tsp baking powder
40g/1½oz/3 tbsp lard (shortening) or vegetable fat
150ml/¼ pint/⅔ cup warm water

1 Mix the flour, salt and baking powder in a bowl. Rub in the fat, stir in the water and knead lightly to a soft dough. Cover with clear film (plastic wrap) and leave to rest for 15 minutes.

2 Divide the dought into 12 equal pieces and shape into balls. Roll out on a lightly floured surface into 15–18cm/6–7in rounds. Cover closely with clear film to keep moist.

3 Heat a heavy frying pan or griddle, add one tortilla and cook for about 1½–2 minutes, turning over as soon as the surface starts to bubble. It should stay flexible. Remove from the pan and wrap in a dishtowel to keep warm while cooking the remaining tortillas in the same way.

Cook's Tips
- Tortillas are delicious either as an accompaniment or filled with roast chicken or cooked minced (ground) meat, refried beans and/or salad to serve as a snack or light lunch.
- To reheat tortillas that have been allowed to cool, wrap in foil and warm in a moderate oven, 180°C/350°F/Gas 4, for about 5 minutes.

BARLEY BANNOCK

Bannocks are flat loaves about the size of a dinner plate. They are traditionally baked on a griddle or girdle (which is the preferred name in Scotland). Barley flour adds a wonderfully earthy flavour to the bread.

MAKES 1 ROUND LOAF

INGREDIENTS
115g/4oz/1 cup barley flour
50g/2oz/½ cup unbleached plain (all-purpose) flour or wholemeal
   (whole-wheat) flour
2.5ml/½ tsp salt
2.5ml/½ tsp cream of tartar
25g/1oz/2 tbsp butter or margarine
175ml/6fl oz/¾ cup buttermilk
2.5ml/½ tsp bicarbonate of soda (baking soda)

1 Wipe the surface of a griddle with a little vegetable oil. Sift the flours, salt and cream of tartar together into a large bowl. Add the butter or margarine and rub into the flour until it resembles fine breadcrumbs.

2 Mix the buttermilk and bicarbonate of soda together. When the mixture starts to bubble add to the flour. Mix together to form a soft dough. Do not over-mix the dough or it will toughen.

3 On a floured surface pat the dough out to form a round about 2cm/¾in thick. Mark the dough into four wedges, using a sharp knife.

4 Heat the griddle until hot. Cook the bannock on the griddle for 8–10 minutes each side over a gentle heat. Do not cook too quickly or the outside will burn before the centre is cooked. Cool slightly on a wire rack and eat warm.

COOK'S TIP
If you cannot locate buttermilk, then use soured milk instead. Stir 5ml/1 tsp lemon juice into 175ml/ 6 fl oz/¾ cup milk and set aside for an hour to sour.

PIADINE

*These soft unleavened Italian breads, cooked directly on the hob, were originally
baked on a hot stone over an open fire. They are best eaten while still warm.
Try them as an accompaniment to soups and dips.*

MAKES 4 PIADINE

INGREDIENTS
175g/6oz/1½ cups unbleached white flour
5ml/1 tsp salt
15ml/1 tbsp olive oil
105ml/7 tbsp lukewarm water

1 Sift the unbleached white flour and salt together into a large bowl, and make a
well in the centre. Add the olive oil and lukewarm water to the well, and
gradually mix to a dough.

2 Knead on a lightly floured surface for 5 minutes until smooth and elastic. Place
in a lightly oiled bowl, cover with oiled clear film (plastic wrap) and leave to
rest for 20 minutes.

3 Heat a griddle over a medium heat. Divide the dough into four equal pieces
and roll each into an 18cm/7in round. Cover until ready to cook.

4 Oil the hot griddle, add one or two piadine and cook for about 2 minutes, or
until they are starting to brown. Turn the piadine over and cook for a further
1–1½ minutes. Serve warm.

COOK'S TIPS
- *If you don't have a griddle, a large heavy frying
pan will work just as well. Keep the cooked
piadine warm while cooking successive batches.*
- *Although not traditional in Italy, these flatbreads
can also be flavoured with herbs. Add 15ml/1 tbsp
of dried oregano. They also taste delicious made
with garlic- or chilli-flavoured olive oil.*

PITTA BREAD

These Turkish breads are a firm favourite in both the eastern Mediterranean and the Middle East, and have now crossed to England and the United States. The versatile soft, flatbread forms a pocket as it cooks, which is perfect for filling with vegetables, salads or meats, such as lamb kebabs.

MAKES 6 PITTA BREADS

INGREDIENTS
225g/8oz/2 cups unbleached white bread flour
5ml/1 tsp salt
15g/½oz fresh yeast
140ml/scant ¼ pint/scant ⅔ cup lukewarm water
10ml/2 tsp extra virgin olive oil

VARIATIONS
To make wholemeal (whole-wheat) pitta breads, replace half the white bread flour with wholemeal bread flour. You can also make smaller round pitta breads about 10cm/4in in diameter as snack breads. Cut in strips, they are very good to eat with dips.

1 Sift the flour and salt together into a bowl. Mix the yeast with the water until dissolved, then stir in the olive oil and pour into a large bowl.

2 Gradually beat the flour into the yeast mixture, then knead the mixture to make a soft dough.

3 Knead on a lightly floured surface for 5 minutes until smooth and elastic. Place in a large clean bowl, cover with lightly oiled clear film (plastic wrap) and leave to rise, in a warm place, for about 1 hour, or until doubled in bulk.

4 Knock back (punch down) the dough. On a lightly floured surface, divide it into six equal pieces and shape into balls. Cover with oiled clear film and leave the balls to rest for 5 minutes.

5 Roll out each ball of dough in turn to an oval about 5mm/¼in thick and 15cm/6in long. Place on a floured dishtowel and cover with lightly oiled clear film. Leave to rise at room temperature for 20–30 minutes.

6 Meanwhile, preheat the oven to 230°C/450°F/Gas 8. Place three baking sheets in the oven to heat at the same time.

7 Place two pitta breads on each baking sheet and bake for 4–6 minutes, or until puffed up; they do not need to brown. If preferred, cook the pitta bread in batches. It is important that the oven has reached the recommended temperature before the pitta breads are baked. This ensures that they puff up.

8 Transfer the pittas to a wire rack to cool until warm, then cover with a dishtowel to keep them soft.

Nut, Fruit & Herb Breads

It is only when you take a close look at the vast number of bread recipes there are that you really appreciate what a truly versatile food this is, and how varied are the potential flavourings. Nuts make an excellent addition to both sweet and savoury breads. In the French *Pain aux Noix*, for instance, walnut pieces add crunch to the crumb, while in the pale golden Cornish Saffron Bread, a subtle flavour is provided by the ground almonds that are added to the flour. Dried fruits are used even more frequently, contributing natural sweetness and moisture, especially when they have been macerated in a spirit such as rum. In savoury breads, herbs are perfect partners, as is evidenced in Dill Bread, Sage Soda Bread, Rosemary Bread, and the attractive Spiral Herb Bread.

PAIN AUX NOIX

This delicious wholemeal bread, enriched with butter and milk, is filled with walnuts. It is the perfect companion for cheese.

MAKES 2 LOAVES

INGREDIENTS
50g/2oz/¼ cup butter
350g/12oz/3 cups wholemeal (whole-wheat) bread flour
115g/4oz/1 cup unbleached white bread flour
15ml/1 tbsp light brown muscovado (molasses) sugar
7.5ml/1½ tsp salt
20g/¾oz fresh yeast
275ml/9fl oz/generous 1 cup lukewarm milk
175g/6oz/1½ cups walnut pieces

1 Grease two baking sheets. Melt the butter until it starts to turn brown, then cool. Mix the flours, sugar and salt in a bowl and make a well in the centre. Cream the yeast with half the milk. Pour into the well, with the remaining milk, then strain in the cool melted butter. Using your hand, mix the liquids together and gradually mix in the flour to make a batter and then a moist dough.

2 Knead on a lightly floured surface for 6–8 minutes. Place in a lightly oiled bowl, cover with lightly oiled clear film (plastic wrap), and leave to rise, in a warm place, for 1 hour, or until doubled in bulk.

3 Turn out the dough on to a lightly floured surface and gently knock back (punch down). Press or roll out to flatten, and then sprinkle over the nuts. Gently press the nuts into the dough, then roll it up. Return to the oiled bowl, re-cover and leave, in a warm place, for 30 minutes.

4 Turn out on to a lightly floured surface, divide in half and shape each piece into a ball. Place on the baking sheets, cover with lightly oiled clear film and leave to rise, in a warm place, for 45 minutes, or until doubled in bulk.

5 Meanwhile, preheat the oven to 220°C/425°F/Gas 7. Using a sharp knife, slash the top of each loaf three times. Bake for about 35 minutes, or until the loaves sound hollow when tapped on the base. Transfer to a wire rack to cool.

MALTED CURRANT BREAD

This spiced currant bread makes a good tea or breakfast bread, sliced and spread with a generous amount of butter. It also makes superb toast.

MAKES 2 LOAVES

INGREDIENTS
50g/2oz/3 tbsp malt extract
30ml/2 tbsp golden (light corn) syrup
50g/2oz/¼ cup butter
450g/1lb/4 cups unbleached white bread flour
5ml/1 tsp mixed (apple pie) spice
20g/¾oz fresh yeast
175ml/6fl oz/¾ cup lukewarm milk
175g/6oz/¾ cup currants, slightly warmed

FOR THE GLAZE
30ml/2 tbsp milk
30ml/2 tbsp caster (superfine) sugar

1 Lightly grease two 450g/1lb loaf pans. Place the malt extract, golden syrup and butter in a pan and heat gently until the butter has melted. Cool. Sift the flour and mixed spice into a large bowl, and make a well in the centre. Cream the yeast with a little of the milk, then blend in the remaining milk. Add to the flour with the malt mixture. Mix to a dough.

2 Knead the dough on a lightly floured surface for 10 minutes. Place in a lightly oiled bowl, cover with lightly oiled clear film (plastic wrap), and leave to rise, in a warm place, for 1½–2 hours, or until doubled in bulk.

3 Turn the dough out on to a lightly floured surface, knock back (punch down), then knead in the currants. Divide the dough in two and shape into two loaves. Place in the prepared pans. Cover with oiled clear film and leave to rise, in a warm place, for 2–3 hours, or until the dough reaches the top of the pans.

4 Preheat the oven to 200°C/400°F/Gas 6. Bake for 35–40 minutes or until golden. Heat the milk and sugar for the glaze in a small pan. Turn out the loaves, brush with the glaze and leave to cool.

WELSH BARA BRITH

This rich, fruity bread – the name literally means "speckled bread" – is a speciality from North Wales. The honey glaze makes a delicious topping.

MAKES 1 LARGE ROUND LOAF

INGREDIENTS
20g/³⁄₄oz fresh yeast
210ml/7fl oz/scant 1 cup lukewarm milk
450g/1lb/4 cups unbleached white bread flour
75g/3oz/6 tbsp butter or lard (shortening)
5ml/1 tsp mixed (apple pie) spice
2.5ml/½ tsp salt
50g/2oz/⅓ cup light brown sugar
1 egg, lightly beaten
115g/4oz/⅔ cup seedless raisins, slightly warmed
75g/3oz/scant ½ cup currants, slightly warmed
40g/1½oz/¼ cup mixed chopped (candied) peel
15–30ml/1–2 tbsp clear honey, for glazing

VARIATIONS
- If you prefer, the bara brith can be baked in a 1.5–1.75 litre/2½–3 pint/6¼–7½ cup loaf pan or a deep round or square cake pan.
- For a more wholesome loaf, replace half the white flour with wholemeal (whole-wheat) bread flour.

1 Grease a baking sheet. In a jug (pitcher), blend the yeast with a little of the milk, then stir in the remainder. Set aside for 10 minutes, until frothy.

2 Sift the flour into a large bowl and rub in the butter or lard until the mixture resembles breadcrumbs. Stir in the mixed spice, salt and light brown sugar, and make a well in the centre.

3 Add the yeast mixture and beaten egg to the centre of the flour. Gradually mix in the surrounding flour to make a rough dough.

4 Turn out the dough on to a lightly floured surface and knead for about 10 minutes until smooth and elastic. Place in a lightly oiled bowl, cover with lightly oiled clear film (plastic wrap), and leave to rise, in a warm place, for 1½ hours, or until doubled in bulk.

5 Turn out the dough on to a lightly floured surface, knock back (punch down), and knead in the dried fruits and peel. Shape into a round and place on the prepared baking sheet. Cover with oiled clear film and leave to rise, in a warm place, for 1 hour, or until the dough doubles in size.

6 Meanwhile, preheat the oven to 200°C/400°F/Gas 6. Bake for 30 minutes or until the bread sounds hollow when tapped on the base. If the bread starts to over-brown, cover it loosely with foil for the last 10 minutes. Transfer the bread to a wire rack, brush with honey and leave to cool.

MONKEY BREAD

This American favourite is also known as bubble bread. The pieces of dough are tossed in a heavenly coating of butter, nuts, cinnamon and rum-soaked fruit.

MAKES 1 LOAF

INGREDIENTS
450g/1lb/4 cups unbleached white bread flour
2.5ml/½ tsp salt
15ml/1 tbsp caster (superfine) sugar
7g/¼oz sachet easy-blend (rapid-rise) dried yeast
120ml/4fl oz/ ½ cup lukewarm milk
120ml/4fl oz/ ½ cup lukewarm water
1 egg, lightly beaten

FOR THE COATING
75g/3oz/ ½ cup sultanas (golden raisins)
45ml/3 tbsp rum or brandy
115g/4oz/1 cup walnuts, finely chopped
10ml/2 tsp ground cinnamon
115g/4oz/⅔ cup soft light brown sugar
50g/2oz/ ¼ cup butter, melted

> VARIATION
> *Replace the easy-blend dried yeast with 20g/¾oz fresh yeast. Mix with the liquid until creamy before adding to the flour.*

1 Lightly grease a 23cm/9in spring-form ring cake pan. Mix the flour, salt and caster sugar together in a large bowl, then stir in the dried yeast. Make a well in the centre.

2 Add the milk, water and egg to the centre of the flour, and mix together to a soft dough. Turn out on to a lightly floured surface, and knead for about 10 minutes until smooth and elastic. Place in a lightly oiled bowl, cover with lightly oiled clear film (plastic wrap) and leave to rise, in a warm place, for 45–60 minutes, or until doubled in bulk.

3 Place the sultanas in a small pan, pour over the rum or brandy and heat for 1–2 minutes, or until warm. Take care not to overheat. Remove from the heat and set aside. Mix the walnuts, cinnamon and sugar in a small bowl.

4 Turn out the dough on to a lightly floured surface and knead gently. Divide into 30 equal pieces and shape into small balls. Dip the balls, one at a time into the melted butter, then roll them in the walnut mixture. Place half in the prepared pan, spaced slightly apart. Sprinkle over all the soaked sultanas.

5 Top with the remaining dough balls, dipping and coating as before. Sprinkle over any remaining walnut mixture and melted butter. Cover with lightly oiled clear film or slide the pan into a lightly oiled polythene bag and leave to rise, in a warm place, for about 45 minutes, or until the dough reaches the top of the tin.

6 Meanwhile, preheat the oven to 190°C/375°F/Gas 5. Bake for 35–40 minutes, or until well risen and golden. Turn out on to a wire rack to cool.

CORNISH SAFFRON BREAD

Often called saffron cake, this light, delicately spiced bread contains strands of saffron and is made in a loaf pan. Whatever the name, the flavour and texture are superb. The simple milk and sugar glaze can be omitted, but it does give the loaves a lovely gloss.

MAKES 2 LOAVES

INGREDIENTS
300ml/½ pint/1¼ cups milk
2.5ml/½ tsp saffron strands
400g/14oz/3½ cups unbleached white bread flour
25g/1oz fresh yeast
50g/2oz/½ cup ground almonds
2.5ml/½ tsp grated nutmeg
2.5ml/½ tsp ground cinnamon
50g/2oz/¼ cup caster (superfine) sugar
2.5ml/½ tsp salt
75g/3oz/6 tbsp butter, softened
50g/2oz/⅓ cup sultanas (golden raisins)
50g/2oz/¼ cup currants

FOR THE GLAZE
30ml/2 tbsp milk
15ml/1 tbsp caster (superfine) sugar

1 Lightly grease two 900g/2lb loaf pans. Heat half the milk until almost boiling. Place the saffron strands in a small heatproof bowl and pour over the milk. Stir gently, then leave to infuse (steep) for 30 minutes.

2 Heat the remaining milk gently in the same pan until it is just lukewarm. Place 50g/2oz/½ cup flour in a small bowl, crumble in the yeast and stir in the milk. Mix well, then leave for about 15 minutes until frothy.

3 Mix the remaining flour, ground almonds, spices, sugar and salt together in a large bowl, and make a well in the centre. Add the saffron infusion, yeast mixture and softened butter to the centre of the flour and mix to a very soft dough.

4 Turn out on to a lightly floured surface and knead for 5 minutes until smooth and elastic. Place the dough in a lightly oiled bowl, cover with lightly oiled clear film (plastic wrap), and leave to rise, in a warm place, for 1½–2 hours, or until it has doubled in bulk.

5 Turn the dough out on to a lightly floured surface, knock back (punch down), and knead in the sultanas and currants. Divide in two and shape into two loaves. Place in the prepared pans. Cover with oiled clear film and leave to rise, in a warm place, for 1½ hours, or until the dough reaches the top of the pans.

6 Meanwhile, preheat the oven to 220°C/425°F/Gas 7. Bake the loaves for about 10 minutes, then reduce the oven temperature to 190°C/375°F/Gas 5 and bake for 15–20 minutes or until golden.

7 While the loaves are baking, make the glaze. Heat the milk and sugar in a small pan, stirring until the sugar has dissolved. As soon as the loaves come out of the oven, brush them with the glaze, leave in the pans for 5 minutes, then turn out on to a wire rack to cool.

DILL BREAD

Cottage cheese and eggs enrich the dough for this tasty bread, which owes its distinctive flavour to dill. It is delicious with sliced salmon or rollmop herrings.

MAKES 2 LOAVES

INGREDIENTS
60ml/4 tbsp olive oil
½ onion, chopped
800–900g/1¾–2lb/7–8 cups strong white bread flour
10ml/2 tsp salt
15ml/1 tbsp caster (superfine) sugar
2 × 7g/¼oz sachets easy-blend (rapid-rise) dried yeast
1 large bunch fresh dill, finely chopped
2 eggs, lightly beaten
115g/4oz/½ cup cottage cheese
475ml/16fl oz/2 cups hand-hot water
milk, for glazing

1 Heat 15ml/1 tbsp of the olive oil in a small frying pan and fry the onion until soft. Set aside to cool. Lightly grease a large baking sheet.

2 Combine the flour, salt, sugar and yeast in a large mixing bowl. Make a well in the centre and add the onion (with the cooking oil), dill, eggs, cottage cheese and remaining oil. Stir in enough of the hand-hot water to make a soft dough.

3 Knead the dough on a lightly floured surface for 5–8 minutes until smooth and elastic. Divide in half and shape each piece into a round.

4 Place the rounds of dough on the baking sheet, cover loosely with oiled clear film (plastic wrap), and leave to rise in a warm place for about 1 hour or until doubled in bulk. Preheat the oven to 190°C/375°F/Gas 5.

5 Score the tops of the loaves, glaze with milk and bake for about 45 minutes, until browned. Allow the loaves to cool slightly on a wire rack before serving.

SAGE SODA BREAD

Soda bread is quick and easy to make; perfect for impromptu picnics or suppers. This one is flecked with sage, but you could use another herb if you prefer.

MAKES 1 LOAF

INGREDIENTS
225g/8oz/2 cups wholemeal (whole-wheat) flour
115g/4oz/1 cup strong white bread flour
2.5ml/½ tsp salt
5ml/1 tsp bicarbonate of soda (baking soda)
30ml/2 tbsp shredded fresh sage leaves
300–450ml/½–¾ pint/1¼–1¾ cups buttermilk

1 Preheat the oven to 220°C/425°F/Gas 7. Lightly oil a baking sheet. Sift both types of flour into a bowl, then tip in any bran remaining in the sieve. Stir in the salt, bicarbonate of soda and shredded sage leaves.

2 Add enough of the buttermilk to make a soft dough, mixing just enough to combine the ingredients. Shape into a round and place on the baking sheet.

3 Cut a deep cross in the top of the loaf. Bake for 40 minutes, or until the loaf is well risen and sounds hollow when rapped underneath. Cool on a wire rack. Serve warm, with butter.

COOK'S TIP
Buttermilk is sold in cartons and is widely available from supermarkets. If you have difficulty locating it, however, you can substitute milk, soured with the addition of 15ml/1 tbsp lemon juice.

ROSEMARY BREAD

An unusual and very tasty bread, this tastes very good with chargrilled lamb chops.
Wrap the cooked loaf in foil and warm it at the side of the oven or barbecue.

MAKES 1 LOAF

INGREDIENTS
25g/1oz/2 tbsp butter
300ml/ ½ pint/1¼ cups milk
175g/6oz/1½ cups white self-raising (self-rising) flour
175g/6oz/1½ cups wholemeal (whole-wheat) flour
15ml/1 tbsp caster (superfine) sugar
5ml/1 tsp salt
10g/ ¼oz sachet easy-blend (rapid-rise) dried yeast
15ml/1 tbsp sesame seeds
15ml/1 tbsp dried chopped onion
15ml/1 tbsp chopped fresh rosemary leaves
115g/4oz/1 cup mature (sharp) Cheddar cheese, cubed
coarse sea salt and rosemary sprigs, to garnish

1 Add the butter to the milk in a small saucepan and allow to melt over a gentle heat. Allow the mixture to cool until hand-hot. Combine the self-raising and wholemeal flours with the sugar, salt and yeast in a large mixing bowl, and make a well in the centre.

2 Add the milk mixture, with the sesame seeds, dried chopped onion and rosemary leaves. Mix to a dough, then transfer to a lightly floured surface and knead for about 8 minutes, until smooth.

3 Flatten the dough, then add the cheese cubes, kneading them in until well distributed. Lightly grease a 450g/1lb loaf pan. Shape the dough into a loaf, place it in the pan and cover loosely. Leave to rise in a warm place for about 1 hour, until doubled in bulk. Preheat the oven to 190°C/375°F/Gas 5.

4 Bake the loaf for 30 minutes, covering it with foil towards the end of cooking if it starts to become too brown. Cool on a wire rack. Scatter coarse sea salt and a few rosemary sprigs on top, to serve.

Spiral Herb Bread

When you cut this bread you are in for a surprise. The spring onion, garlic and herb filling swirls attractively through every slice.

MAKES 2 LOAVES

INGREDIENTS
350g/12oz/3 cups strong white bread flour
350g/12oz/3 cups wholemeal (whole-wheat) flour
15ml/1 tbsp salt
2 × 7g/¼oz sachets easy-blend (rapid-rise) dried yeast
600ml/1 pint/2½ cups hand-hot water
25g/1oz/2 tbsp butter
1 bunch spring onions (scallions), finely chopped
1 garlic clove, crushed
1 large bunch fresh parsley, finely chopped
salt and ground black pepper
milk, for glazing

1 Sift the flours into a large mixing bowl, then stir in the salt and yeast. Make a well in the centre and add enough of the hand-hot water to make a rough dough. Knead on a lightly floured surface for about 10 minutes, until smooth.

2 Melt the butter in a small frying pan and fry the spring onions and garlic until soft. Stir in the chopped fresh parsley, with salt and pepper to taste.

3 Lightly grease two 450g/1lb loaf pans. Divide the dough in half. Roll out each piece in turn to a 35 × 23cm/14 × 9in rectangle. Spread each rectangle with half the herb mixture, taking it just to the edges of the dough.

4 Roll up each rectangle loosely from a short side. Pinch the ends of each roll to seal. Place each roll in a loaf pan, cover loosely with oiled clear film (plastic wrap), and leave to rise in a warm place for about 1 hour, until the loaves have doubled in bulk. Meanwhile, preheat the oven to 190°C/375°F/Gas 5.

5 Glaze the loaves with milk. Bake for about 50 minutes or until they are golden and sound hollow when rapped underneath. Cool on a wire rack.

SMALL BREADS

The cook's creativity is given full rein when it comes to making rolls, breadsticks, pretzels and the aptly named New England Fantans. Shaping these small breads is great fun, and excellent practice for making larger braids, batons and cottage loaves. Detailed instructions are given in the recipe for Shaped Dinner Rolls. Also in this chapter are several griddle cakes, including Scottish Oatcakes – a good choice for those who prefer to limit the amount of fat they consume – and Crumpets, although the latter are not quite such a healthy option, especially if you obey the injunction to serve them with lashings of butter. Making Pretzels could prove a knotty problem, but Grissini are very straightforward, and they taste truly delectable.

Scottish Morning Rolls

These rolls are best served warm, as soon as they are baked. In Scotland they are a firm favourite for breakfast and are often served with a fried egg and bacon.

Makes 10 rolls

Ingredients
450g/1lb/4 cups unbleached plain (all-purpose) white flour, plus extra for dusting
10ml/2 tsp salt
20g/¾oz fresh yeast
150ml/¼ pint/⅔ cup lukewarm milk
150ml/¼ pint/⅔ cup lukewarm water
30ml/2 tbsp milk, for glazing

1 Grease two baking sheets. Sift the flour and salt together into a large bowl and make a well in the centre. Mix the yeast with the milk, then mix in the water. Add to the centre of the flour and mix together to form a soft dough.

2 Knead the dough lightly in the bowl, shape into a round, then cover with lightly oiled clear film (plastic wrap). Leave to rise, in a warm place, for 1 hour, or until doubled in bulk. Turn the dough out on to a lightly floured surface and knock back (punch down).

3 Divide the dough into 10 equal pieces. Knead lightly and, using a rolling pin, shape each piece to a flat oval measuring 10 × 7.5cm/4 × 3in or a flat round with a diameter of 9cm/3½in.

4 Transfer to the prepared baking sheets, spaced well apart, and cover with oiled clear film. Leave to rise, in a warm place, for about 30 minutes.

5 Meanwhile, preheat the oven to 200°C/400°F/Gas 6. Press each roll in the centre with the three middle fingers to equalize the air bubbles and to help prevent blistering. Brush with milk and dust with flour. Bake for 15–20 minutes or until lightly browned. Dust with more flour and cool slightly on a wire rack. Serve the rolls warm.

Scottish Oatcakes

The crunchy texture of these tempting oatcakes makes them difficult to resist.
Serve solo, with butter or with a good, flavoursome cheese.

MAKES 8 OATCAKES

INGREDIENTS
115g/4oz/1 cup medium or fine oatmeal
1.5ml/¼ tsp salt
pinch of bicarbonate of soda (baking soda)
15ml/1 tbsp melted butter or lard (shortening)
45–60ml/3–4 tbsp hot water

1 Very lightly oil a griddle or heavy frying pan. Mix the oatmeal, salt and soda together in a bowl. Add the melted butter or lard and sufficient hot water to make a dough. Lightly knead on a surface dusted with oatmeal until it is smooth. Cut the dough in half.

2 On an oatmeal-dusted surface roll each piece of dough out as thinly as possible into a round about 15cm/6in across and 5mm/¼in thick. Cut each round into four quarters or farls. Heat the griddle over a medium heat until warm. Transfer four farls, using a metal spatula or fish slice, to the griddle and cook over a low heat for 4–5 minutes. The edges may start to curl.

3 Using the spatula or slice, carefully turn the farls over and cook for about 1–2 minutes. If preferred the second side can be cooked under a preheated grill (broiler) until crisp, but not brown. Transfer to a wire rack to cool. Repeat with the remaining farls.

COOK'S TIP
Oatcakes are traditionally cooked on the griddle, but they can also be cooked in the oven at 180°C/350°F/Gas 4 for about 20 minutes, or until pale golden in colour.

SHAPED DINNER ROLLS

These professional-looking rolls are perfect for entertaining. You can always make double the amount of dough and freeze half, tightly wrapped. Just thaw, glaze and bake as required.

MAKES 12 ROLLS

INGREDIENTS
450g/1lb/4 cups unbleached white bread flour
10ml/2 tsp salt
2.5ml/½ tsp caster (superfine) sugar
7g/¼oz sachet easy-blend (rapid-rise) dried yeast
50g/2oz/¼ cup butter or margarine
250ml/8fl oz/1 cup lukewarm milk
1 egg, beaten

FOR THE TOPPING
1 egg yolk
15ml/1 tbsp water
poppy seeds and sesame seeds, for sprinkling

1 Lightly grease two baking sheets. Sift the flour and salt together into a large bowl and stir in the sugar and yeast. Add the butter or margarine and rub in until the mixture resembles fine breadcrumbs.

2 Make a well in the centre. Add the milk and egg to the well and mix to a dough. Knead on a lightly floured surface for 10 minutes until smooth and elastic. Place in a lightly oiled bowl, cover with lightly oiled clear film (plastic wrap) and leave to rise, in a warm place, for 1 hour, or until doubled in bulk.

3 Turn the dough out on to a lightly floured surface, knock back (punch down) and knead for 2–3 minutes. Divide the dough into 12 equal pieces and shape into rolls as described in steps 4–8.

4 To make plaits (braids): divide each piece of dough into three equal pieces. Working on a lightly floured surface, roll each piece to a sausage, keeping the lengths and widths even. Pinch three strips together at one end. Plait them neatly but not too tightly. Pinch the ends together and tuck under the plait.

5 To make trefoils: divide each piece of dough into three and roll into balls. Place the three balls together in a triangular shape.

6 To make batons: shape each piece of dough into an oblong and slash the surface of each with diagonal cuts just before baking.

7 To make cottage rolls: divide each piece of dough into two-thirds and one-third and shape into rounds. Place the small one on top of the large one and make a hole through the centre with the floured handle of a wooden spoon.

8 To make knots: shape each piece of dough into a long roll and tie a single knot, pulling the ends through.

9 Place the dinner rolls on the prepared baking sheets, spacing them well apart, cover the rolls with oiled clear film and leave to rise, in a warm place, for about 30 minutes, or until doubled in bulk.

10 Meanwhile, preheat the oven to 220°C/425°F/Gas 7. Mix the egg yolk and water together for the glaze and brush over the rolls. Sprinkle some with poppy seeds and some with sesame seeds. Bake for 15–18 minutes or until golden. Lift the rolls off the sheet using a metal spatula, and transfer to a wire rack to cool.

CRUMPETS

Home-made crumpets are less doughy and not as heavy as most supermarket versions. Serve them lightly toasted, oozing with butter.

MAKES ABOUT 20 CRUMPETS

INGREDIENTS
225g/8oz/2 cups unbleached plain (all-purpose) flour
225g/8oz/2 cups unbleached white bread flour
10ml/2 tsp salt
600ml/1 pint/2½ cups milk and water mixed
30ml/2 tbsp sunflower oil
15ml/1 tbsp caster (superfine) sugar
15g/½oz fresh yeast
2.5ml/½ tsp bicarbonate of soda (baking soda)
120ml/4fl oz/½ cup lukewarm water

1 Lightly grease a griddle or heavy frying pan and four 8cm/3¼in plain pastry (cookie) cutters or crumpet rings.

2 Sift the flours and salt together into a large bowl and make a well in the centre. Heat the milk and water mixture, oil and sugar until lukewarm. Mix the yeast with 150ml/¼ pint/⅔ cup of this liquid.

3 Add the yeast mixture and remaining liquid to the centre of the flour and beat vigorously for about 5 minutes until smooth and elastic. Cover with lightly oiled clear film (plastic wrap) and leave to rise, in a warm place, for about 1½ hours, or until the mixture is bubbly and about to fall.

4 Dissolve the soda in the lukewarm water and stir into the batter. Re-cover and leave to rise for 30 minutes.

5 Place the cutters or crumpet rings on the griddle and warm over a medium heat. Fill the cutters or rings a generous 1cm/½in deep. Cook over a gentle heat for 6–7 minutes. The tops should be dry, with a mass of tiny holes.

6 Carefully remove the cutters or rings and turn the crumpets over. Cook for 1–2 minutes or until pale golden. Repeat with remaining batter. Serve warm.

ENGLISH MUFFINS

Perfect served warm, split open and buttered for afternoon tea; or try these favourites toasted, split and topped with ham and eggs for brunch.

MAKES 9 MUFFINS

INGREDIENTS
450g/1lb/4 cups unbleached white bread flour
7.5ml/1½ tsp salt
350–375ml/12–13fl oz/1½–1⅔ cups lukewarm milk
2.5ml/½ tsp caster (superfine) sugar
15g/½oz fresh yeast
15ml/1 tbsp melted butter or olive oil
rice flour or semolina, for dusting

1 Generously flour a non-stick baking sheet. Very lightly grease a griddle. Sift the flour and salt together into a large bowl and make a well in the centre. Blend 150ml/¼ pint/⅔ cup of the milk, sugar and yeast together. Stir in the remaining milk and butter or oil.

2 Add the yeast mixture to the centre of the flour and beat for 4–5 minutes until smooth and elastic. The dough will be soft but just hold its shape. Cover with lightly oiled clear film (plastic wrap) and leave to rise, in a warm place, for 45–60 minutes, or until doubled in bulk.

3 Turn out the dough on a well floured surface and knock back (punch down). Roll out evenly to about 1cm/½in thick. Using a floured 7.5cm/3in plain cutter, cut out 9 rounds. Dust with rice flour or semolina and place on the prepared baking sheet. Cover and leave to rise, in a warm place, for about 20–30 minutes.

4 Warm the griddle over a medium heat. Carefully transfer the muffins in batches to the griddle. Cook slowly for about 7 minutes on each side or until golden brown. Transfer to a wire rack to cool.

COOK'S TIP
If you'd like to serve the muffins warm, transfer them to a wire rack to cool slightly before serving.

PETIT PAIN AU LAIT

These classic French round milk rolls have a soft crust and a light, slightly sweet crumb. They won't last long!

MAKES 12 ROLLS

INGREDIENTS
450g/1lb/4 cups unbleached white bread flour
10ml/2 tsp salt
15ml/1 tbsp caster (superfine) sugar
50g/2oz/¼ cup butter, softened
15g/½oz fresh yeast
280ml/9fl oz/generous 1 cup lukewarm milk, plus 15ml/1 tbsp extra milk, for glazing

1 Lightly grease two baking sheets. Sift the flour and salt together into a large bowl. Stir in the sugar. Rub the softened butter into the flour. Cream the yeast with 60ml/4 tbsp of the milk. Stir in the remaining milk. Pour into the flour mixture and mix to a soft dough.

2 Knead on a lightly floured surface for 8–10 minutes until smooth and elastic. Place in a lightly oiled bowl, cover with lightly oiled clear film (plastic wrap) and leave to rise, in a warm place, for 1 hour, or until doubled in bulk.

3 Turn out the dough on to a lightly floured surface and gently knock back (punch down). Divide into 12 equal pieces. Shape into balls and space on the prepared baking sheets. Using a sharp knife, cut a cross in the top of each roll. Cover with lightly oiled clear film and leave to rise, in a warm place, for about 20 minutes, or until the rolls have doubled in size.

4 Preheat the oven to 200°C/400°F/Gas 6. Brush the rolls with milk and bake for 20–25 minutes, or until golden. Transfer to a wire rack to cool.

VARIATION
These can also be made into long rolls. To shape, flatten each ball of dough and fold in half. Roll back and forth to form a 13cm/5in long roll, tapered at either end. Slash the tops horizontally several times.

FRENCH DIMPLED ROLLS

A French and Belgian speciality, these attractive rolls are distinguished by the split down the centre. They have a crusty finish while remaining soft and light inside.

MAKES 10 ROLLS

INGREDIENTS
400g/14oz/3½ cups unbleached white bread flour
7.5ml/1½ tsp salt
5ml/1 tsp caster (superfine) sugar
15g/½oz fresh yeast
120ml/4fl oz/½ cup lukewarm milk
175ml/6fl oz/¾ cup lukewarm water

1 Lightly grease two baking sheets. Sift the flour and salt into a large bowl. Stir in the sugar and make a well in the centre. Cream the yeast with the milk until dissolved, then pour into the centre of the flour mixture. Sprinkle over a little of the flour from around the edge. Leave at room temperature for 15–20 minutes, or until the mixture starts to bubble.

2 Add the water and gradually mix in the flour to form a fairly moist, soft dough. Turn out on to a lightly floured surface and knead for 8–10 minutes until smooth and elastic. Place in a lightly oiled bowl, cover with lightly oiled clear film (plastic wrap) and leave to rise, at room temperature, for about 1½ hours, or until doubled in bulk.

3 Turn out on to a lightly floured surface and knock back (punch down). Re-cover and leave to rest for 5 minutes. Divide the dough into 10 pieces. Shape into balls by rolling the dough under a cupped hand, then roll until oval. Lightly flour the tops. Space well apart on the baking sheets, cover with lightly oiled clear film and leave to rise, at room temperature, for about 30 minutes, or until almost doubled in size.

4 Lightly oil the side of your hand and press the centre of each roll to make a deep split. Re-cover and leave to rest for 15 minutes. Meanwhile, place a roasting pan in the bottom of the oven and preheat the oven to 230°C/450°F/ Gas 8. Pour 250ml/8fl oz/1 cup water into the pan. Bake the rolls for 15 minutes, or until golden. Cool on a wire rack.

SESAME STUDDED GRISSINI

These crisp, pencil-like breadsticks are easy to make and far more delicious than the commercially manufactured grissini. Be warned, however. Once you start to nibble one, it could be very difficult to stop.

MAKES 20 GRISSINI

INGREDIENTS
225g/8oz/2 cups unbleached white bread flour
7.5ml/1½ tsp salt
15g/½oz fresh yeast
135ml/4½fl oz/scant ⅔ cup lukewarm water
30ml/2 tbsp extra virgin olive oil, plus extra for brushing
sesame seeds, for coating

1 Lightly oil two baking sheets. Sift the flour and salt together into a large bowl and make a well in the centre.

2 In a jug (pitcher), cream the yeast with the water. Pour into the centre of the flour, add the olive oil and mix to a soft dough. Turn out on to a lightly floured surface and knead for 8–10 minutes until smooth and elastic.

3 Roll the dough into a rectangle about 15 × 20cm/6 × 8in. Brush with olive oil, cover with lightly oiled clear film (plastic wrap), and leave to rise, in a warm place, for about 1 hour, or until doubled in bulk.

4 Preheat the oven to 200°C/400°F/Gas 6. Spread out the sesame seeds. Cut the dough in two 7.5 × 10cm/3 × 4in rectangles. Cut each piece into ten 7.5cm/3in strips. Stretch each strip gently until it is about 30cm/12in long.

5 Roll each grissini, as it is made, in the sesame seeds. Place the grissini on the prepared baking sheets, spaced well apart. Lightly brush with olive oil. Leave to rise, in a warm place, for 10 minutes.

6 Bake the grissini for 15–20 minutes turning over halfway through baking and changing the position of the baking sheets, so they brown evenly. Transfer to a wire rack to cool.

SAFFRON & BASIL BREADSTICKS

Saffron lends its delicate aroma and flavour, as well as its rich yellow colour, to these tasty breadsticks. They are delicious on their own, but taste even better with a dip, such as hummus or tzatziki.

MAKES 32 BREADSTICKS

INGREDIENTS
generous pinch of saffron threads
30ml/2 tbsp boiling water
450g/1lb/4 cups strong white bread flour
5ml/1 tsp salt
10ml/2 tsp easy-blend (rapid-rise) dried yeast
300ml/½ pint/1¼ cups lukewarm water
45ml/3 tbsp olive oil
45ml/3 tbsp chopped fresh basil

1 Lightly oil three or four baking sheets. Put the saffron threads in a cup and pour over 30ml/2 tbsp of the boiling water. Leave to infuse for 10 minutes. Meanwhile, sift the flour and salt into a large bowl. Add the yeast. Make a well in the centre.

2 When the saffron liquid has cooled to lukewarm, add it to the well in the flour with the remaining lukewarm water, oil and basil. Mix to a soft dough. Knead on a lightly floured surface for 8–10 minutes until smooth and elastic.

3 Place the dough in a lightly oiled bowl, cover with lightly oiled clear film (plastic wrap) and leave in a warm place, for 1 hour, or until doubled in bulk.

4 Divide the dough into 32 pieces and shape into long sticks. Place well apart on the baking sheets. Cover with lightly oiled clear film and leave to rise for 15–20 minutes, until puffy.

5 Bake for 15 minutes, until the breadsticks are crisp and golden. Cool briefly on a wire rack. These are best served warm.

PRETZELS

Pretzels or brezeln, *as they are known in Germany, are said to be derived from the Latin* bracellae *or arms, referring to the crossed "arms" of dough inside the oval shape. This shape is also used for biscuits in Germany and Austria, and in Alsace the pretzel shape is part of the wrought iron emblem of quality that bakers display outside their shops.*

MAKES 12 PRETZELS

INGREDIENTS

FOR THE YEAST SPONGE
7g/¼oz fresh yeast
75ml/5 tbsp water
15ml/1 tbsp unbleached plain (all-purpose) white flour

FOR THE DOUGH
7g/¼oz fresh yeast
150ml/¼ pint/⅔ cup lukewarm water
75ml/5 tbsp lukewarm milk
400g/14oz/3½ cups unbleached white bread flour
7.5ml/1½ tsp salt
25g/1oz/2 tbsp butter, melted

FOR THE TOPPING
1 egg yolk
15ml/1 tbsp milk
sea salt or caraway seeds, for sprinkling

1 Lightly flour a baking sheet. Also grease two baking sheets. In a bowl, cream the yeast for the yeast sponge with the water, then mix in the flour, cover with clear film (plastic wrap) and leave to stand at room temperature for 2 hours.

2 Mix the yeast for the dough with the water until dissolved, then stir in the milk. Sift 350g/12oz/3 cups of the flour and the salt into a large bowl. Add the yeast sponge mixture and the butter; mix for 3–4 minutes. Turn out on to a lightly floured surface and knead in the remaining flour to make a medium firm dough. Place in a lightly oiled bowl, cover with lightly oiled clear film and leave to rise, in a warm place, for 30 minutes, or until almost doubled in bulk.

3 Turn out on to a lightly floured surface and knock back (punch down) the dough. Knead into a ball, return to the bowl, replace the clear film cover and leave to rise for 30 minutes.

4 Turn out the dough on to a lightly floured surface. Divide it equally into 12 pieces and form into balls. Take one ball of dough and cover the remainder with a dishtowel. Roll into a thin stick 46cm/18in long and about 1cm/½in thick in the middle and thinner at the ends. Bend each end of the dough stick into a horseshoe. Cross over and place the ends on top of the thick part of the pretzel. Repeat with the remaining dough balls.

5 Place on the floured baking sheet to rest for 10 minutes. Meanwhile, preheat the oven to 190°C/375°F/Gas 5. Bring a large pan of water to the boil, then reduce to a simmer. Add pretzels to the simmering water in batches, two or three at a time, and poach for about 1 minute. Drain the pretzels on a dishtowel and place on the greased baking sheets, spaced well apart.

6 Mix the egg yolk and milk together and brush this glaze over the pretzels. Sprinkle with sea salt or caraway seeds, and bake the pretzels for 25 minutes, or until they are deep golden. Transfer to a wire rack to cool.

BAGELS

Bagels are eaten in many countries, especially where there is a Jewish community, and are very popular in the United States. They can be made from white, wholemeal or rye flour, and finished with a variety of toppings, including caraway, poppy seeds, sesame seeds and onion.

MAKES 10 BAGELS

INGREDIENTS
350g/12oz/3 cups unbleached white bread flour
10ml/2 tsp salt
7g/¼oz sachet easy-blend (rapid-rise) dried yeast
5ml/1 tsp malt extract
210ml/7½fl oz/scant 1 cup lukewarm water

FOR POACHING
2.5 litres/4 pints/2½ quarts water
15ml/1 tbsp malt extract

FOR THE TOPPING
1 egg white
10ml/2 tsp cold water
30ml/2 tbsp poppy, sesame or caraway seeds

1 Oil two baking sheets. Sift the flour and salt together into a large bowl. Stir in the dried yeast. Make a well in the centre. Mix the malt extract and water, add to the centre of the flour and mix to a dough. Knead on a floured surface for 8–10 minutes until smooth and elastic.

2 Place in a lightly oiled bowl, cover with lightly oiled clear film (plastic wrap) and leave to rise, in a warm place, for about 1 hour, or until doubled in bulk.

3 Turn out on to a lightly floured surface and knock back (punch down). Knead for 1 minute, then divide into 10 equal pieces. Shape into balls, cover with clear film and leave to rest for 5 minutes.

4 Gently flatten each ball and make a hole through the centre with your thumb. Enlarge the hole slightly. Place the bagels on a floured tray; re-cover and leave in a warm place, for 10–20 minutes, or until they begin to rise.

5 Meanwhile, preheat the oven to 220°C/425°F/Gas 7. Place the water and malt extract for poaching in a large pan, bring to the boil, then reduce to a simmer. Place the bagels in the water two or three at a time and poach for about 1 minute. They will sink and then rise again when first added to the pan. Using a large slotted spoon, turn over and cook for 30 seconds. Remove and drain on a dishtowel. Repeat with the remaining bagels.

6 Place five bagels on each prepared baking sheet, spacing them well apart. Beat the egg white with the water for the topping, brush the mixture over the top of each bagel and sprinkle with poppy, sesame or caraway seeds. Bake for 20–25 minutes, or until golden brown. Transfer to a wire rack to cool.

BLINIS

Blinis are the celebrated leavened Russian pancakes. Traditionally served with sour cream and caviar, they have a very distinctive flavour and a fluffy, light texture.

MAKES ABOUT 10 BLINIS

INGREDIENTS
50g/2oz/½ cup buckwheat flour
50g/2oz/½ cup unbleached plain (all-purpose) flour
2.5ml/½ tsp freshly ground black pepper
5ml/1 tsp salt
15g/½oz fresh yeast
200ml/7fl oz/scant 1 cup lukewarm milk
1 egg, separated

1 Mix the buckwheat flour, plain flour, pepper and salt together in a large bowl. In a separate, smaller bowl, cream the yeast with 60ml/4 tbsp of the milk, then mix in the remaining milk.

2 Make a well in the centre of the flour mixture. Add the egg yolk and yeast mixture and gradually whisk in the flour to form a smooth batter. Cover with clear film (plastic wrap), and leave to stand in a warm place for 1 hour.

3 Whisk the egg white until it forms soft peaks and fold into the batter. Lightly oil a heavy frying pan and heat it.

4 Add about 45ml/3 tbsp of the batter to the pan to make a 10cm/4in round pancake. Cook until the surface begins to dry out, then turn the pancake over using a metal spatula and cook for 1–2 minutes. Make more blinis with the remaining batter. Serve warm.

VARIATION
You can use all buckwheat flour, which will give the blinis a stronger flavour.

NEW ENGLAND FANTANS

These fantail rolls look stylish and are so versatile that they are equally suitable for a simple snack or a gourmet dinner party.

MAKES 9 ROLLS

INGREDIENTS

15g/½oz fresh yeast
75ml/5 tbsp buttermilk, at room temperature
10ml/2 tsp caster (superfine) sugar
75ml/5 tbsp milk
65g/2½oz/5 tbsp butter
375g/13oz/3¼ cups unbleached white bread flour
5ml/1 tsp salt
1 egg, lightly beaten

1 Grease a nine 7.5cm/3in cup muffin pan or use foil cases. Mix the yeast with the buttermilk and sugar and then leave to stand for 15 minutes. Meanwhile, pour the milk into a pan, add 40g/1½oz/3 tbsp of the butter and heat until the butter has melted. Cool until lukewarm.

2 Sift the flour and salt together into a large bowl. Add the yeast mixture, milk mixture and egg, and mix to a soft dough. Turn out on to a lightly floured surface and knead for 5–8 minutes until smooth and elastic. Place in a lightly oiled bowl, cover with lightly oiled clear film (plastic wrap) and leave to rise, in a warm place, for about 1 hour, until doubled in size.

3 Turn out on to a lightly floured surface, knock back (punch down) and knead until smooth and elastic. Roll into an oblong measuring 45 × 30cm/18 × 12in and about 5mm/¼in thick. Melt the remaining butter, brush over the dough and cut it lengthways into five equal strips. Stack on top of each other and cut across into nine equal 5cm/2in strips.

4 Pinch one side of each layered strip together, then place pinched side down into a prepared muffin cup or foil case. Cover with lightly oiled clear film, and leave to rise, in a warm place, for 30–40 minutes, or until the fantans have almost doubled in size. Meanwhile, preheat the oven to 200°C/400°F/Gas 6. Bake for 20 minutes, or until golden. Turn out on to a wire rack to cool.

Sourdough & Grain Breads

Based on a natural leaven, sometimes with a little added yeast, sourdough breads have a distinctive, slightly acid flavour. The method exploits the fact that any flour and water dough or batter of vegetable origin will begin to ferment spontaneously in the right conditions. The process begins with a small quantity of dough or batter, called, appropriately enough, the starter. Over the next few days, the starter is fed – or "refreshed" – with flour and water at regular intervals before being mixed into the final dough. Sometimes a mixture of flours is used, as in German Sourdough Bread, which includes both wholemeal (whole-wheat) and rye flour. Rye is also used in dense, delicious breads like Pumpernickel, Sunshine Loaf and Pain Bouillie.

German Sourdough Bread

This bread includes rye, wholemeal and plain flours for a superb depth of flavour. Serve in thick slices, with butter or a strongly flavoured cheese.

Makes 1 loaf

Ingredients

For the sourdough starter
75g/3oz/¾ cup rye flour
80ml/3fl oz/⅓ cup warm water
pinch caraway seeds

For the dough
15g/½oz fresh yeast
315ml/11fl oz/1⅓ cups lukewarm water
275g/10oz/2½ cups rye flour
150g/5oz/1¼ cups wholemeal (whole-wheat) bread flour
150g/5oz/1¼ cups unbleached white bread flour
10ml/2 tsp salt

1 Mix the rye flour, warm water and caraway seeds for the starter in a bowl. Use your fingertips to mix to a soft paste. Cover with a damp dishtowel and leave in a warm place for about 36 hours. Stir after 24 hours.

2 Lightly grease a baking sheet. Mix the yeast for the dough with the lukewarm water, then stir into the starter. Mix all the flours with the salt in a large bowl. Make a well in the centre, add the yeast liquid and mix to a smooth dough.

3 Knead on a lightly floured surface for 8–10 minutes until smooth. Place in a lightly oiled bowl, cover with lightly oiled clear film (plastic wrap) and leave to rise, in a warm place, for 1½ hours, or until nearly doubled in bulk.

4 Knock back (punch down) and knead gently. Shape into a round and place, seam up, in a floured basket or couronne. Cover with lightly oiled clear film, and leave to rise, in a warm place, for 2–3 hours.

5 Meanwhile, preheat the oven to 200°C/400°F/Gas 6. Turn out the loaf on to the prepared baking sheet and bake for 35–40 minutes. Cool on a wire rack.

PUMPERNICKEL

This famous German rye bread is extremely dense and dark, with an intense flavour.
It is baked very slowly, and it is more like a steamed bread than a baked one.

MAKES 2 LOAVES

INGREDIENTS
450g/1lb/4 cups rye flour
225g/8oz/2 cups wholemeal (whole-wheat) flour
115g/4oz/⅔ cup bulgur wheat
10ml/2 tsp salt
30ml/2 tbsp molasses
850ml/1 pint 8fl oz/3½ cups warm water
15ml/1 tbsp vegetable oil

1 Lightly oil two 18 × 9cm/7 × 3½in loaf pans. Mix the rye flour, wholemeal (whole-wheat) flour, bulgur wheat and salt together in a large bowl. Mix the molasses with the warm water. Add the oil to the flours. Mix to a dense mass.

2 Place in the prepared pans, pressing well into the corners. Cover with lightly oiled clear film (plastic wrap), and leave in a warm place for 18–24 hours.

3 Preheat the oven to 110°C/225°F/Gas ¼. Cover the pans tightly with foil. Fill a roasting pan with boiling water and place a rack above it. Place the pans on top of the rack and transfer carefully to the oven. Bake the loaves for 4 hours.

4 Increase the oven temperature to 160°C/325°F/Gas 3. Top up the water in the roasting pan if necessary, uncover the loaves and bake for a further 30–45 minutes, or until the loaves feel firm and the tops are crusty.

5 Leave to cool in the pans for 5 minutes, then turn out on to a wire rack to cool completely. Serve cold, very thinly sliced, with cold meats.

COOK'S TIP
This bread improves on keeping. Keep for at least
24 hours double-wrapped inside a plastic bag or
greaseproof (waxed) paper and foil before slicing.

POLISH RYE BREAD

This rye bread is made with half white flour, which gives it a lighter, more open texture than a traditional rye loaf. Serve thinly sliced with cold meats and fish.

MAKES 1 LOAF

INGREDIENTS
225g/8oz/2 cups rye flour
225g/8oz/2 cups unbleached white bread flour
10ml/2 tsp caraway seeds
10ml/2 tsp salt
20g/¾oz fresh yeast
140ml/scant ¼ pint/scant ⅔ cup lukewarm milk
5ml/1 tsp clear honey
140ml/scant ¼ pint/scant ⅔ cup lukewarm water
wholemeal (whole-wheat) flour, for dusting

1 Lightly grease a baking sheet. Mix the flours, caraway seeds and salt in a large bowl and make a well in the centre. In a bowl or measuring jug (cup), cream the yeast with the milk and honey. Pour into the centre of the flour, add the water and gradually incorporate the surrounding flour and caraway mixture until a dough forms.

2 Knead the dough on a lightly floured surface for 8–10 minutes until smooth. Place in a lightly oiled bowl, cover with lightly oiled clear film (plastic wrap) and leave to rise, in a warm place, for about 3 hours, or until doubled in bulk.

3 Turn out the dough on to a lightly floured surface and knock back (punch down). Shape into an oval loaf and place on the prepared baking sheet. Dust with wholemeal (whole-wheat) flour, cover with lightly oiled clear film and leave to rise, in a warm place, for 1–1½ hours, or until doubled in size. Meanwhile, preheat the oven to 220°C/425°F/Gas 7.

4 Using a sharp knife, slash the loaf with two long cuts about 2.5cm/1in apart. Bake for 30–35 minutes, or until the loaf sounds hollow when tapped on the base. Transfer the loaf to a wire rack and set aside to cool.

FINNISH BARLEY BREAD

In Northern Europe breads are often made using cereals such as barley and rye,
which produce very satisfying, tasty breads.

MAKES 1 SMALL LOAF

INGREDIENTS
225g/8oz/2 cups barley flour
5ml/1 tsp salt
10ml/2 tsp baking powder
25g/1oz/2 tbsp butter, melted
120ml/4fl oz/½ cup single (light) cream
60ml/4 tbsp milk

1 Lightly grease a baking sheet. Preheat the oven to 200°C/400°F/Gas 6. Sift the dry ingredients into a bowl. Add the butter, cream and milk. Mix to a dough.

2 Turn out the dough on to a lightly floured surface and shape into a flat round about 1cm/½in thick.

3 Transfer to the prepared baking sheet and using a sharp knife, lightly mark the top into six equal sections.

4 Prick the surface of the round evenly with a fork. Bake for 15–18 minutes, or until pale golden. Cut into wedges and serve warm.

COOK'S TIPS
- *This flatbread tastes very good with cottage cheese, especially cottage cheese with chives.*
- *For a citrusy tang, add 10–15ml/2–3 tsp finely grated lemon, lime or orange rind to the flour mixture in step 1.*

SUNSHINE LOAF

Scandinavia, Land of the Midnight Sun, has numerous breads based on rye. This splendid table centrepiece is made with a blend of rye and white flours, the latter helping to lighten the bread.

MAKES 1 LARGE LOAF

INGREDIENTS

FOR THE STARTER
60ml/4 tbsp lukewarm milk
60ml/4 tbsp lukewarm water
7g/¼oz fresh yeast
100g/3¾oz/scant 1 cup unbleached white bread flour

FOR THE DOUGH
15g/½oz fresh yeast
500ml/17fl oz/generous 2 cups lukewarm water
450g/1lb/4 cups rye flour
225g/8oz/2 cups unbleached white bread flour
15ml/1 tbsp salt
milk, for glazing
caraway seeds, for sprinkling

> ### VARIATION
> This bread can be shaped into one large round or oval loaf, if you prefer.

1 Combine the milk and water for the starter in a large bowl. Mix in the yeast until dissolved. Gradually add the bread flour, stirring it with a metal spoon.

2 Cover the bowl with clear film (plastic wrap) and leave the mixture in a warm place for 3–4 hours, or until well risen, bubbly and starting to collapse.

3 Mix the yeast for the dough with 60ml/4 tbsp of the water until creamy, then stir in the remaining water. Gradually mix into the starter to dilute it. Gradually mix in the rye flour to form a smooth batter. Cover with lightly oiled clear film and leave in a warm place, for 3–4 hours, or until well risen.

4 Stir the bread flour and salt into the batter to form a dough. Turn on to a lightly floured surface and knead for 5 minutes until smooth and elastic. Place in a lightly oiled bowl, cover with lightly oiled clear film and leave to rise, in a warm place, for about 1 hour, or until doubled in bulk.

5 Knock back (punch down) on a lightly floured surface. Using a sharp knife, cut the dough into five equal pieces. Roll one piece into a 50cm/20in "sausage" and roll up into a spiral shape.

6 Cut the remaining pieces of dough in half and shape each one into a 20cm/8in rope. Place in a circle on a large baking sheet, spaced equally apart, like rays of the sun, and curl the ends round, leaving a small gap in the centre. Place the spiral shape on top. Cover with lightly oiled clear film and leave to rise, in a warm place, for 30 minutes.

7 Meanwhile, preheat the oven to 230°C/450°F/Gas 8. Brush the bread with a little milk, sprinkle with caraway seeds and bake for 30 minutes, or until lightly browned. Transfer to a wire rack to cool.

Pain Bouillie

This is an old-fashioned style of rye bread. Rye flour is mixed with boiling water like a porridge and left overnight to ferment.

MAKES 2 LOAVES

INGREDIENTS

FOR THE PORRIDGE
225g/8oz/2 cups rye flour
450ml/¾ pint/1¾ cups boiling water
5ml/1 tsp clear honey

FOR THE DOUGH
7g/¼oz fresh yeast
30ml/2 tbsp lukewarm water
5ml/1 tsp caraway seeds, crushed
10ml/2 tsp salt
350g/12oz/3 cups unbleached white bread flour
olive oil, for brushing

COOK'S TIP
Serve very thinly sliced, with a little butter, or as an accompaniment to cold meats and cheeses.

---

1 Lightly grease a 23.5 × 13cm/9¼ × 5in loaf pan. Place the rye flour for the porridge in a large bowl. Pour over the boiling water and leave to stand for 5 minutes. Stir in the honey. Cover with clear film (plastic wrap) and leave in a warm place for about 12 hours.

2 Make the dough. Put the yeast in a measuring jug (cup) and blend in the water. Stir the mixture into the porridge with the crushed caraway seeds and salt. Add the white flour a little at a time, mixing first with a wooden spoon and then with your hands, until the mixture forms a firm dough.

3 Turn out on to a lightly floured surface and knead for 6–8 minutes until smooth and elastic. Return to the bowl, cover with lightly oiled clear film and leave to rise, in a warm place, for 1½ hours, or until doubled in bulk.

4 Turn out the dough on to a lightly floured surface and knock back (punch down). Using a sharp knife, cut the dough into two equal pieces and roll each piece into a rectangle 38 × 12cm/15 × 4½in. Fold the bottom third up and the top third down and seal the edges. Turn over.

5 Brush one side of each piece of folded dough with olive oil, and place side by side in the prepared pan, oiled edges next to each other. Cover with lightly oiled clear film and leave to rise, in a warm place, for 1 hour, or until the dough reaches the top of the pan.

6 Meanwhile, preheat the oven to 220°C/425°F/Gas 7. Brush the tops of the loaves with olive oil, and using a sharp knife, slash with one or two cuts. Bake for 30 minutes, then reduce the oven temperature to 190°C/375°F/Gas 5 and bake for a further 25–30 minutes. Turn out on to a wire rack to cool.

ENRICHED BREADS

Butter is the ingredient most often added to doughs when a richer result is sought, but cheese, milk, sour cream and eggs may also be used. Occasionally, lard or shortening is included in the dough instead of butter, as is the case with the English harvest bread, Lardy Cake. In yeast pastries like Croissants, the butter or other fat is added after the basic dough has been made, in much the same way as butter is incorporated in puff pastry. This results in gloriously light layers that melt in the mouth.

Another rich ingredient that can be added to bread dough is chocolate, either as cocoa powder or pieces of slab chocolate. In one memorable bread – the Italian Pane al Cioccolato – both types are used. Slices of this moreish loaf taste even more delicious when topped with mascarpone.

VIRGINIA SPOON BREAD

According to legend, spoon bread originated when too much water was added to a corn bread batter; the baked bread had to be spooned out of the tin. It is delicious.

MAKES 1 LARGE LOAF

INGREDIENTS
450ml/¾ pint/1¾ cups milk
75g/3oz/⅔ cup cornmeal
15g/½oz/1 tbsp butter
75g/3oz/¾ cup grated mature (sharp) Cheddar cheese
1 garlic clove, crushed
3 eggs, separated
75g/3oz/½ cup whole corn kernels (optional)
salt and ground black pepper

1 Preheat the oven to 180°C/350°F/Gas 4. Grease a 1.5 litre/2½ pint/6 cup soufflé dish. Place the milk in a large heavy pan. Heat gently, then gradually add the cornmeal, stirring. Add salt and slowly bring to the boil, stirring all the time. Cook for 5–10 minutes, stirring frequently, until thick and smooth.

2 Remove from the heat and stir in the butter, Cheddar cheese, garlic and egg yolks. Season to taste. In a bowl, whisk the egg whites until they form soft peaks. Stir one-quarter into the cornmeal mixture and then gently fold in the remainder. Fold in the well-drained corn, if using.

3 Spoon the mixture into the prepared soufflé dish and bake for 45–50 minutes, or until puffed and beginning to brown. Serve at once.

VARIATIONS
Add 115g/4oz fried chopped bacon or 5–10ml/ 1–2 tsp finely chopped green chilli for different flavoured spoon breads.

SALLY LUNN

Sally Lunn is traditionally served warm sliced into three layers horizontally, spread with clotted cream or butter and re-assembled. It looks fantastic.

MAKES 1 ROUND LOAF

INGREDIENTS
25g/1oz/2 tbsp butter, plus extra for greasing
150ml/¼ pint/⅔ cup milk or double (heavy) cream
15ml/1 tbsp caster (superfine) sugar
15g/½oz fresh yeast
275g/10oz/2½ cups unbleached white bread flour
2.5ml/½ tsp salt
finely grated rind of ½ lemon

FOR THE GLAZE
15ml/1 tbsp milk
15ml/1 tbsp caster (superfine) sugar

1 Lightly butter a 15cm/6in round cake pan, 7.5cm/3in deep. Dust lightly with flour. Melt the butter and stir in the milk or cream and sugar. Cool to tepid then stir in the yeast and leave for 10 minutes, or until frothy.

2 Sift the flour and salt together into a large bowl. Stir in the lemon rind and make a well in the centre. Add the yeast mixture and mix to a soft dough.

3 Knead the dough on a lightly floured surface for about 10 minutes until smooth. Shape into a ball and place in the prepared pan. Cover with lightly oiled clear film (plastic wrap) and leave to rise, in a warm place, for 1¼–1½ hours.

4 Preheat the oven to 220°C/425°F/Gas 7. Bake for 15–20 minutes or until light golden. Heat the milk and sugar for the glaze in a small pan until the sugar has dissolved, then bring to the boil. Brush the glaze over the bread, cool in the pan for 10 minutes, then cool slightly on a wire rack before slicing and filling.

LARDY CAKE

This special rich fruit bread was originally made throughout many counties of England for celebrating the harvest. Using lard rather than butter or margarine makes an authentic lardy cake.

MAKES 1 LARGE LOAF

INGREDIENTS
450g/1lb/4 cups unbleached white bread flour
5ml/1 tsp salt
15g/½oz/1 tbsp lard (shortening)
25g/1oz/2 tbsp caster (superfine) sugar
20g/¾oz fresh yeast
300ml/½ pint/1¼ cups lukewarm water

FOR THE FILLING
75g/3oz/6 tbsp lard
75g/3oz/6 tbsp soft light brown sugar
115g/4oz/½ cup currants, slightly warmed
75g/3oz/½ cup sultanas (golden raisins), slightly warmed
25g/1oz/3 tbsp mixed chopped (candied) peel
5ml/1 tsp mixed (apple pie) spice

FOR THE GLAZE
10ml/2 tsp sunflower oil
15–30ml/1–2 tbsp caster sugar

1 Grease a 25 × 20cm/10 × 8in shallow roasting pan. Sift the flour and salt into a large bowl and rub in the lard. Stir in the sugar and make a well in the centre.

2 In a bowl, cream the yeast with half of the water, then blend in the remainder. Add to the centre of the flour and mix to a smooth dough.

3 Knead on a lightly floured surface for about 10 minutes until smooth and elastic. Place in a lightly oiled bowl, cover with lightly oiled clear film (plastic wrap) and leave to rise, in a warm place, for 1 hour, or until doubled in bulk.

4 Turn the dough out on to a lightly floured surface and knock back (punch down). Knead for 2–3 minutes. Roll into a rectangle about 5mm/¼in thick.

5 Using half the lard for the filling, cover the top two-thirds of the dough with flakes of lard. Sprinkle over half the sugar, half the dried fruits and peel, and half the mixed spice. Fold the bottom third up and the top third down, sealing the edges with the rolling pin.

6 Turn the dough by 90°. Repeat the rolling and cover with the remaining lard, fruit and peel and mixed spice. Fold, seal and turn as before. Roll out the dough to fit the prepared pan. Cover with lightly oiled clear film and leave to rise, in a warm place, for 30–45 minutes, or until doubled in size.

7 Meanwhile, preheat the oven to 200°C/400°F/Gas 6. Brush the top of the lardy cake with sunflower oil and sprinkle with caster sugar.

8 Score a criss-cross pattern on top using a sharp knife, then bake for 30–40 minutes until golden. Turn out on to a wire rack to cool slightly. Serve warm, cut into slices or squares.

CROISSANTS

Golden layers of flaky pastry, puffy, light and flavoured with butter is how the best croissants should be. Serve warm on the day of baking.

MAKES 14 CROISSANTS

INGREDIENTS
350g/12oz/3 cups unbleached white bread flour
115g/4oz/1 cup fine French plain flour
5ml/1 tsp salt
25g/1oz/2 tbsp caster (superfine) sugar
15g/½oz fresh yeast
225ml/scant 8fl oz/scant 1 cup lukewarm milk
1 egg, lightly beaten
225g/8oz/1 cup butter

FOR THE GLAZE
1 egg yolk
15ml/1 tbsp milk

> COOK'S TIP
> *Make sure that the block of butter and the dough are about the same temperature when combining, to ensure the best results.*

1 Sift the flours and salt together into a large bowl. Stir in the sugar. Make a well in the centre. Cream the yeast with 45ml/3 tbsp of the milk, then stir in the remainder. Add the yeast mixture to the centre of the flour, then add the egg and gradually beat in the flour until it forms a dough.

2 Turn out on to a lightly floured surface and knead for 3–4 minutes. Place in a large lightly oiled bowl, cover with lightly oiled clear film (plastic wrap), and leave to rise, in a warm place, for about 1 hour, or until doubled in bulk.

3 Knock back (punch down), re-cover and chill in the refrigerator for 1 hour. Meanwhile, flatten the butter into a block about 2cm/¾in thick. Knock back the dough and turn out on to a lightly floured surface.

4 Roll out the dought into a rough 25cm/10in square, rolling the edges thinner than the centre. Place the block of butter diagonally in the centre and fold the corners of the dough over the butter like an envelope, tucking in the edges to completely enclose the butter.

5 Roll the dough into a rectangle about 2cm/¾in thick, approximately twice as long as it is wide. Fold the bottom third up and the top third down and seal the edges with a rolling pin. Wrap in clear film and chill for 20 minutes.

6 Repeat the rolling, folding and chilling twice more, turning the dough by 90° each time. Roll out on a floured surface into a 63 × 33cm/25 × 13in rectangle; trim the edges to leave a 60 × 30cm/24 × 12in rectangle. Cut in half lengthways. Cut crossways into 14 equal triangles with 15cm/6in bases.

7 Place the dough triangles on two baking sheets, cover with clear film and chill for 10 minutes. To shape the croissants, place each one with the wide end at the top, hold each side and pull gently to stretch the top of the triangle a little, then roll towards the point, finishing with the pointed end tucked underneath. Curve the ends towards the pointed end to make a crescent. Place on the two baking sheets, spaced well apart.

8 Mix together the egg yolk and milk for the glaze. Lightly brush a little glaze over the croissants, avoiding the cut edges of the dough. Cover the croissants loosely with lightly oiled clear film (plastic wrap). Leave them to rise, in a warm place, for about 30 minutes, or until they have almost doubled in size.

9 Meanwhile, preheat the oven to 220°C/425°F/Gas 7. Brush the croissants with the remaining glaze and bake for 15–20 minutes, or until crisp and golden. Transfer to a wire rack to cool slightly before serving warm.

BRIOCHE

Rich and buttery yet light and airy, this wonderful loaf captures the essence of the classic French enriched bread.

MAKES 1 LOAF

INGREDIENTS
350g/12oz/3 cups unbleached white bread flour
2.5ml/½ tsp salt
15g/½oz fresh yeast
60ml/4 tbsp lukewarm milk
3 eggs, lightly beaten
175g/6oz/¾ cup butter, softened
25g/1oz/2 tbsp caster (superfine) sugar

FOR THE GLAZE
1 egg yolk
15ml/1 tbsp milk

COOK'S TIP
Although not as popular as croissants outside of France, brioche makes a perfect bread for breakfast. It tastes wonderful served with marmalade or a fruit conserve. Savoury brioche, made using cheese in place of some of the butter, is delicious, too. Baked in a loaf shape, the middle can be hollowed out and filled with wild mushrooms or grilled peppers.

1 Sift the flour and salt together into a large bowl and make a well in the centre. Put the yeast in a measuring jug (cup) and stir in the milk. Add the yeast mixture to the centre of the flour with the eggs and mix together to form a soft dough.

2 Using your hand, beat the dough for 4–5 minutes until smooth and elastic. Cream the butter and sugar together. Gradually add the butter mixture to the dough in small amounts, making sure it is incorporated before adding more. Beat until smooth, shiny and elastic.

3 Cover the bowl with lightly oiled clear film (plastic wrap) and leave the dough to rise, in a warm place, for 1–2 hours or until doubled in bulk. Lightly knock back (punch down) the dough, then re-cover and place in the refrigerator for 8–10 hours or overnight.

4 Lightly grease a 1.6 litre/2¾ pint/scant 7 cup brioche mould. Turn the dough out on to a lightly floured surface. Cut off almost a quarter and set aside. Shape the rest into a ball and place in the prepared mould. Shape the reserved dough into an elongated egg shape. Using two or three fingers, make a hole in the centre of the large ball of dough and gently insert the narrow end of the egg-shaped dough.

5 Mix together the egg yolk and milk for the glaze, and brush a little over the brioche. Cover with lightly oiled clear film and leave to rise, in a warm place, for 1½–2 hours, or until the dough nearly reaches the top of the mould.

6 Meanwhile, preheat the oven to 230°C/450°F/Gas 8. Brush the brioche with the remaining glaze and bake for 10 minutes. Reduce the oven temperature to 190°C/375°F/Gas 5 and bake for a further 20–25 minutes, or until golden. Turn out on to a wire rack to cool.

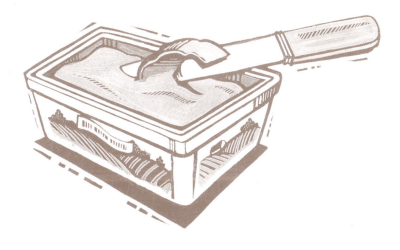

SWISS BRAID

This plaited, attractively tapered loaf is known as Zupfe in Switzerland. Often eaten at the weekend, it is has a glossy crust and a wonderfully light crumb.

MAKES 1 LOAF

INGREDIENTS
350g/12oz/3 cups unbleached white bread flour
5ml/1 tsp salt
20g/¾oz fresh yeast
30ml/2 tbsp lukewarm water
150ml/¼ pint/⅔ cup sour cream
1 egg, lightly beaten
50g/2oz/¼ cup butter, softened

FOR THE GLAZE
1 egg yolk
15ml/1 tbsp water

COOK'S TIP
If you prefer, use a 7g/¼oz sachet of easy-blend (rapid-rise) yeast. Add directly to the flour with the salt, then add the warmed sour cream and water and mix together.

---

1 Lightly grease a baking sheet. Sift the flour and salt together into a large bowl and make a well in the centre. Mix the yeast with the water in a jug (pitcher).

2 Gently warm the sour cream in a small pan until it reaches blood heat (35–38°C/95–100°F). Add to the yeast mixture and mix together. Add the yeast mixture and egg to the centre of the flour and gradually mix to a dough. Beat in the softened butter.

3 Turn out on to a lightly floured surface and knead for 5 minutes until smooth and elastic. Place in a lightly oiled bowl, cover with lightly oiled clear film (plastic wrap) and leave to rise, in a warm place, for about 1½ hours, or until doubled in size.

4 Turn out on to a lightly floured surface and knock back (punch down). Cut in quarters and shape each piece of dough into a long rope making all the ropes the same length. Arrange the ropes side by side and pinch together at one end.

5 Starting at pinched end, cross second rope from left over the rope to its right. Cross the far right rope over the two ropes to its left, then the far left rope over the two ropes to its right. Repeat until the braid is complete, then tuck the ends under. Cover with oiled clear film and leave to rise, in a warm place, for 40 minutes.

6 Meanwhile, preheat the oven to 190°C/ 375°F/Gas 5. Mix the egg yolk and water for the glaze, and brush over the loaf. Bake the bread for 30–35 minutes, or until golden. Cool on a wire rack.

PANE AL CIOCCOLATO

This slightly sweet chocolate bread from Italy is often served with creamy mascarpone cheese as a dessert or snack.

MAKES 1 LOAF

INGREDIENTS

350g/12oz/3 cups unbleached white bread flour
25ml/1½ tbsp cocoa powder (unsweetened)
2.5ml/½ tsp salt
25g/1oz/2 tbsp caster (superfine) sugar
15g/½oz fresh yeast
250ml/8fl oz/1 cup lukewarm water
25g/1oz/2 tbsp butter, softened
75g/3oz plain (semisweet) Continental chocolate, coarsely chopped
melted butter, for brushing

1 Lightly grease a 15cm/6in round deep cake pan. Sift the flour, cocoa powder and salt into a large bowl. Stir in the sugar. Make a well in the centre.

2 Cream the yeast with 60ml/4 tbsp of the water, then stir in the rest. Add to the centre of the flour mixture and gradually mix to a dough. Knead in the butter, then knead on a floured surface until smooth and elastic.

3 Place in a lightly oiled bowl, cover with lightly oiled clear film (plastic wrap). Leave to rise, in a warm place, for about 1 hour, or until doubled in bulk.

4 Turn out on to a lightly floured surface and knock back (punch down). Gently knead in the chocolate, then re-cover and leave to rest for 5 minutes.

5 Shape the dough into a round and place in the pan. Cover with lightly oiled clear film and leave to rise, in a warm place, for 45 minutes, or until doubled in size; the dough should reach the top of the pan.

6 Preheat the oven to 220°C/425°F/Gas 7. Bake for 10 minutes, then reduce the oven temperature to 190°C/375°F/Gas 5 and bake for a further 25–30 minutes. Brush the top with melted butter and leave to cool on a wire rack.

BUCHTY

Popular in both Poland and Germany as special breakfast treats, these are also excellent split and toasted, and served with cured meats.

MAKES 16 ROLLS

INGREDIENTS
450g/1lb/4 cups unbleached white bread flour
5ml/1 tsp salt
50g/2oz/¼ cup caster (superfine) sugar
90g/3½oz/scant ½ cup butter
120ml/4fl oz/½ cup milk
20g/¾oz fresh yeast
3 eggs, lightly beaten

1 Grease a 20cm/8in square loose-bottomed cake pan. Sift the flour and salt together into a large bowl and stir in the sugar. Make a well in the centre.

2 Melt 50g/2oz/¼ cup of the butter in a small pan, then remove from the heat and stir in the milk. Leave to cool until lukewarm. Stir the yeast into the milk mixture until it has dissolved. Pour into the centre of the flour and stir in sufficient flour to form a thick batter. Sprinkle with a little of the surrounding flour, cover and leave in a warm place for 30 minutes.

3 Gradually beat in the eggs and remaining flour to form a soft, smooth dough. This will take about 10 minutes. Cover with lightly oiled clear film (plastic wrap). Leave to rise, in a warm place, for about 1½ hours, or until doubled in bulk.

4 Turn out the dough on to a lightly floured surface and knock back (punch down). Divide into 16 equal pieces and shape into rounds. Melt the remaining butter in a saucepan. Dip the rounds into the melted butter, then place, slightly apart, in the cake pan. Re-cover and leave to rise, in a warm place, for about 1 hour, or until doubled in size.

5 Meanwhile, preheat the oven to 190°C/375°F/Gas 5. Spoon any remaining melted butter evenly over the rolls and bake for 25 minutes, or until golden brown. Turn out on to a wire rack to cool, then separate into rolls.

CHALLAH

Challah is an egg-rich, light-textured bread baked for the Jewish Sabbath and to celebrate religious holidays. It is usually braided with three or four strands of dough, but eight strands or more may be used to create especially festive loaves.

MAKES 1 LARGE LOAF

INGREDIENTS
500g/1¼lb/5 cups unbleached white bread flour
10ml/2 tsp salt
20g/¾oz fresh yeast
200ml/7fl oz/scant 1 cup lukewarm water
30ml/2 tbsp caster (superfine) sugar
2 eggs
75g/3oz/6 tbsp butter or margarine, melted

FOR THE GLAZE
1 egg yolk
15ml/1 tbsp water
10ml/2 tsp poppy seeds, for sprinkling

COOK'S TIP
If you prefer, divide the dough in half and make two smaller challah, keeping the braids quite simple. Decorate with poppy seeds or leave plain. Reduce the baking time by about 10 minutes.

1 Lightly grease a baking sheet. Sift the flour and salt together into a large bowl and make a well in the centre. Mix the yeast with the water and sugar, add to the centre of the flour with the eggs and melted butter or margarine, and gradually mix in the surrounding flour to form a soft dough.

2 Turn out on to a lightly floured surface and knead for 10 minutes until smooth and elastic. Place in a lightly oiled bowl, cover with lightly oiled clear film (plastic wrap) and leave to rise, in a warm place, for 1 hour, or until doubled in bulk. Knock back (punch down), re-cover and leave to rise again for 1 hour.

3 Knock back, turn out on to a lightly floured surface and knead gently. Divide into four equal pieces. Roll each into a rope about 45cm/18in long. Line up next to each other. Pinch the ends together at one end.

4 Starting from the right, lift the first rope over the second and the third rope over the fourth. Take the fourth rope and place it between the first and second ropes. Repeat, starting from the right, and continue until plaited.

5 Tuck the ends under and place the loaf on the prepared baking sheet. Cover with lightly oiled clear film and leave to rise in a warm place, for about 30–45 minutes, or until doubled in size. Meanwhile, preheat the oven to 200°C/400°F/Gas 6. Beat the egg yolk and water together for the glaze.

6 Brush the egg glaze gently over the loaf. Sprinkle evenly with the poppy seeds and bake for 35–40 minutes, or until the challah is a deep golden brown. Transfer to a wire rack and leave to cool before slicing.

FESTIVE BREADS

Special breads have always been associated with celebrations, whether because of their shape, as is the case with the Harvest Festival Sheaf, or because they contain charms or novelties, like the dried bean that is traditionally hidden inside Twelfth Night Bread. In the West, the two festivals that are most often marked with the baking of specific loaves are Christmas and Easter. In Italy, it is customary to bake Panettone at Christmas time, and this rich yet light fruit bread has become a popular choice in other countries too, possibly as an alternative to richer, darker fruit cakes. Stollen is the traditional German Christmas bread. With its almond filling, it is perennially popular. Easter in Greece is marked with Tsoureki, a braided bread topped with scarlet-painted eggs.

TSOUREKI

Topped with brightly coloured eggs, this braided enriched bread is an important part of the Greek Easter celebrations, when it spells the end of the Lenten fast. It looks very impressive with its decoration of edible gold leaf and split almonds, and is great fun to make. Children especially enjoy preparing the scarlet eggs and burying them in the dough.

MAKES 1 LOAF

INGREDIENTS

FOR THE EGGS
3 eggs
1.5ml/¼ tsp bright red food colouring paste
15ml/1 tbsp white wine vinegar
5ml/1 tsp water
5ml/1 tsp olive oil

FOR THE DOUGH
450g/1lb/4 cups unbleached white bread flour
2.5ml/½ tsp salt
5ml/1 tsp ground allspice
2.5ml/½ tsp ground cinnamon
2.5ml/½ tsp caraway seeds
20g/¾oz fresh yeast
175ml/6fl oz/¾ cup lukewarm milk
50g/2oz/¼ cup butter
40g/1½oz/3 tbsp caster (superfine) sugar
2 eggs

FOR THE GLAZE
1 egg yolk
5ml/1 tsp clear honey
5ml/1 tsp water

FOR THE DECORATION
50g/2oz/½ cup split almonds, slivered
edible gold leaf, optional

1 Lightly grease a baking sheet. Place the eggs in a pan of water and bring to the boil. Boil gently for 10 minutes. Meanwhile, mix the red food colouring, vinegar and water together in a shallow bowl. Remove the eggs from the boiling water, place on a wire rack for a few seconds to dry, then roll in the colouring mixture. Return to the rack to cool and dry completely.

2 When cold, drizzle the olive oil on to absorbent kitchen paper, lift up each egg in turn and rub all over with the oiled paper.

3 To make the dough, sift the flour, salt, allspice and cinnamon into a large bowl. Stir in the caraway seeds.

4 In a jug (pitcher), mix the yeast with the milk. In a bowl, cream the butter and sugar together, then beat in the eggs. Add the creamed mixture to the flour with the yeast mixture and gradually mix to a dough. Turn out the dough on to a lightly floured surface and knead until smooth and elastic.

5 Place in a lightly oiled bowl, cover with lightly oiled clear film (plastic wrap) and leave to rise, in a warm place, for about 2 hours, or until doubled in bulk.

6 Knock back (punch down) the dough and knead for 2–3 minutes. Return to the bowl, re-cover and leave to rise again, in a warm place, for about 1 hour, or until doubled in bulk.

7 Knock back and turn out on to a lightly floured surface. Divide the dough into three equal pieces; roll each into a 38–50cm/15–20in long rope. Plait (braid) these together from the centre to the ends.

8 Place on the prepared baking sheet and push the dyed eggs into the loaf. Cover and leave to rise, in a warm place, for about 1 hour.

9 Meanwhile, preheat the oven to 190°C/375°F/Gas 5. Mix the egg yolk, honey and water together for the glaze, and brush over the loaf. Sprinkle with almonds and edible gold leaf, if using. Bake for 40–45 minutes, or until golden and sounding hollow when tapped on the base. Transfer to a wire rack to cool.

Harvest Festival Sheaf

This is one of the most visually stunning breads. Celebratory loaves can be seen in various forms in churches and in the windows of many bakeries throughout Britain around the time of the September harvest.

MAKES 1 LARGE LOAF

INGREDIENTS
900g/2lb/8 cups unbleached white bread flour
15ml/1 tbsp salt
15g/½oz fresh yeast
75ml/5 tbsp lukewarm milk
400ml/14fl oz/1⅔ cups cold water

FOR THE GLAZE
1 egg
15ml/1 tbsp milk

COOK'S TIPS
- *Check the bread occasionally while baking, and cover the ends with foil after the first 15 minutes if they start to over-brown.*
- *Harvest loaves are often baked for display, rather than for eating. If you'd like to do this, leave the baked loaf in the oven, reducing the temperature to 120°C/250°F/Gas ½, for several hours until the dough dries out.*

---

1 Lightly grease a large baking sheet, at least 38 × 33cm/15 × 13in. Sift the flour and salt together into a large bowl, and make a well in the centre.

2 Cream the yeast with the milk in a jug (pitcher). Add to the centre of the flour with the water and mix to a stiff dough. Turn out on to a lightly floured surface, and knead for about 10–15 minutes until smooth and elastic.

3 Place in a lightly oiled bowl, cover with lightly oiled clear film (plastic wrap) and leave to rise, at room temperature, for 2 hours, or until doubled in bulk.

4 Turn the dough out on to a lightly floured surface, knock back (punch down) and knead for about 1 minute. Cover and leave to rest for 10 minutes.

5 Divide the dough in two. Roll out one piece to a 35 × 25cm/14 × 10in oblong. Fold loosely in half lengthways. Cut out a half mushroom shape for the sheaf (leave the folded edge uncut). Make the stalk "base" about 18cm/7in long.

6 Place the dough on the prepared baking sheet and open out. Prick all over with a fork and brush with water to prevent a skin from forming. Reserve 75g/3oz of the trimmings for the tie. Cover and set aside. Divide the remaining dough in two pieces and mix the rest of the trimmings with one half. Cover and set aside. Beat together the egg and milk for the glaze.

7 Roll out the remaining dough on a lightly floured surface to a neat rectangle, 28 × 18cm/11 × 7in, and cut into 30–35 thin strips 18cm/7in long. Place side by side lengthways on the base, as close as possible, to represent wheat stalks.

8 Brush the wheat stalks with some glaze. Take the larger piece of reserved dough and divide into four. Divide each piece into about 25 and shape into oblong rolls to make about 100 wheat ears. Make each roll pointed at one end. Using scissors, snip along either side of each roll, towards the centre, to make wheat ear shapes.

9 Preheat the oven to 220°C/425°F/Gas 7. Arrange the ears around the outer edge of the top of the mushroom shape, overlapping on to the baking sheet. Repeat a second row lower down, placing the row between the first ears. Repeat until they are all used. Brush with some glaze as you proceed, to prevent the dough from drying out.

10 Divide the smaller piece of reserved dough into six pieces and roll each to a 43cm/17in strip. Make two plaits (braids) each with three strips. Place across the wheat stalks to make a tied bow. Brush with some glaze. Prick between the wheat ears and stalks using a sharp knife and bake the sheaf for 15 minutes.

11 Reduce the oven temperature to 180°C/350°F/Gas 4. Brush the bread with the remaining glaze and bake for a further 30–35 minutes, or until golden and firm. Leave to cool on the baking sheet.

PANETTONE

This classic Italian bread was once found only in its country of origin, except at Christmas time, when the festive breads, in their familiar gift boxes, would find their way into grocery stores and supermarkets everywhere. Today, you can buy Panettone all year round. It is a surprisingly light bread even though it is rich with butter and dried fruit.

MAKES 1 LOAF

INGREDIENTS
400g/14oz/3½ cups unbleached white bread flour
2.5ml/½ tsp salt
15g/½oz fresh yeast
120ml/4fl oz/½ cup lukewarm milk
2 eggs
2 egg yolks
75g/3oz/6 tbsp caster (superfine) sugar
150g/5oz/⅔ cup butter, softened
115g/4oz/⅔ cup mixed chopped (candied) peel
75g/3oz/½ cup raisins
melted butter, for brushing

> COOK'S TIP
> *Once the dough has been enriched with butter, do not prove it in too warm a place or the loaf will become greasy.*

1 Using a double layer of baking parchment, line and butter a 15cm/6in deep cake pan or soufflé dish. Extend the paper 7.5cm/3in above the top of the pan or soufflé dish.

2 Sift the flour and salt together into a large bowl. Make a well in the centre. Cream the yeast with 60ml/4 tbsp of the milk, then mix in the remainder.

3 Pour the yeast mixture into the centre of the flour, add the whole eggs and mix in sufficient flour to make a thick batter. Sprinkle a little of the remaining flour over the top and leave to "sponge", in a warm place, for 30 minutes.

4 Add the egg yolks and sugar, and mix to a soft dough. Work in the softened butter, then turn out on to a lightly floured surface and knead for 5 minutes until smooth and elastic. Place in a lightly oiled bowl, cover with lightly oiled clear film (plastic wrap), and leave to rise, in a slightly warm place, for 1½–2 hours, or until the dough has doubled in bulk.

5 Knock back (punch down) the dough and turn out on to a lightly floured surface. Gently knead in the peel and raisins. Shape into a ball and place in the prepared pan or dish. Cover with lightly oiled clear film and leave to rise, in a slightly warm place, for about 1 hour, or until doubled in size.

6 Meanwhile, preheat the oven to 190°C/375°F/Gas 5. Brush the surface with melted butter and cut a cross in the top using a sharp knife. Bake for 20 minutes, then reduce the oven temperature to 180°C/350°F/Gas 4. Brush the top with butter again and bake for a further 25–30 minutes, or until golden. Cool in the pan or dish for 5–10 minutes, then turn out on to a wire rack to cool.

STOLLEN

This German bread, made for the Christmas season, is rich with rum-soaked fruits and is wrapped around a moist almond filling. The folded shape of the dough over the filling represents the baby Jesus wrapped in swaddling clothes.

MAKES 1 LARGE LOAF

INGREDIENTS
75g/3oz/½ cup sultanas (golden raisins)
50g/2oz/¼ cup currants
45ml/3 tbsp rum
375g/13oz/3¼ cups unbleached white bread flour
2.5ml/½ tsp salt
50g/2oz/¼ cup caster (superfine) sugar
1.5ml/¼ tsp ground cardamom
2.5ml/½ tsp ground cinnamon
40g/1½oz fresh yeast
120ml/4fl oz/½ cup lukewarm milk
50g/2oz/¼ cup butter, melted
1 egg, lightly beaten
50g/2oz/⅓ cup mixed chopped (candied) peel
50g/2oz/⅓ cup blanched whole almonds, chopped
melted butter, for brushing
icing (confectioners') sugar, for dusting

FOR THE ALMOND FILLING
115g/4oz/1 cup ground almonds
50g/2oz/¼ cup caster sugar
50g/2oz/½ cup icing sugar
2.5ml/½ tsp lemon juice
½ egg, lightly beaten

1 Lightly grease a baking sheet. Preheat the oven to 180°C/350°F/Gas 4. Put the sultanas and currants in a heatproof bowl and warm for 3–4 minutes. Pour over the rum and set aside.

2 Sift the flour and salt together into a large bowl. Stir in the sugar and spices. Make a well in the centre of the dry ingredients.

3 Mix the yeast with the milk until creamy. Pour into the flour and mix a little of the flour from around the edge into the milk mixture to make a thick batter. Sprinkle some of the remaining flour over the top of the batter, then cover with clear film (plastic wrap) and leave in a warm place for 30 minutes.

4 Add the melted butter and egg and mix to a soft dough. Turn out the dough on to a lightly floured surface and knead for 8–10 minutes until smooth and elastic. Place in a lightly oiled bowl, cover with lightly oiled clear film, and leave to rise, in a warm place, for 2–3 hours, or until doubled in bulk.

5 Mix the ground almonds and sugars together for the filling. Add the lemon juice and sufficient egg to knead to a smooth paste. Shape into a 20cm/8in long "sausage", cover and set aside.

6 Turn out the dough on to a lightly floured surface and knock back (punch down). Pat out the dough into a rectangle about 2.5cm/1in thick and sprinkle over the sultanas, currants, mixed chopped peel and almonds. Fold and knead the dough to incorporate the fruit and nuts.

7 Roll out the dough into an oval about 30 × 23cm/12 × 9in. Roll the centre slightly thinner than the edges. Place the almond paste filling along the centre and fold over the dough to enclose it, making sure that the top of the dough doesn't completely cover the base. The top edge should be slightly in from the bottom edge. Press down to seal.

8 Place the loaf on the prepared baking sheet, cover with lightly oiled clear film and leave to rise, in a warm place, for 45–60 minutes, or until doubled in size.

9 Meanwhile, preheat the oven to 200°C/400°F/Gas 6. Bake the loaf for about 30 minutes, or until it sounds hollow when tapped on the base. Brush the top with melted butter and transfer to a wire rack to cool. Dust with icing sugar just before serving.

Danish Julekage

In Scandinavia, special slightly sweet holiday breads containing fragrant cardamom seeds are common. This exotic bread, enriched with butter and a selection of glacé and dried fruits or "jewels", is traditionally served over the Christmas period with cups of hot spiced punch.

MAKES 1 LOAF

INGREDIENTS
25g/1oz fresh yeast
75ml/5 tbsp lukewarm milk
450g/1lb/4 cups unbleached white bread flour
10ml/2 tsp salt
75g/3oz/6 tbsp butter
15 cardamom pods
2.5ml/½ tsp vanilla essence (extract)
50g/2oz/⅓ cup soft light brown sugar
grated rind of ½ lemon
2 eggs, lightly beaten
50g/2oz/¼ cup ready-to-eat dried apricots, chopped
50g/2oz/¼ cup glacé (candied) pineapple pieces, chopped
50g/2oz/¼ cup red and green glacé (candied) cherries, chopped
25g/1oz/3 tbsp dried dates, chopped
25g/1oz/2 tbsp crystallized stem ginger, chopped

FOR THE GLAZE
1 egg white
10ml/2 tsp water

FOR THE DECORATION
15ml/1 tbsp caster (superfine) sugar
2.5ml/½ tsp ground cinnamon
8 pecan nuts or whole blanched almonds

1 Lightly grease a 23 × 13cm/9 × 5in loaf pan. In a measuring jug (cup), cream the yeast with the milk and set aside until frothy.

2 Sift the flour and salt together into a large bowl. Add the butter and rub in. Make a well in the centre. Add the yeast mixture to the centre of the flour and butter mixture and stir in sufficient flour to form a thick batter. Sprinkle over a little of the remaining flour and set aside in a warm place for 15 minutes.

3 Remove the seeds from the cardamom pods. Put them in a mortar or strong bowl and crush with a pestle or the end of a rolling pin. Add the crushed seeds to the batter with the vanilla essence, sugar, grated lemon rind and beaten eggs, then mix to a soft dough.

4 Knead on a lightly floured surface for 8–10 minutes until smooth and elastic. Place in a lightly oiled bowl, cover with lightly oiled clear film (plastic wrap) and leave to rise, in a warm place, for 1–1½ hours, or until doubled in bulk.

5 Knock back (punch down) the dough and turn it out on to a lightly floured surface. Flatten into a rectangle and sprinkle over half of the apricots, pineapple, cherries, dates and ginger. Fold the sides into the centre and then fold in half to contain the fruit. Flatten into a rectangle again and sprinkle over the remaining fruit. Fold and knead gently to distribute the fruit. Cover the fruited dough with lightly oiled clear film and leave to rest for 10 minutes.

6 Roll the fruited dough into a rectangle 38 × 25cm/15 × 10in. With a short side facing you, fold the bottom third up lengthways and the top third down, tucking in the sides, to form a 23 × 13cm/9 × 5in loaf. Place in the prepared pan, seam side down. Cover with lightly oiled clear film and leave to rise, in a warm place, for 1 hour, or until the dough has reached the top of the pan.

7 Meanwhile, preheat the oven to 180°C/350°F/Gas 4. Using a sharp knife, slash the top of the loaf lengthways and then make diagonal slits on either side.

8 Mix together the egg white and water for the glaze, and brush over the top. Mix the sugar and cinnamon in a bowl, then sprinkle over the top. Decorate with pecan nuts or almonds. Bake for 45–50 minutes, or until risen and browned. Transfer to a wire rack to cool.

TWELFTH NIGHT BREAD

January 6th, Epiphany or the Day of the Three Kings, is celebrated in Spain as a time to exchange Christmas presents. Historically this date was when the Three Wise Men arrived bearing gifts. An ornamental bread ring is specially baked for the occasion. The traditional version contains a silver coin, china figure or dried bean hidden inside. The lucky recipient is declared King of the festival.

MAKES 1 LARGE LOAF

INGREDIENTS
450g/1lb/4 cups unbleached white bread flour
2.5ml/½ tsp salt
25g/1oz fresh yeast
140ml/scant ¼ pint/scant ⅔ cup mixed lukewarm milk and water
75g/3oz/6 tbsp butter
75g/3oz/6 tbsp caster (superfine) sugar
10ml/2 tsp finely grated lemon rind
10ml/2 tsp finely grated orange rind
2 eggs, beaten
15ml/1 tbsp brandy
15ml/1 tbsp orange flower water
silver coin or dried bean (optional)
1 egg white, lightly beaten, for glazing

FOR THE DECORATION
a mixture of candied and glacé fruit slices
flaked (sliced) almonds

> COOK'S TIP
> This bread can be baked in a lightly greased 24cm/9½in ring-shaped cake pan or a savarin mould. Place the dough seam-side down into the pan or mould and seal the ends together.

1 Lightly grease a large baking sheet. Sift the flour and salt together into a large bowl. Make a well in the centre.

2 In a bowl, mix the yeast with the milk and water until the yeast has dissolved. Pour the yeast mixture into the centre of the flour and stir in enough of the flour from around the sides of the well to make a thick batter.

3 Sprinkle a little of the remaining flour over the top of the batter and leave to "sponge", in a warm place, for about 15 minutes or until frothy.

4 Using an electric whisk or a wooden spoon, beat the butter and sugar together in a bowl until soft and creamy, then set aside.

5 Add the citrus rinds, eggs, brandy and orange flower water to the flour mixture and use a wooden spoon to mix to a sticky dough.

6 Using one hand, beat the mixture until it forms a fairly smooth dough. Gradually beat in the reserved butter mixture and beat for a few minutes until the dough is smooth and elastic. Cover with lightly oiled clear film (plastic wrap) and leave to rise, in a warm place, for about 1½ hours, or until doubled in bulk.

7 Knock back (punch down) the dough and turn out on to a lightly floured surface. Gently knead for 2 or 3 minutes. Sterilize the lucky coin or bean in boiling water, if using, and work into the dough.

8 Using a rolling pin lightly dusted with flour, roll out the dough into a long strip measuring about 66 × 13cm/26 × 5in.

9 Roll up the dough from one long side like a Swiss roll to make a long "sausage" shape. Place seam side down on the prepared baking sheet and seal the ends together to make a ring. Cover with lightly oiled clear film and leave to rise, in a warm place, for 1–1½ hours, or until doubled in size.

10 Meanwhile, preheat the oven to 180°C/350°F/Gas 4. Brush the dough ring with lightly beaten egg white and decorate with the candied and glacé fruit slices, pushing them slightly into the dough. Sprinkle the top with almond flakes and bake for 30–35 minutes, or until risen and golden. Turn the loaf out on to a wire rack to cool.

KUGELHOPF

This inviting, fluted ring-shaped bread originates from Alsace, although Germany, Hungary and Austria all have their own variations. Kugelhopf can be sweet or savoury; this version is richly flavoured with nuts, onion and bacon.

MAKES 1 LOAF

INGREDIENTS
150g/5oz/²⁄₃ cup unsalted (sweet) butter, softened
12 walnut halves
675g/1½lb/6 cups unbleached white bread flour
7.5ml/1½ tsp salt
20g/¾oz fresh yeast
300ml/10fl oz/1¼ cups milk
15ml/1 tbsp vegetable oil
115g/4oz smoked bacon, diced
1 onion, finely chopped
5 eggs, beaten
freshly ground black pepper

> VARIATION
> *If you wish to make a sweet kugelhopf replace the walnuts with whole almonds and the bacon and onion with 115g/4oz/²⁄₃ cup raisins and 50g/2oz/ ¹⁄₃ cup mixed chopped (candied) peel. Add 50g/ 2oz/¼ cup caster (superfine) sugar to the flour in step 2 and omit the black pepper.*

1 Use 25g/1oz/2 tbsp of the butter to grease a 23cm/9in kugelhopf mould. Place 8 walnut halves around the base and chop the remainder.

2 Sift the flour and salt together into a large bowl and season with pepper. Make a well in the centre. In a jug (pitcher), cream the yeast with 45ml/3 tbsp of the milk. Pour into the centre of the flour with the remaining milk. Mix in a little flour to make a thick batter. Sprinkle a little of the remaining flour over the top of the batter, cover with clear film (plastic wrap) and leave to rise in a warm place for 20–30 minutes until the yeast mixture bubbles.

3 Meanwhile, heat the oil in a frying pan and cook the bacon and onion over a medium heat until the onion is pale golden. Set aside to cool.

4 Add the eggs to the flour mixture and gradually beat in the flour, using your hand. Gradually beat in the remaining softened butter to form a soft dough. Cover with lightly oiled clear film and leave to rise, in a warm place, for 45–60 minutes, or until almost doubled in bulk. Preheat the oven to 200°C/400°F/Gas 6.

5 Knock back (punch down) the dough and gently knead in the bacon, onion and nuts. Place in the mould, cover with lightly oiled clear film and leave to rise, in a warm place, for about 1 hour, or until it has risen to the top of the mould.

6 Bake for 40–45 minutes, or until the loaf has browned and sounds hollow when tapped on the base. Cool in the mould for 5 minutes, then on a wire rack.

MACHINE-MADE BREADS

If making bread by hand is a labour of love, using a bread machine is a liberating labour saver. When you're busy, what could be simpler than measuring some liquid into a pan, sprinkling flour over the top, adding salt, sugar and yeast and flicking a switch or two? While you get on with other things, the machine mixes, kneads, rests and proves the dough, then bakes it. The results can be excellent, provided you follow the chosen recipe exactly, and take the time to get to know your own appliance before you begin.

Bread machines vary in capacity, so many of the recipes in this section give ingredients for three different sizes of loaf. Where only one set of ingredients is given, it should be possible to bake the bread in any machine, but check your handbook to make sure.

Using a bread machine doesn't confine you to the simpler breads, either. Rich breads, shaped loaves and fancy rolls are all feasible. Just use the machine to make the dough, then shape it by hand and bake it in a conventional oven.

BASIC BREADS

Having a daily supply of really fresh bread has never been easier. In less time than it would take you to visit the baker's shop, you can assemble the ingredients and set up the machine. If you have a delay mechanism, you can even do this just before going to bed. Time the machine to finish baking just after your alarm clock goes off, so you can place the bread on a rack to cool while you get ready, and sit down to a breakfast of warm bread before you face the day. In this section you'll find the daily breads that everyone enjoys, from white to wholemeal (whole-wheat) and a Granary Bread that is perfect for those who like a bit of texture in their bread. For a light, velvety crumb, try the Milk Loaf, but don't make this one ahead of baking. If you wish to use the delay switch, choose the Farmhouse Loaf, which uses powdered milk instead of fresh.

WHITE BREAD

This is a simple, all-purpose white bread recipe, which makes the perfect basis for experimenting. Try using different brands of flours and be prepared to make minor alterations to quantities if necessary, to find the optimum recipe for your machine.

MAKES 1 LOAF

SMALL
210ml/7½fl oz/scant 1 cup water
375g/13oz/3¼ cups unbleached white
   bread flour
7.5ml/1½ tsp salt
15ml/1 tbsp granulated sugar
25g/1oz/2 tbsp butter
5ml/1 tsp easy-blend (rapid-rise)
   dried yeast
unbleached white bread flour,
   for dusting

MEDIUM
320ml/11¼fl oz/generous 1⅓ cups
   water
500g/1lb 2oz/4½ cups unbleached
   white bread flour
7.5ml/1½ tsp salt
15ml/1 tbsp granulated sugar
25g/1oz/2 tbsp butter
5ml/1 tsp easy-blend (rapid-rise)
   dried yeast
unbleached white bread flour,
   for dusting

LARGE
420ml/15fl oz/generous 1¾ cups water
675g/1½lb/6 cups unbleached white
   bread flour
10ml/2 tsp salt
22ml/1½ tbsp granulated sugar
40g/1½oz/3 tbsp butter
7.5ml/1½ tsp easy-blend (rapid-rise)
   dried yeast
unbleached white bread flour,
   for dusting

COOK'S TIP
To give the crust a richer golden appearance, add skimmed milk powder (non fat dry milk) to the flour. For a small loaf, you will need 15ml/1 tbsp; medium, 22ml/1½ tbsp and large, 30ml/2 tbsp.

1 Pour the water into the bread machine pan. However, if the instructions for your machine specify that the yeast is to be placed in the pan first, reverse the order in which you add the liquid and dry ingredients.

2 Sprinkle over the flour, ensuring that it covers the water. Add the salt, sugar and butter in separate corners of the bread pan. Make a small indent in the centre of the flour (but not down as far as the liquid) and add the yeast.

3 Close the lid. Set the bread machine to the basic/normal setting and select medium crust. Press Start.

4 Remove the bread pan at the end of the baking cycle and turn out the loaf on to a wire rack to cool.

Light Wholemeal Bread

A tasty, light wholemeal loaf which can be cooked on the quicker basic or normal setting. This bread toasts very well.

Makes 1 loaf

Small
280ml/10fl oz/1¼ cups water
250g/9oz/2¼ cups wholemeal
　(whole-wheat) bread flour
125g/4½oz/generous 1 cup white
　bread flour
7.5ml/1½ tsp salt
7.5ml/1½ tsp granulated sugar
20g/¾oz/1½ tbsp butter
5ml/1 tsp easy-blend (rapid-rise)
　dried yeast

Medium
350ml/12fl oz/1½ cups water
350g/12oz/3 cups wholemeal
　(whole-wheat) bread flour
150g/5½oz/1⅓ cups white bread flour
10ml/2 tsp salt
10ml/2 tsp granulated sugar
25g/1oz/2 tbsp butter
7.5ml/1½ tsp easy-blend (rapid-rise)
　dried yeast

Large
450ml/16fl oz/scant 2 cups water
475g/1lb 1oz/4¼ cups wholemeal
　(whole-wheat) bread flour
200g/7oz/1¾ cups white bread flour
10ml/2 tsp salt
15ml/1 tbsp granulated sugar
25g/1oz/2 tbsp butter
10ml/2 tsp easy-blend (rapid-rise)
　dried yeast

Variation
This is a fairly light brown loaf as it contains a mixture of white and wholemeal (whole-wheat) bread flour. For an even lighter brown bread, replace the wholemeal bread flour with brown bread flour. This contains less bran and wheatgerm than wholemeal flour, and will produce a slightly lighter bread.

1 Pour the water into the bread machine pan. If the instructions for your bread machine specify that the yeast is to be placed in the pan first, reverse the order in which you add the liquid and dry ingredients to the pan.

2 Sprinkle over each type of flour in turn, ensuring that the water is completely covered. Add the salt, sugar and butter in separate corners of the bread pan. Make a small indent in the centre of the flour and add the yeast.

3 Close the lid. Set the bread machine to the basic/normal setting and select the medium crust. Press Start.

4 Remove the bread pan at the end of the baking cycle and turn out the loaf on to a wire rack to cool.

MILK LOAF

Adding milk results in a soft, velvety grained loaf with a beautifully browned crust.
It is important to use milk at room temperature.

MAKES 1 LOAF

SMALL
180ml/6½fl oz/generous ¾ cup milk
60ml/2fl oz/¼ cup water
375g/13oz/3¼ cups unbleached white
   bread flour
7.5ml/1½ tsp salt
10ml/2 tsp granulated sugar
20g/¾oz/1½ tbsp butter
2.5ml/½ tsp easy-blend dried
   (rapid-rise) yeast

LARGE
280ml/10fl oz/1¼ cups milk
130ml/4½fl oz/½ cup + 1 tbsp water
675g/1½lb/6 cups unbleached white
   bread flour
10ml/2 tsp salt
15ml/1 tbsp granulated sugar
25g/1oz/2 tbsp butter
7.5ml/1½ tsp easy-blend dried
   (rapid-rise) yeast

MEDIUM
200ml/7fl oz/⅞ cup milk
100ml/3½fl oz/7 tbsp water
450g/1lb/4 cups unbleached white
   bread flour
7.5ml/1½ tsp salt
10ml/2 tsp granulated sugar
25g/1oz/2 tbsp butter
5ml/1 tsp easy-blend dried
   (rapid-rise) yeast

1 Pour the milk and water into the bread machine pan. If the instructions for your machine specify that the yeast is to be placed in the pan first, reverse the order in which you add the liquid and dry ingredients. Sprinkle over the flour, covering the water. Add the salt, sugar and butter in separate corners of the pan. Make a small indent in the centre of the flour and add the yeast.

2 Close the lid. Set the bread machine to the basic/normal setting and select the medium crust. Press Start.

3 Remove the bread pan at the end of the baking cycle and turn out the loaf on to a wire rack to cool.

GRANARY BREAD

Granary flour – like Malthouse flour – is a blend, and contains malted wheat grain which gives a crunchy texture to this loaf.

MAKES 1 LOAF

SMALL
240ml/8½fl oz/generous 1 cup
   water
375g/13oz/3¼ cups Granary
   (whole-wheat) bread flour
5ml/1 tsp salt
10ml/2 tsp granulated sugar
20g/¾oz/1½ tbsp butter
2.5ml/½tsp easy-blend (rapid-rise)
   dried yeast

MEDIUM
350ml/12fl oz/1½ cups water
500g/1lb 2oz/4½ cups Granary
   (whole-wheat) bread flour
7.5ml/1½ tsp salt
15ml/1 tbsp granulated sugar
25g/1oz/2 tbsp butter
7.5ml/1½ tsp easy-blend (rapid-rise)
   dried yeast

LARGE
400ml/14fl oz/generous 1⅔ cups water
675g/1½lb/6 cups Granary
   (whole-wheat) bread flour
10ml/2 tsp salt
15ml/1 tbsp granulated sugar
25g/1oz/2 tbsp butter
7.5ml/1½ tsp easy-blend (rapid-rise)
   dried yeast

1 Add the water to the bread machine pan. If the instructions for your machine specify that the yeast is to be placed in the pan first, simply reverse the order in which you add the liquid and dry ingredients. Sprinkle over the flour, covering the water. Add the salt, sugar and butter in separate corners of the pan. Make a small indent in the centre of the flour and add the yeast.

2 Close the lid. Set the bread machine to the wholemeal or multi-grain setting and select the medium crust. Press Start.

3 Remove the bread pan at the end of the baking cycle, and turn out the loaf on to a wire rack to cool.

FARMHOUSE LOAF

The flour-dusted split top gives a charmingly rustic look to this tasty wholemeal-enriched white loaf. It is perfect for everyday meals.

MAKES 1 LOAF

SMALL

210ml/7½fl oz/scant 1 cup water

350g/12oz/3 cups unbleached white bread flour, plus extra for dusting

25g/1oz/¼ cup wholemeal (whole-wheat) bread flour

15ml/1 tbsp skimmed milk powder (non fat dry milk)

7.5ml/1½ tsp salt

7.5ml/1½ tsp granulated sugar

15g/½oz/1 tbsp butter

4ml/¾ tsp easy-blend (rapid-rise) dried yeast

water, for glazing

MEDIUM

320ml/11¼fl oz/generous 1⅓ cups water

425g/15oz/3¾ cups unbleached white bread flour, plus extra for dusting

75g/3oz/¾ cup wholemeal (whole-wheat) bread flour

22ml/1½ tbsp skimmed milk powder (non fat dry milk)

7.5ml/1½ tsp salt

7.5ml/1½ tsp granulated sugar

25g/1oz/2 tbsp butter

5ml/1 tsp easy-blend (rapid-rise) dried yeast

water, for glazing

LARGE

420ml/15fl oz/generous 1¾ cups water

600g/1lb 5oz/5¼ cups unbleached white bread flour, plus extra for dusting

75g/3oz/¾ cup wholemeal (whole-wheat) bread flour

30ml/2 tbsp skimmed milk powder (non fat dry milk)

10ml/2 tsp salt

10ml/2 tsp granulated sugar

25g/1oz/2 tbsp butter

7.5ml/1½ tsp easy-blend (rapid-rise) dried yeast

water, for glazing

1 Pour the water into the bread pan. If the instructions for your machine specify that the yeast is to be placed in the pan first, reverse the order in which you add the liquid and dry ingredients.

2 Sprinkle over both the flours, covering the water completely. Add the skimmed milk powder. Add the salt, sugar and butter in separate corners of the bread pan. Make a small indent in the centre of the flour (but not down as far as the liquid) and then add the yeast.

3 Close the lid. Set the bread machine to the basic/normal setting and select the medium crust. Press Start.

4 Ten minutes before the baking time commences, brush the top of the loaf with water and dust with a little white bread flour. Slash the top of the bread with a sharp knife.

5 Remove the bread pan at the end of the baking cycle and turn out the loaf on to a wire rack to cool.

COOK'S TIP
Try this rustic bread using Granary (whole-wheat) or Malthouse flour instead of wholemeal bread flour for added texture.

FRENCH BREAD

It is traditional for French bread to have a crisp crust and light, chewy crumb.
Use the French bread setting on your bread machine to achieve this unique texture.

MAKES 1–4 LOAVES

SMALL
MAKES 1 LOAF
150ml/5fl oz/⅔ cup water
225g/8oz/2 cups unbleached white
  bread flour
5ml/1 tsp salt
7.5ml/1½ tsp easy-blend (rapid-rise)
  dried yeast

MEDIUM
MAKES 2–3 LOAVES
315ml/11fl oz/1⅓ cups water
450g/1lb/4 cups unbleached white
  bread flour
7.5ml/1½ tsp salt
7.5ml/1½ tsp easy-blend (rapid-rise)
  dried yeast

LARGE
MAKES 3–4 LOAVES
500ml/17½fl oz/2⅛ cups water
675g/1½lb/6 cups unbleached white
  bread flour
10ml/2 tsp salt
10ml/2 tsp easy-blend (rapid-rise)
  dried yeast

COOK'S TIP
Use the French bread baking setting if you do not
have a French bread dough setting. Remove the
dough before the final rising stage and shape as
directed in the recipe.

1 Add the water to the bread machine pan. If the instructions for your machine specify that the yeast is to be placed in the pan first, simply reverse the order in which you add the liquid and dry ingredients to the pan.

2 Sprinkle over the flour, to cover the water. Add the salt in a corner. Make an indent in the centre of the flour and add the yeast. Close the lid. Select the French bread dough setting (see Cook's Tip). Press Start.

3 When the dough cycle has finished, remove the dough from the machine, place it on a lightly floured surface and knock it back (punch it down). Divide it into two or three equal portions if using the medium quantity or three or four portions if using the large quantity.

4 On a floured surface shape each piece of dough into a ball, then roll out to a rectangle measuring 18–20 × 7.5cm/7–8 × 3in. Fold one-third up lengthways and one-third down, then press. Repeat twice more, leaving the dough to rest between foldings to avoid tearing. Shape each ball in the same way.

5 Gently roll and stretch each piece to a 28–33cm/11–13in loaf, depending on whether you aim to make smaller or larger loaves. Place each loaf in a floured banneton or between the folds of a floured and pleated dishtowel, so that the French bread shape is maintained during rising.

6 Cover with lightly oiled clear film (plastic wrap) and leave in a warm place for 30–45 minutes. Preheat the oven to 230°C/450°F/Gas 8.

7 Roll the loaf or loaves on to a baking sheet, spacing them well apart. Slash the top of each loaf several times with a sharp knife. Place at the top of the oven, spray the inside of the oven with water and bake for 15–20 minutes, or until golden. Transfer the French bread sticks to a wire rack to cool.

SAVOURY BREADS

Anyone who imagines a bread machine is only good for the most ordinary of breads should take a glance at the recipes in this chapter. Ciabatta, Caramelized Onion Bread and Marbled Pesto Bread are just three of the specialized breads described here. For many of the breads, the machine is used merely to prepare the dough, with the final shaping done by hand. However, Grainy Mustard & Beer Loaf is entirely made within the machine, as is the very tasty Sun-Dried Tomato Bread. If you're seeking to impress dinner party guests, consider making Venison Tordu, a twisted bread, which has strips of smoked venison running through it. This gives the bread a gamey flavour, which is underlined by the crushed juniper berries that are also included.

CIABATTA

This popular Italian flat loaf is irregularly shaped and typically has large air holes in the crumb. The dough for this bread is extremely wet. Do not be tempted to add more flour – it's meant to be that way.

MAKES 2 LOAVES

INGREDIENTS

FOR THE *BIGA*
200ml/7fl oz/⅞ cup water
175g/6oz/1½ cups unbleached white bread flour
2.5ml/½ tsp easy-blend (rapid-rise) dried yeast

FOR THE CIABATTA DOUGH
200ml/7fl oz/⅞ cup water
30ml/2 tbsp milk
30ml/2 tbsp extra virgin olive oil
325g/11½oz/scant 3 cups unbleached white bread flour, plus extra for dusting
7.5ml/1½ tsp salt
2.5ml/½ tsp granulated sugar
1.5ml/¼ tsp easy-blend (rapid-rise) dried yeast

1 Pour the water for the *biga* into the bread pan. If necessary, reverse the order in which you add the liquid and dry ingredients. Sprinkle over the flour, covering the water. Make an indent in the centre of the flour and add the yeast. Close the lid and set the bread machine to the dough setting, choosing the basic dough setting if there is more than one alternative. Press Start. Mix for 5 minutes, then switch off the machine.

2 Leave the *biga* in the bread machine, or place in a large mixing bowl covered with lightly oiled clear film (plastic wrap), leaving it undisturbed, overnight or for at least 12 hours, until the dough has risen and is just starting to collapse.

3 Return the *biga* to the pan, if necessary. Add the water, milk and oil for the ciabatta dough. Sprinkle over the flour. Add the salt and sugar in separate corners. Make a small indent in the centre of the flour and add the yeast.

4 Set the bread machine to the dough setting, choosing the basic dough setting, if there is more than one alternative. Press Start.

5 When the cycle has finished, transfer the dough to a bowl and cover with oiled clear film. Leave to rise for about 1 hour, until the dough has tripled in size. Sprinkle two baking sheets with flour.

6 Using a spoon or a dough scraper, divide the dough into two portions. Carefully tip one portion of the dough on to one of the prepared baking sheets, trying to avoid knocking the air out of the dough. Using well-floured hands shape the dough into a rectangular loaf about 2.5cm/1in thick, pulling and stretching as necessary. Repeat with the remaining piece of dough.

7 Sprinkle both loaves with flour. Leave them, uncovered, in a warm place for about 20–30 minutes. The dough will spread and rise. Meanwhile, preheat the oven to 220°C/425°F/Gas 7.

8 Bake the ciabatta for 25–30 minutes, or until both loaves have risen, are light golden in colour and sound hollow when tapped on the base. Transfer them to a wire rack to cool before serving with butter, or olive oil for dipping.

FETA & OLIVE LOAF

This bread has a delicious flavour, thanks to the Mediterranean ingredients, and it will conjure up memories of summer holidays in Greece.

MAKES 1 LOAF

INGREDIENTS
210ml/7½fl oz/scant 1 cup water
350g/12oz/3 cups unbleached white bread flour
25g/1oz/¼ cup wholemeal (whole-wheat) bread flour
15ml/1 tbsp skimmed milk powder (non-fat dry milk)
5ml/1 tsp salt
7.5ml/1½ tsp granulated sugar
5ml/1 tsp easy-blend (rapid-rise) dried yeast
40g/1½oz/scant ½ cup well drained, pitted black olives, chopped
50g/2oz feta cheese, crumbled
15ml/1 tbsp olive oil, for brushing

1 Pour the water into the bread pan. If necessary, reverse the order in which you add the liquid and dry ingredients. Sprinkle over the unbleached white bread and wholemeal flours, covering the water completely. Add the skimmed milk powder. Place the salt and sugar in separate corners of the bread pan. Make an indent in the flour, and add the yeast.

2 Set the bread machine to the dough setting, choosing basic raisin dough if available. Press Start. Lightly oil a 18–20cm/7–8in deep round cake pan.

3 Add the olives and feta cheese when the bread machine beeps or 5 minutes before the end of the kneading cycle. Once the dough cycle has finished, place the dough on a lightly floured surface and knock back (punch down) gently.

4 Shape the dough into a plump ball, the same diameter as the pan. Place in the prepared pan, cover with oiled clear film (plastic wrap) and leave to rise for 30–45 minutes. Preheat the oven to 200°C/400°F/Gas 6.

5 Remove the clear film and brush the olive oil over the top of the loaf. Bake in the oven for 35–40 minutes, or until golden. Turn the bread out on to a wire rack to cool.

LEEK & PANCETTA BREAD

What could be tastier than this tray bread, topped with leeks and pancetta in a savoury custard? Serve it sliced, with a simple salad of dressed leaves.

MAKES 1 LOAF

INGREDIENTS
90ml/6 tbsp water
1 egg
225g/8oz/2 cups unbleached white bread flour
5ml/1 tsp salt
25g/1oz butter
5ml/1 tsp easy-blend (rapid-rise) dried yeast

FOR THE FILLING
575g/1¼lb/4–5 leeks, thinly sliced
30ml/2 tbsp sunflower oil
75g/3oz sliced pancetta or streaky (fatty) bacon, cut into strips
140ml/5fl oz/⅝ cup sour cream
70ml/2½fl oz/5 tbsp milk
2 eggs, lightly beaten
15ml/1 tbsp chopped fresh basil leaves
salt and ground black pepper

1 Pour the water and egg into the bread machine pan, reversing the order in which you add wet and dry ingredients if necessary. Sprinkle over the flour, covering the liquid, then add the salt and butter in separate corners. Make an indent in the centre of the flour and add the yeast. Set the bread machine to the dough setting choosing basic or pizza dough setting if available. Press Start.

2 Lightly oil a 20 × 30cm/8 × 12in Swiss (jelly) roll tin (pan), about 1cm/½in deep. Fry the leeks in a frying pan in the oil until softened but not browned. When the dough is ready, knock back (punch down), then roll it out to fit the pan, covering the base and sides evenly. Preheat the oven to 190°C/375°F/Gas 5.

3 Scatter the leeks and pancetta over the dough. Mix the sour cream, milk, eggs, basil, salt and pepper and pour over the leeks. Bake for 30–35 minutes, or until the filling has set and the edges of the bread are golden. Serve hot or warm.

Venison Tordu

This pretty twisted bread is punctuated with strips of smoked venison, black pepper and crushed juniper berries. It tastes delicious on its own, perhaps with a glass of red wine. Alternatively, cut the bread into thick slices and serve it with olives and salted nuts as a precursor to an Italian meal.

Makes 1 loaf

Ingredients
230ml/8fl oz/1 cup water
350g/12oz/3 cups unbleached white bread flour
5ml/1 tsp granulated sugar
5ml/1 tsp salt
5ml/1 tsp easy-blend (rapid-rise) dried yeast
40g/1½oz smoked venison, cut into strips
5ml/1 tsp freshly ground black pepper
5ml/1 tsp juniper berries, crushed
unbleached white bread flour, for dusting

Cook's Tip
Try using cured and smoked venison, marinated in olive oil and herbs, for this recipe. The olive oil and herbs add an extra flavour which beautifully complements this bread. Alternatively, sprinkle 5ml/1 tsp of dried herbs such as rosemary, thyme, sage or oregano over the dough in step 4.

1 Pour the water into the bread machine pan. If the instructions for your bread machine specify that the yeast is to be placed in the pan first, simply reverse the order in which you add the water and dry ingredients to the pan.

2 Sprinkle over the white bread flour, ensuring that it completely covers the water. Add the sugar and salt, placing them in separate corners of the bread pan. Make a shallow indent in the centre of the flour (but not down as far as the liquid) and add the easy-blend (rapid-rise) dried yeast.

3 Close the lid. Set the bread machine to the dough setting, choosing the basic dough setting if available. Press Start. Lightly oil a baking sheet.

4 When the dough cycle has finished, remove the dough from the bread machine pan and place it on a lightly floured surface. Knock back (punch down) gently. Shape the dough into a ball and flatten the top slightly.

5 Roll the dough out to a round, about 2cm/¾in thick. Sprinkle the top of the dough with venison strips, black pepper and juniper berries. Leave a 1cm/½in clear border around the edge.

6 Fold one side of the dough to the centre, then repeat on the other side. Press the folds gently with a rolling pin to seal them, then fold the flavoured dough again along the centre line. Press the seam gently to seal, then roll the dough backwards and forwards to make a loaf about 65cm/26in long.

7 Using the side of your hand, press across the centre of the loaf to make an indentation. Bring both ends towards each other to make an upside down "U" shape and twist together.

8 Place the venison tordu on the prepared baking sheet. Cover the loaf with lightly oiled clear film (plastic wrap) and leave to rise in a warm place for 30 minutes, or until it has almost doubled in size. Meanwhile, preheat the oven to 220°C/425°F/Gas 7. Remove the clear film and dust the top of the twisted loaf with white bread flour.

9 Bake for 25–30 minutes, or until the bread is golden and sounds hollow when tapped on the base. Turn out on to a wire rack to cool. Serve freshly baked, while the bread is still slightly warm.

GRAINY MUSTARD & BEER LOAF

For a ploughman's lunch par excellence, serve chunks of this wonderful bread with mature cheeses and pickles. Add a few celery sticks for extra crunch.

MAKES 1 LOAF

SMALL
180ml/6½fl oz/generous ¾ cup
 flat beer
15ml/1 tbsp vegetable oil
30ml/2 tbsp wholegrain mustard
250g/9oz/2¼ cups unbleached white
 bread flour
125g/4½oz/generous 1 cup wholemeal
 (whole-wheat) bread flour
15ml/1 tbsp skimmed milk powder
 (non fat dry milk)
5ml/1 tsp salt
7.5ml/1½ tsp granulated sugar
5ml/1 tsp easy-blend (rapid-rise)
 dried yeast

MEDIUM
280ml/10fl oz/1¼ cups flat beer
15ml/1 tbsp vegetable oil
45ml/3 tbsp wholegrain mustard
350g/12oz/3 cups unbleached white
 bread flour
150g/5½oz/1⅓ cups wholemeal
 (whole-wheat) bread flour
22ml/1½ tbsp skimmed milk powder
 (non fat dry milk)
7.5ml/1½ tsp salt
10ml/2 tsp granulated sugar
5ml/1 tsp easy-blend (rapid-rise)
 dried yeast

LARGE
360ml/12½fl oz/generous 1½ cups
 flat beer
30ml/2 tbsp vegetable oil
60ml/4 tbsp wholegrain mustard
475g/1lb 1oz/4¼ cups unbleached
 white bread flour
200g/7oz/1¾ cups wholemeal
 (whole-wheat) bread flour
30ml/2 tbsp skimmed milk powder
 (non-fat dry milk)
7.5ml/1½ tsp salt
15ml/1 tbsp granulated sugar
7.5ml/1½ tsp easy-blend (rapid-rise)
 dried yeast

COOK'S TIP
Use pale ale for a more subtle taste or brown ale if you prefer a stronger flavour to your bread. Open at least 1 hour before using, to make sure it is flat.

1 Pour the beer and oil into the bread machine pan. Add the mustard. If the instructions for your machine specify that the yeast is to be placed in the pan first, reverse the order in which you add the liquid and dry ingredients.

2 Sprinkle over the white and wholemeal (whole-wheat) flours, ensuring that the liquid is completely covered. Add the skimmed milk powder. Add the salt and sugar, placing them in separate corners of the bread pan. Make a small indent in the centre of the flour (but not down as far as the liquid) and add the yeast.

3 Close the lid. Set the bread machine to the basic/normal setting and select the medium crust. Press Start.

4 Remove the bread pan at the end of the baking cycle and turn out the loaf on to a wire rack to cool.

Caramelized Onion Bread

The unmistakable, mouthwatering flavour of golden fried onions is captured in this Coburg-shaped bread. Serve with soup, cheeses or salad.

Makes 1 loaf

Ingredients
50g/2oz/¼ cup butter
2 onions, chopped
280ml/10fl oz/1¼ cups water
15ml/1 tbsp clear honey
450g/1lb/4 cups unbleached white bread flour
7.5ml/1½ tsp salt
2.5ml/½ tsp freshly ground black pepper
7.5ml/1½ tsp easy-blend (rapid-rise) dried yeast

1 Melt the butter in a frying pan and sauté the onions over a low heat until soft and golden. Remove the pan from the heat and let the onions cool slightly. Place a sieve over the bread machine pan, then tip the contents of the frying pan into it, so that the butter and cooking juices fall into the pan. Set the onions aside to cool completely.

2 Add the water and honey to the bread pan. Reverse the order in which you add the wet and dry ingredients if necessary. Sprinkle over the flour, covering the liquid. Place the salt and pepper in separate corners. Make a shallow indent in the centre of the flour and add the yeast. Close the lid.

3 Set the bread machine to the dough setting, choosing the basic raisin dough setting if available. Press Start. Add the onions when the machine beeps or in the last 5 minutes of kneading. Lightly flour a baking sheet.

4 When the cycle has finished, remove the dough from the bread pan and place on a lightly floured surface. Knock back (punch down) the dough gently, then shape into a ball. Place it on the baking sheet and cover with oiled clear film (plastic wrap). Leave to rise for about 45 minutes.

5 Preheat the oven to 200°C/400°F/Gas 6. Slash a 1cm/½in deep cross in the top of the loaf. Bake for 35–40 minutes. Turn out on to a wire rack to cool.

THREE-CHEESES BREAD

A tempting trio of Italian cheeses – mascarpone, Gorgonzola and Parmesan – is responsible for the marvellous flavour of this round loaf.

MAKES 1 LOAF

180ml/6½fl oz/generous ¾ cup water
1 egg, beaten
100g/3½oz/5 tbsp mascarpone cheese
400g/14oz/3½ cups unbleached white bread flour
50g/2oz/½ cup Granary (whole-wheat) flour
10ml/2 tsp granulated sugar
5ml/1 tsp salt
7.5ml/1½ tsp easy-blend (rapid-rise) dried yeast
75g/3oz Mountain Gorgonzola cheese, cut into small dice
75g/3oz/1 cup freshly grated Parmesan cheese
45ml/3 tbsp chopped fresh chives

FOR THE TOPPING
1 egg yolk
15ml/1 tbsp water
15ml/1 tbsp wheat flakes

1 Add the water, egg and mascarpone to the machine pan. If the instructions for your machine specify that the yeast is to be placed in the pan first, reverse the order in which you add the liquid and dry ingredients. Sprinkle over all the flour, covering the water. Add the sugar and salt in separate corners. Make a small indent in the flour (but not down as far as the liquid) and add the yeast. Close the lid and select the dough setting, choosing basic raisin dough if available. Press Start.

2 Add the Gorgonzola, Parmesan and chives when the machine beeps or during the last 5 minutes of kneading. When the dough is ready, place it on a floured surface. Knock back (punch down) gently, then shape into a 20cm/8in round loaf.

3 Cover with oiled clear film (plastic wrap). Leave to rise in a warm place for 30–45 minutes. Preheat the oven to 200°C/400°F/Gas 6 and lightly oil a baking sheet. Brush with the egg yolk and water, and sprinkle with wheat flakes. Score the bread into 8. Bake for 30 minutes, or until golden and hollow sounding. Cool.

Sun-dried Tomato Bread

The dense texture and highly concentrated flavour of sun-dried tomatoes makes them perfect for flavouring bread dough, and when Parmesan cheese is added, the result is an exceptionally tasty loaf that everyone will enjoy.

Makes 1 loaf

Small

15g/½oz/¼ cup sun-dried tomatoes

130ml/4½fl oz/½ cup + 1 tbsp water

70ml/2½fl oz/¼ cup + 1 tbsp milk

15ml/1 tbsp extra virgin olive oil

325g/11½oz/scant 3 cups unbleached white bread flour

50g/2oz/½ cup wholemeal (whole-wheat) bread flour

40g/1½oz/½ cup freshly grated Parmesan cheese

5ml/1 tsp salt

5ml/1 tsp granulated sugar

4ml/¾ tsp easy-blend (rapid-rise) dried yeast

Medium

25g/1oz/½ cup sun-dried tomatoes

190ml/6¾fl oz/scant ⅞ cup water

115ml/4fl oz/½ cup milk

30ml/2 tbsp extra virgin olive oil

425g/15oz/3¾ cups unbleached white bread flour

75g/3oz/¾ cup wholemeal (whole-wheat) bread flour

50g/2oz/⅔ cup freshly grated Parmesan cheese

7.5ml/1½ tsp salt

10ml/2 tsp granulated sugar

5ml/1 tsp easy-blend (rapid-rise) dried yeast

Large

40g/1½oz/¾ cup sun-dried tomatoes

240ml/8½fl oz/generous 1 cup water

140ml/5fl oz/⅝ cup milk

45ml/3 tbsp extra virgin olive oil

575g/1¼lb/5 cups unbleached white bread flour

115g/4oz/1 cup wholemeal (whole-wheat) bread flour

75g/3oz/1 cup freshly grated Parmesan cheese

10ml/2 tsp salt

10ml/2 tsp granulated sugar

7.5ml/1½ tsp easy-blend (rapid-rise) dried yeast

1 Place the sun-dried tomatoes in a small bowl and pour over enough warm water to cover them. Leave to soak for 15 minutes, then tip into a sieve which you have placed over a measuring jug (cup). Allow the tomatoes to drain thoroughly, then chop them finely.

2 Check the quantity of tomato water against the amount of water required for the loaf, and add more water if this is necessary. Pour it into the bread machine pan, then add the milk and olive oil. If the instructions for your machine specify that the yeast is to be placed in the pan first, then simply reverse the order in which you add the liquid and dry ingredients.

3 Sprinkle over both types of flour, ensuring that the liquid is completely covered. Sprinkle over the Parmesan, then add the salt and sugar, placing them in separate corners of the bread pan. Make a small indent in the centre of the flour (but not down as far as the liquid) and add the yeast.

4 Close the lid. Set the bread machine to the basic/normal setting, choosing the raisin setting, if available, and select the medium crust. Press Start. Add the tomatoes at the beep or during the last 5 minutes of kneading. Remove the bread pan at the end of the baking cycle, and turn out the loaf on to a wire rack to cool.

Marbled Pesto Bread

Using ready-made pesto sauce means that this scrumptious bread is very easy to make. Use a good quality sauce – or, if you have the time, make your own – so that the flavours of garlic, basil, pine nuts and Parmesan cheese can be clearly discerned.

Makes 1 loaf

Ingredients
140ml/scant 5fl oz/⅝ cup milk
150ml/5fl oz/scant ⅔ cup water
30ml/2 tbsp extra virgin olive oil
450g/1lb/4 cups unbleached white bread flour
7.5ml/1½ tsp granulated sugar
7.5ml/1½ tsp salt
7.5ml/1½ tsp easy-blend (rapid-rise) dried yeast
100g/3½oz/7 tbsp ready-made pesto sauce

For the topping
15ml/1 tbsp extra virgin olive oil
10ml/2 tsp coarse sea salt

> ### Cook's Tip
> For a really luxurious twist to this bread, make your own pesto filling. Put 75g/3oz basil leaves, 1 clove garlic, 30ml/2 tbsp pine nuts, salt and pepper, and 90ml/3fl oz olive oil in a mortar and crush to a paste with a pestle, or alternatively, place in a blender and blend until creamy. Work in 50g/2oz freshly grated Parmesan cheese. Any leftover pesto can be kept for up to 2 weeks in the refrigerator.

1 Remove the milk from the refrigerator 30 minutes before using, to bring it to room temperature. Pour the water, milk and extra virgin olive oil into the bread machine pan. If the instructions for your bread machine specify that the yeast is to be placed in the pan first, then simply reverse the order in which you add the liquid and dry ingredients.

2 Sprinkle over the flour, ensuring that it covers the liquid mixture completely. Add the sugar and salt, placing them in separate corners of the bread pan. Make a small indent in the centre of the flour (but do not go down as far as the liquid) and add the dried yeast to the hollow.

3 Close the lid. Set the bread machine to the dough setting; if your machine has a choice of settings use the basic dough setting. Select the medium crust. Press Start. Lightly oil a 25 × 10cm/10 × 4in loaf pan.

4 When the dough cycle has finished, remove the dough from the machine and place it on a lightly floured surface. Knock back (punch down) gently, then roll it out to a rectangle about 2cm/¾in thick and 25cm/10in long. Cover with oiled clear film (plastic wrap) and leave to relax for a few minutes, if the dough proves difficult to roll out.

5 Spread the pesto sauce over the dough. Leave a clear border of 1cm/½in along one long edge. Roll up the dough lengthways, Swiss (jelly) roll fashion, tuck the ends under and place seam down in the prepared pan. Cover with oiled clear film and set aside in a warm place to rise for 45 minutes or until the dough has more than doubled in size and almost reaches the top of the loaf pan. Meanwhile, preheat the oven to 220°C/425°F/Gas 7.

6 Remove the clear film and brush the olive oil over the top of the loaf. Use a sharp knife to score the top with four diagonal cuts. Repeat the cuts in the opposite direction to make a criss-cross pattern. Sprinkle with the sea salt. Bake for 25–30 minutes, or until the bread is golden and sounds hollow when tapped on the base. Turn out on to a wire rack to cool.

Spinach & Parmesan Bloomer

This pretty pale green loaf is flavoured with spinach, onion and Parmesan cheese.
Whole pine nut kernels are dispersed through the dough of this perfect summertime
bread. Serve it with a dressed salad or a chilled soup.

MAKES 1 LOAF

INGREDIENTS
15ml/1 tbsp olive oil
1 onion, chopped
115g/4oz fresh young spinach leaves
120ml/4fl oz/ ½ cup water
1 egg, beaten
450g/1lb/4 cups unbleached white bread flour
2.5ml/ ½ tsp freshly grated nutmeg
50g/2oz/ ⅔ cup freshly grated Parmesan cheese
7.5ml/1½ tsp salt
5ml/1 tsp granulated sugar
7.5ml/1½ tsp easy-blend (rapid-rise) dried yeast
30ml/2 tbsp pine nuts

> ### VARIATION
> *Use Swiss chard instead of spinach, if you prefer.*
> *Choose young leaves, stripping them off the ribs.*
> *If fresh spinach is unavailable you could replace it*
> *with thawed frozen spinach. Make sure any excess*
> *water has been squeezed out first, before placing it*
> *in the bread machine. It may be worth holding a*
> *little of the water back and checking the dough as*
> *it starts to mix in step 5.*

1 Heat the olive oil in a frying pan, add the chopped onion and sauté until a light
golden colour. Add the spinach, stir well to combine and cover the pan very
tightly. Remove from the heat and leave to stand for 5 minutes. Then stir again
and leave the pan uncovered, to cool.

2 Tip the spinach mixture into the bread machine pan. Add the water and egg. If the instructions for your machine specify that the yeast is to be placed in the pan first, reverse the order in which you add the liquid mixture and dry ingredients.

3 Sprinkle over the white bread flour, ensuring that it completely covers the liquid mixture in the bread pan. Sprinkle the grated nutmeg and the Parmesan cheese over the flour. Place the salt and sugar in separate corners of the bread pan. Make a small indent in the centre of the flour (but not down as far as the liquid) and add the easy-blend (rapid-rise) dried yeast.

4 Close the lid. Set the bread machine to the dough setting, choosing the basic raisin dough setting (if available). Press Start. Lightly flour two baking sheets. Add the pine nuts to the dough when the machine beeps or during the last 5 minutes of the kneading process.

5 When the dough cycle has finished, remove the dough from the machine and place it on a lightly floured work surface. Gently knock the dough back (punch it down), then carefully roll it out to a rectangle about 2.5cm/1in thick. Roll up the rectangle of dough from one long side to form a thick baton shape, with a square end.

6 Place the baton on the prepared baking sheet, seam side up, cover it with lightly oiled clear film (plastic wrap) and leave to rest for 15 minutes.

7 Turn the bread over and place on the second baking sheet. Plump up the dough by tucking the ends and sides under. Cover it with lightly oiled clear film again and leave it to rise in a warm place for 30 minutes. Meanwhile, preheat the oven to 220°C/425°F/Gas 7.

8 Using a sharp knife, slash the top of the bloomer with five diagonal slashes. Bake it for 30–35 minutes, or until it is golden and the bottom sounds hollow when tapped. Turn the bread out on to a wire rack to cool.

CHILLI BREAD

There's a surprise waiting for anyone who bites into this tasty wholemeal bread. Fresh chillies are speckled throughout the crumb. Use Kenyan chillies for a milder flavour, or Scotch Bonnets for a fiery taste.

MAKES 1 LOAF

SMALL
15ml/1 tbsp sunflower oil
1–2 fresh chillies, chopped
210ml/7½fl oz/scant 1 cup water
250g/9oz/2¼ cups unbleached white
   bread flour
125g/4½oz/generous 1 cup wholemeal
   (whole-wheat) bread flour
7.5ml/1½ tsp salt
7.5ml/1½ tsp granulated sugar
25g/1oz/2 tbsp butter
5ml/1 tsp easy-blend (rapid-rise)
   dried yeast

MEDIUM
15ml/1 tbsp sunflower oil
2–3 fresh chillies, chopped
320ml/11¼fl oz/generous 1⅓ cups
   water
350g/12oz/3 cups unbleached white
   bread flour

150g/5½oz/1⅓ cups wholemeal
   (whole-wheat) bread flour
10ml/2 tsp salt
10ml/2 tsp granulated sugar
25g/1oz/2 tbsp butter
5ml/1 tsp easy-blend (rapid-rise)
   dried yeast

LARGE
30ml/2 tbsp sunflower oil
3–4 fresh chillies, chopped
420ml/15fl oz/generous 1¾ cups water
475g/1lb 1oz/4¼ cups unbleached
   white bread flour
200g/7oz/1¾ cups wholemeal
   (whole-wheat) bread flour
10ml/2 tsp salt
15ml/1 tbsp granulated sugar
40g/1½oz/3 tbsp butter
7.5ml/1½ tsp easy-blend (rapid-rise)
   dried yeast

VARIATION
Use chilli flakes instead of fresh chillies, if you prefer. You will need 10–20 ml/2–4 tsp, depending on the size of the loaf and how hot you wish to make the bread. Err on the side of caution the first time you try this, just to be safe!

1 Heat the oil in a small frying pan. Add the chillies and sauté them over a medium heat for 3–4 minutes until softened. Set aside to cool.

2 Tip the chillies and their oil into the bread machine pan. Pour in the water. Reverse the order in which you add the wet and dry ingredients if necessary.

3 Sprinkle over both types of flour, ensuring that the liquid is covered. Place the salt, sugar and butter in separate corners of the bread machine pan. Make an indent in the flour (but not down as far as the liquid) and add the yeast.

4 Close the lid. Set the bread machine to the basic/normal setting and select the medium crust. Press Start.

5 Remove the bread pan at the end of the baking cycle, and turn out the loaf on to a wire rack to cool.

FLATBREADS

One of the many good things about owning a bread machine is that it encourages you to experiment with making the more unusual types of bread. Making dough by hand is very fulfilling, but it can be a messy business. As anyone who has ever cleaned a table or board after using it to knead dough will know, it is amazing how far bits of flour will travel, and how hard they stick. If you have a bread machine, the dough is made in a contained area, and all you need to do is shape and cook it. Have a go at making Garlic & Coriander Naan, for instance, or make your own Pitta Breads, ready for splitting and filling. If you really want to show off, Carta di Musica is the perfect choice. This crisp bread resembles sheets of music manuscript paper.

GARLIC & CORIANDER NAAN

Indian restaurants the world over have introduced us to several differently flavoured examples of this leavened flatbread. This version is particularly delicious and is sure to become a great favourite. The bread is traditionally made in a tandoor oven, but this method has been developed to give almost identical results.

MAKES 3

INGREDIENTS
100ml/3½ fl oz/7 tbsp water
60ml/4 tbsp natural (plain) yogurt
280g/10oz/2½ cups unbleached white bread flour
1 garlic clove, finely chopped
5ml/1 tsp black onion seeds
5ml/1 tsp ground coriander
5ml/1 tsp salt
10ml/2 tsp clear honey
15ml/1 tbsp melted ghee or butter, plus 30–45ml/2–3 tbsp melted ghee or butter, for brushing
5ml/1 tsp easy-blend (rapid-rise) dried yeast
15ml/1 tbsp chopped fresh coriander (cilantro)

> VARIATION
> *For a basic naan omit the coriander, garlic and black onion seeds. Include a little ground black pepper or chilli powder for a slightly piquant note.*

1 Mix the water and natural yogurt, then pour into the bread machine pan. If the instructions for your bread machine specify that the easy-blend dried yeast is to be placed in the pan first, then simply reverse the order in which you add the liquid and dry ingredients.

2 Sprinkle over the flour, ensuring that it covers the liquid completely. Add the garlic, black onion seeds and ground coriander. Add the salt, honey and the 15ml/1 tbsp melted ghee or butter in separate corners of the bread pan. Make a small indent in the centre of the flour (but not down as far as the liquid) and add the easy-blend (rapid-rise) dried yeast.

3 Close the lid. Set the bread machine to the dough setting, choosing the basic or pizza dough setting if available. Press Start.

4 When the dough cycle has finished, preheat the oven to its highest setting. Place three baking sheets in the oven to heat. Remove the risen dough from the breadmaking machine and place it on a lightly floured surface.

5 Gently knock back (punch down) the naan dough, and then knead in the chopped fresh coriander. Divide the dough into three equal pieces.

6 Shape each piece into a ball and cover two of the pieces with oiled clear film (plastic wrap). Roll out the remaining piece of dough into a large teardrop shape, making it about 5–8mm/¼–⅓in thick. Cover with oiled clear film while you roll out the remaining two pieces of dough to make two more naan.

7 Preheat the grill (broiler) to its highest setting. Place the naan on the preheated baking sheets and then bake them for 4–5 minutes, until puffed up.

8 Remove the baking sheets from the oven and place them under the hot grill for a few seconds, until the naan start to brown and blister. Brush the naan with melted ghee or butter and serve warm.

LAVASH

These Middle Eastern flatbreads puff up slightly during cooking, to make a bread which is crispy, but not as dry and crisp as a cracker.

MAKES 10

INGREDIENTS
250ml/generous 8½fl oz/generous 1 cup water
45ml/3 tbsp natural (plain) yogurt
350g/12oz/3 cups unbleached white bread flour
115g/4oz/1 cup wholemeal (whole-wheat) bread flour
5ml/1 tsp salt
5ml/1 tsp easy-blend (rapid-rise) dried yeast

FOR THE TOPPING
30ml/2 tbsp milk
30ml/2 tbsp millet seeds

1 Pour the water and yogurt into the bread machine pan, reversing the order in which you add wet and dry ingredients if necessary. Sprinkle over all the flour, covering the liquid, then add the salt in one corner. Make an indent in the centre of the flour (but not down as far as the liquid) and add the yeast. Close the lid. Set the bread machine to the dough setting, choosing basic or pizza dough setting if available. Press Start.

2 When the dough is ready, knock it back (punch it down), place on a lightly floured surface, then divide it into 10 pieces. Shape each to a ball, then flatten to a disc. Cover with oiled clear film (plastic wrap) and leave to rest for 5 minutes. Preheat the oven to 230°C/450°F/Gas 8. Place four baking sheets in the oven.

3 Roll each ball of dough out very thinly, then stretch it over the backs of your hands, to shape the lavash. If the dough starts to tear, leave it to rest for a few minutes after rolling. Stack the lavash between layers of oiled clear film and cover to keep moist.

4 Place as many lavash as will fit comfortably on each baking sheet, brush with milk and sprinkle with millet seeds. Bake for 5–8 minutes, or until puffed and starting to brown. Transfer to a wire rack and cook the remaining lavash.

PITTA BREADS

These are easy to make and extremely versatile. Serve them warm with dips or soups, or split them in half and stuff the pockets with your favourite filling.

MAKES 6–10

INGREDIENTS
210ml/7½fl oz/scant 1 cup water
15ml/1 tbsp olive oil
350g/12oz/3 cups unbleached white bread flour, plus extra for sprinkling
7.5ml/1½ tsp salt
5ml/1 tsp granulated sugar
5ml/1 tsp easy-blend (rapid-rise) dried yeast

1 Pour the water and olive oil into the bread machine pan. If your instructions specify that the yeast is to be placed in the pan first, reverse the order in which you add the liquid and dry ingredients. Add the flour, ensuring that it covers the liquid in the pan.

2 Add the salt and sugar in separate corners. Make a shallow indent in the centre of the flour (but not down as far as the liquid) and add the yeast. Close the lid. Set the bread machine to the dough setting, choosing basic or pizza dough setting if available. Press Start.

3 When the dough cycle has finished, remove the dough. Place it on a lightly floured surface and knock back (punch down) gently. Divide it into six or 10 pieces of equal size, and shape each piece to a ball.

4 Cover the balls of dough with oiled clear film (plastic wrap) and leave them to rest for about 10 minutes. Preheat the oven to 230°C/450°F/Gas 8. Place three baking sheets in the oven to heat.

5 Flatten each piece of dough slightly, and then roll out into an oval or round, about 5mm/¼in thick. Lightly sprinkle with flour. Cover with oiled clear film and leave to rest for 10 minutes.

6 Place the pittas on the baking sheets and bake for 5–6 minutes, or until they are puffed up and lightly browned. Allow to cool on wire racks.

CARTA DI MUSICA

This crunchy, crisp bread looks like sheets of music manuscript paper, which is how it came by its name. It originated in Sardinia, and can be found throughout southern Italy, where it is eaten not only as a bread, but as a substitute for pasta in lasagne. It also makes a good pizza base.

MAKES 8

INGREDIENTS
280ml/10fl oz/1¼ cups water
450g/1lb/4 cups unbleached white bread flour
7.5ml/1½ tsp salt
5ml/1 tsp granulated sugar
5ml/1 tsp easy-blend (rapid-rise) dried yeast

> COOK'S TIP
> *Cutting the partially cooked breads in half is quite tricky. You may find it easier to divide the dough into six or eight pieces, and roll these as thinly as possible before baking.*

1 Pour the water into the bread machine pan. If the instructions for your machine specify that the yeast should be placed in the pan first, simply reverse the order in which you add the liquid and dry ingredients to the pan.

2 Sprinkle over the white bread flour, ensuring that it covers the water. Add the salt in one corner of the bread pan and the sugar in another corner. Make a small indent in the centre of the flour (but not down as far as the liquid) and add the easy-blend (rapid-rise) dried yeast.

3 Close the lid. Set the bread machine to the dough setting, choosing the basic dough setting if available. Press Start.

4 When the dough cycle has finished, remove the dough from the machine and place it on a lightly floured surface. Knock back (punch down) gently and divide it into 4 equal pieces. Shape each piece of dough into a ball, then roll a piece out until about 3mm/⅛in thick.

5 Now roll out the other three pieces. If the dough starts to tear, cover it with oiled clear film (plastic wrap) and leave it to rest for 2–3 minutes.

6 When all the dough has been rolled out, cover with oiled clear film and leave to rest on the floured surface for 10–15 minutes. Preheat the oven to 230°C/450°F/Gas 8. Place 2 baking sheets in the oven to heat.

7 Keeping the other dough rounds covered, place one round on each baking sheet. Bake for 5 minutes, or until they have puffed up.

8 Remove from the oven and cut each round in half horizontally to make two thinner breads. Place these cut-side up on the baking sheets, return them to the oven and bake for 5–8 minutes more, until crisp. Turn out on to a wire rack and cook the remaining breads.

PIDE

A traditional Turkish ridged flatbread, this is often baked plain, but can also be sprinkled with aromatic black nigella seeds, which taste rather like oregano.

MAKES 3

INGREDIENTS
240ml/8½fl oz/generous 1 cup water
30ml/2 tbsp olive oil
450g/1lb/4 cups unbleached white bread flour
5ml/1 tsp salt
5ml/1 tsp sugar
5ml/1 tsp easy-blend (rapid-rise) dried yeast
1 egg yolk mixed with 10ml/2 tsp water, for glazing
nigella or poppy seeds, for sprinkling

1 Pour the water and oil into the bread machine pan, reversing the order in which you add the wet and dry ingredients if necessary. Sprinkle over the flour, covering the liquid. Add the salt in one corner and the sugar in another. Make an indent in the centre of the flour (but not down as far as the liquid) and add the yeast.

2 Close the lid. Set the bread machine to the dough setting, choosing the basic dough setting if available. Press Start.

3 When the dough is ready, knock back (punch down) gently on a lightly floured surface. Divide it into three pieces of equal size. Shape each into a ball.

4 Roll each ball of dough into a round, about 15cm/6in in diameter. Cover with oiled clear film (plastic wrap) and leave to rise for 20 minutes. Meanwhile, preheat the oven to 230°C/450°F/Gas 8.

5 Using your fingers, ridge the bread, while enlarging it until it is 5mm/¼in thick. Start from the top of the round, pressing your fingers down and away from you, into the bread. Repeat a second row beneath the first, and so on.

6 Turn the bread by 90° and repeat the pressing to give a criss-cross ridged effect. Place the pide on floured baking sheets, brush with egg glaze and sprinkle with seeds. Bake for 9–10 minutes, or until puffy and golden. Serve immediately.

OLIVE FOUGASSE

A French hearth bread, fougasse is traditionally baked on the floor of the hot bread oven, just after the fire has been raked out.

MAKES 1 FOUGASSE

INGREDIENTS
210ml/7½fl oz/scant 1 cup water
15ml/1 tbsp olive oil, plus extra for brushing
350g/12oz/3 cups unbleached white bread flour
5ml/1 tsp salt
5ml/1 tsp granulated sugar
5ml/1 tsp easy-blend (rapid-rise) dried yeast
50g/2oz/½ cup pitted black olives, chopped

1 Pour the water and the olive oil into the bread machine pan. Reverse the order in which you add the wet and dry ingredients if necessary. Sprinkle over the flour, covering the liquid. Add the salt in one corner and the sugar in another. Make a small indent in the centre of the flour (but not down as far as the liquid) and add the yeast.

2 Close the lid. Set the bread machine to the dough setting, choosing the basic or pizza dough setting if available. Press Start. When the cycle has finished, remove the dough from the machine and place it on a lightly floured surface. Knock the dough back (punch it down) gently and flatten it slightly. Sprinkle over the olives and fold over the dough two or three times to incorporate them.

3 Flatten the dough and roll it into an oblong, about 30cm/12in long. Make four or five parallel cuts diagonally through the body of the dough, leaving the edges intact. Gently stretch the dough so that it resembles a ladder.

4 Lightly oil a baking sheet, then place the shaped dough on it. Cover with oiled clear film (plastic wrap) and leave to rise in a warm place for about 30 minutes, or until the dough has nearly doubled in bulk.

5 Preheat the oven to 220°C/425°F/Gas 7. Brush the top of the fougasse with olive oil, place in the oven and bake about for 20–25 minutes, or until the bread is golden. Turn out on to a wire rack to cool.

ONION FOCACCIA

Focaccia, with its characteristic texture and dimpled surface, has become hugely popular in recent years. This version has a delectable red onion and fresh sage topping. It tastes good enough to serve on its own, or with a salad.

MAKES 1 FOCACCIA

INGREDIENTS
210ml/7½fl oz/scant 1 cup water
15ml/1 tbsp olive oil
350g/12oz/3 cups unbleached white bread flour
2.5ml/½ tsp salt
5ml/1 tsp granulated sugar
5ml/1 tsp easy-blend (rapid-rise) dried yeast
15ml/1 tbsp chopped fresh sage
15ml/1 tbsp chopped red onion

FOR THE TOPPING
30ml/2 tbsp olive oil
½ red onion, thinly sliced
5 fresh sage leaves
10ml/2 tsp coarse sea salt
coarsely ground black pepper

1 Pour the water and oil into the bread pan. Reverse the order in which you add the wet and dry ingredients if necessary.

2 Sprinkle over the flour, ensuring that it covers the liquid. Add the salt and sugar in separate corners. Make a small indent in the flour (but not down as far as the liquid) and add the yeast.

3 Close the lid. Set the bread machine to the dough setting. If your machine has a choice of settings use the basic or pizza dough setting. Press Start.

4 Lightly oil a 25–28cm/10–11in shallow round cake pan or pizza pan. When the cycle has finished, remove the dough from the pan and place it on a surface lightly dusted with flour.

5 Knock the dough back (punch it down) and flatten it slightly. Sprinkle over the sage and red onion and knead gently to incorporate.

6 Shape the dough into a ball, flatten it, then roll it into a round of about 25–28cm/10–11in. Place in the prepared pan. Cover with oiled clear film (plastic wrap) and leave to rise in a warm place for 20 minutes.

7 Meanwhile, preheat the oven to 200°C/400°F/Gas 6. Uncover the risen focaccia, and, using your fingertips, poke the dough to make deep dimples over the surface. Cover and leave to rise for 10–15 minutes, or until the dough has doubled in bulk.

8 Drizzle over the olive oil and sprinkle with the onion, sage leaves, sea salt and black pepper. Bake for 20–25 minutes, or until golden. Turn out on to a wire rack to cool slightly. Serve warm.

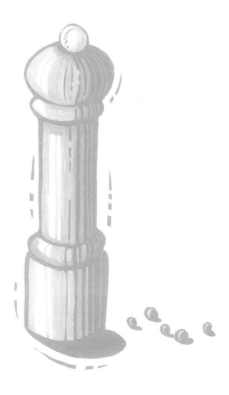

NUT, FRUIT & HERB BREADS

Some of the bread machine recipes in this half of the book are duplicated in the section that deals with handmade breads, so the keen baker can experiment with both methods. These nut, fruit and herb recipes are unique, however, and so delicious that it is worth buying a bread machine to make any one of them. Hazelnut & Fig Bread, with its combination of juicy dried figs, toasted wheatgerm and roasted nuts, is a sure winner, unless of course you prefer something a little more savoury, like Garlic & Herb Walnut Bread. The combination of rum and raisins has long been the basis of a popular ice cream. Here's your chance to try it in a bread. Spiced with ginger and glazed with honey, it is very good indeed.

Hazelnut & Fig Bread

This healthy, high-fibre bread, flavoured with figs and hazelnuts, is an excellent choice for breakfast. Serve it solo or with butter and honey or fig conserve.

Makes 1 loaf

Small
25g/1oz/3 tbsp hazelnuts
230ml/8fl oz/1 cup water
5ml/1 tsp lemon juice
280g/10oz/2½ cups white bread flour
75g/3oz/¾ cup brown bread flour
45ml/3 tbsp toasted wheatgerm
15ml/1 tbsp skimmed milk powder
  (non fat dry milk)
5ml/1 tsp salt
10ml/2 tsp granulated sugar
20g/¾oz/1½ tbsp butter
5ml/1 tsp easy-blend (rapid-rise)
  dried yeast
25g/1oz/3 tbsp ready-to-eat dried figs

Medium
40g/1½oz/⅓ cup hazelnuts
280ml/10fl oz/1¼ cups water
7.5ml/1½ tsp lemon juice
350g/12oz/3 cups white bread flour
100g/3½oz/scant 1 cup brown
  bread flour
60ml/4 tbsp toasted wheatgerm
30ml/2 tbsp skimmed milk powder

(non fat dry milk)
7.5ml/1½ tsp salt
15ml/1 tbsp granulated sugar
25g/1oz/2 tbsp butter
7.5ml/1½ tsp easy-blend (rapid-rise)
  dried yeast
40g/1½oz/¼ cup ready-to-eat
  dried figs

Large
50g/2oz/½ cup hazelnuts
450ml/16fl oz/scant 2 cups water
10ml/2 tsp lemon juice
500g/1lb 2oz/4½ cups unbleached
  white bread flour
115g/4oz/1 cup brown bread flour
75ml/5 tbsp toasted wheatgerm
45ml/3 tbsp skimmed milk powder
  (non fat dry milk)
10ml/2 tsp salt
20ml/4 tsp granulated sugar
40g/1½oz/3 tbsp butter
7.5ml/1½ tsp easy-blend (rapid-rise)
  dried yeast
50g/2oz/⅓ cup ready-to-eat dried figs

Cook's Tip
Nuts contain natural oils which turn rancid if stored too warm or for too long. Buy in small quantities and store in an air-tight container in a cool place.

1 Spread out the hazelnuts in a grill (broiler) pan and roast them under a medium grill for 3–4 minutes, until the skins darken. Watch them closely and do not let them burn. Remove from the heat and, when cool enough to handle, rub off the skins. Chop the hazelnuts roughly.

2 Pour the water and the lemon juice into the bread machine pan. If the instructions for your machine specify that the yeast is to be placed in the pan first, reverse the order in which you add the liquid and dry ingredients.

3 Sprinkle over the flours, then the wheatgerm, covering the water. Add the milk powder. Add the salt, sugar and butter in separate corners. Make an indent in the flour and add the yeast.

4 Close the lid. Set the bread machine to the basic/normal setting, choosing the raisin setting if available. Select the medium crust and press Start. Coarsely chop the dried figs. Add the hazelnuts and the figs to the bread pan when the machine beeps or after the first kneading has finished.

5 Remove the bread pan at the end of the baking cycle, and turn the loaf out on to a wire rack. Leave it to cool completely before slicing.

GARLIC & HERB WALNUT BREAD

Walnut bread is very popular in France. This delicious variation includes both garlic and basil for additional flavour.

MAKES 1 LOAF

SMALL
150ml/5fl oz/⅔ cup milk
60ml/2fl oz/4 tbsp water
30ml/2 tbsp extra virgin olive oil
325g/11½oz/scant 3 cups unbleached
  white bread flour
40g/1½oz/scant ⅓ cup rolled oats
40g/1½oz/⅓ cup chopped walnuts
1 garlic clove, finely chopped
5ml/1 tsp dried oregano
5ml/1 tsp drained fresh basil in
  sunflower oil
5ml/1 tsp salt
7.5ml/1½ tsp granulated sugar
2.5ml/½ tsp easy-blend (rapid-rise)
  dried yeast

MEDIUM
180ml/6½fl oz/generous ¾ cup milk
105ml/7 tbsp water
45ml/3 tbsp extra virgin olive oil
450g/1lb/4 cups unbleached white
  bread flour
50g/2oz/½ cup rolled oats
50g/2oz/½ cup chopped walnuts
1½ garlic cloves, finely chopped

7.5ml/1½ tsp dried oregano
7.5ml/1½ tsp drained fresh basil in
  sunflower oil
7.5ml/1½ tsp salt
10ml/2 tsp granulated sugar
5ml/1 tsp easy-blend (rapid-rise)
  dried yeast

LARGE
200ml/7fl oz/⅞ cup milk
140ml/5fl oz/⅝ cup water
60ml/4 tbsp extra virgin olive oil
600g/1lb 5oz/generous 5¼ cups
  unbleached white bread flour
65g/2½oz/scant ⅔ cup rolled oats
65g/2½oz/generous ½ cup
  chopped walnuts
2 garlic cloves, finely chopped
7.5ml/1½ tsp dried oregano
7.5ml/1½ tsp drained fresh basil in
  sunflower oil
10ml/2 tsp salt
10ml/2 tsp granulated sugar
7.5ml/1½tsp easy-blend (rapid-rise)
  dried yeast

COOK'S TIP
A number of herbs are now available freshly chopped and preserved in oil, so you can enjoy the flavour of delicate herbs like basil all year round.

1 Pour the milk, water and olive oil into the bread machine pan. If the instructions for your machine specify that the yeast is to be placed in the pan first, reverse the order in which you add the liquid and dry ingredients.

2 Sprinkle over the flour and rolled oats, ensuring that they completely cover the liquid mixture. Add the chopped walnuts, garlic, oregano and basil. Place the salt and sugar in separate corners of the bread machine pan. Make a small indent in the centre of the flour (but do not go down as far as the liquid) and tip in the easy-blend dried yeast.

3 Close the lid. Set the bread machine to the basic/normal setting and select medium crust. Press Start.

4 Remove the bread pan from the machine at the end of the baking cycle and turn out the loaf on to a wire rack to cool.

Rum & Raisin Loaf

Juicy raisins, plumped up with dark rum, flavour this tea-time loaf. It's more than good enough to serve just as it is, but slices can also be lightly toasted and buttered to ring the changes. For a delicious quick dessert, toast several slices and serve each topped with a scoop of vanilla ice cream and some slices of preserved stem ginger.

MAKES 1 LOAF

SMALL
75g/3oz/generous ½ cup raisins
22ml/1½ tbsp dark rum
1 egg
140ml/5fl oz/scant ⅔ cup milk
350g/12oz/3 cups unbleached white
   bread flour
1.5ml/¼ tsp ground ginger
25g/1oz/2 tbsp caster (superfine) sugar
2.5ml/½ tsp salt
40g/1½oz/3 tbsp butter
5ml/1 tsp easy-blend (rapid-rise)
   dried yeast
10ml/2 tsp clear honey, warmed

MEDIUM
90g/3¼oz/⅔ cup raisins
30ml/2 tbsp dark rum
1 egg
240ml/8½fl oz/generous 1 cup milk
500g/1lb 2oz/4½ cups unbleached
   white bread flour
2.5ml/½ tsp ground ginger
40g/1½oz/3 tbsp caster
   (superfine) sugar
3.5ml/¾ tsp salt
50g/2oz/¼ cup butter
7.5ml/1½ tsp easy-blend (rapid-rise)
   dried yeast
15ml/1 tbsp clear honey, warmed

LARGE
115g/4oz/⅘ cup raisins
45ml/3 tbsp dark rum
2 eggs, lightly beaten
290ml/10fl oz/1¼ cups milk
675g/1½b/6 cups unbleached white
   bread flour
5ml/1 tsp ground ginger
50g/2oz/¼ cup caster (superfine) sugar
5ml/1 tsp salt
65g/2½oz/5 tbsp butter
7.5ml/1½ tsp easy-blend (rapid-rise)
   dried yeast
15ml/1 tbsp clear honey, warmed

1 Place the raisins and rum in a small bowl and leave to soak for 2 hours, or longer if you can. Add the egg(s) and milk to the bread machine pan. If the instructions for your machine specify that the yeast is to be placed in the pan first, reverse the order in which you add the liquid and dry ingredients.

2 Sprinkle over the flour, ensuring that it covers the liquid completely. Add the ground ginger. Add the caster sugar, salt and butter, placing them in separate corners of the bread machine pan. Make a small indent in the centre of the flour (but not down as far as the liquid) and pour in the dried yeast.

3 Close the lid. Set the bread machine to the basic/normal setting, choosing the raisin setting if available, and select medium crust. Press Start. Add the raisins when the machine beeps to add extra ingredients, or after the first kneading.

4 Remove the bread at the end of the baking cycle and turn out on to a wire rack. Brush the top with honey and leave the loaf to cool.

MUESLI & DATE BREAD

This makes the perfect breakfast or brunch bread. Use your own favourite unsweetened muesli to ring the changes.

MAKES 1 LOAF

INGREDIENTS
260ml/9fl oz/scant 1¼ cups water
30ml/2 tbsp sunflower oil
15ml/1 tbsp clear honey
300g/10½oz/2⅔ cups unbleached white bread flour
75g/3oz/¾ cup wholemeal (whole-wheat) bread flour
150g/5½oz/generous 1½ cups unsweetened fruit and nut muesli (granola)
45ml/3 tbsp skimmed milk powder (non fat dry milk)
7.5ml/1½ tsp salt
7.5ml/1½ tsp easy-blend (rapid-rise) dried yeast
65g/2½oz/scant ½ cup stoned (pitted) dates, chopped

COOK'S TIP
The amount of water required may vary with the type of muesli used. Add another 15ml/1 tbsp water if the dough is too firm.

1 Pour the water, oil and honey into the bread pan. Reverse the order in which you add the wet and dry ingredients if necessary. Sprinkle over the flours, covering the water completely. Add the muesli and skimmed milk powder, then the salt, in a corner of the pan. Make a small indent in the flour and add the yeast.

2 Close the lid. Set the bread machine to the dough setting, choosing the basic raisin dough setting if available. Press Start. Add the dates when the machine beeps or during the last 5 minutes of kneading. Lightly oil a baking sheet.

3 When the dough cycle has finished, remove the dough from the machine and place it on a surface lightly dusted with wholemeal flour. Knock the dough back (punch it down) gently.

4 Shape the dough into a plump round and place it on the prepared baking sheet. Using a sharp knife make three cuts across the top about 1cm/½in deep, to divide the bread into six equal sections.

5 Cover the loaf with lightly oiled clear film (plastic wrap) and leave to rise for 30–45 minutes, or until it has almost doubled in size.

6 Preheat the oven to 200°C/400°F/Gas 6. Bake the loaf for 30–35 minutes until it is golden and hollow sounding. Transfer it to a wire rack to cool.

COOK'S TIP
Wholemeal (whole-wheat) flour does not keep as well as white flour, because it contains the oils in wheat germ. Buy fairly small quantities at a time, and store the flour in a very cool place. The salad drawer of the refrigerator is ideal.

ROSEMARY & RAISIN LOAF

Inspired by a classic Tuscan bread – panmarino – this bread is flavoured with rosemary and raisins and enriched with eggs and olive oil.

MAKES 1 LOAF

SMALL

135ml/4½fl oz/½ cup + 1 tbsp water
45ml/3 tbsp extra virgin olive oil
1 egg
375g/13oz/3¼ cups unbleached white
    bread flour
15ml/1 tbsp skimmed milk powder
    (non fat dry milk)
10ml/2 tsp fresh rosemary, chopped
5ml/1 tsp salt
10ml/2 tsp granulated sugar
5ml/1 tsp easy-blend (rapid-rise)
    dried yeast
75g/3oz/½ cup raisins

MEDIUM

160ml/5½fl oz/generous ⅔ cup water
60ml/4 tbsp extra virgin olive oil
2 eggs
500g/1lb 2oz/4½ cups unbleached
    white bread flour
30ml/2 tbsp skimmed milk powder
    (non fat dry milk)

15ml/1 tbsp fresh rosemary, chopped
7.5ml/1½ tsp salt
10ml/2 tsp granulated sugar
5ml/1 tsp easy-blend (rapid-rise)
    dried yeast
115g/4oz/generous ⅔ cup raisins

LARGE

200ml/7fl oz/⅞ cup water
75ml/5 tbsp extra virgin olive oil
3 eggs
675g/1½lb/6 cups unbleached white
    bread flour
45ml/3 tbsp skimmed milk powder
    (non fat dry milk)
20ml/4 tsp fresh rosemary, chopped
7.5ml/1½ tsp salt
15ml/1 tbsp granulated sugar
7.5ml/1½ tsp easy-blend (rapid-rise)
    dried yeast
150g/5oz/1 cup raisins

VARIATION
This savoury bread can be made with chopped almonds and sultanas (golden raisins) or dried figs, instead of raisins. All are delicious flavours for serving with soft cheese.

1 Pour the water, extra virgin olive oil and egg(s) into the bread machine pan. If the instructions for your machine specify that the yeast is to be placed in the pan first, reverse the order in which you add the liquid and dry ingredients.

2 Sprinkle over the flour, ensuring that it covers the water. Add the skimmed milk powder (non fat dry milk) and rosemary. Add the salt and sugar in separate corners of the bread pan. Make a small indent in the centre of the flour (but not down as far as the liquid) and add the yeast.

3 Close the lid. Set the bread machine to the basic/normal setting, with raisin setting (if available), medium crust. Press Start. Add the raisins when the machine beeps or 5 minutes before the kneading cycle ends.

4 Remove the bread pan from the machine at the end of the baking cycle and turn out the loaf on to a wire rack to cool.

MIXED HERB COTTAGE LOAF

There's something very satisfying about the shape of a cottage loaf, and the flavour of fresh herbs – chives, thyme, tarragon and parsley – adds to the appeal. This loaf makes the perfect centrepiece for the table, for guests to help themselves.

MAKES 1 LOAF

INGREDIENTS
300ml/10½fl oz/1¼ cups water
450g/1lb/4 cups unbleached white bread flour, plus extra for dusting
7.5ml/1½ tsp granulated sugar
7.5ml/1½ tsp salt
7.5ml/1½ tsp easy-blend (rapid-rise) dried yeast
15ml/1 tbsp chopped fresh chives
10ml/2 tsp chopped fresh thyme
15ml/1 tbsp chopped fresh tarragon
30ml/2 tbsp chopped fresh parsley

FOR THE GLAZE
5ml/1 tsp salt
15ml/1 tbsp water

VARIATION
Vary the combination of fresh herbs you use, according to availability and taste. You should aim for just under 75ml/5 tbsp in all, but use more pungent herbs sparingly, so their taste does not become too overpowering.

1 Pour the water into the bread machine pan. If the operating instructions for your bread machine specify that the yeast is to be placed in the pan first, then simply reverse the order in which you add the water and dry ingredients.

2 Sprinkle over the flour, ensuring that it covers the water completely. Add the granulated sugar and the salt, placing them in separate corners of the bread machine pan. Make a small indent in the centre of the flour (but not down as far as the water) and add the easy-blend dried yeast.

3 Close the lid. Set the bread machine to the dough setting, choosing basic raisin dough setting if available. Press Start.

4 Add the chives, thyme, tarragon and parsley when the machine beeps to add extra ingredients, or during the final 5 minutes of kneading. Lightly flour two baking sheets and set them aside.

5 When the dough is ready, remove it from the machine. Place it on a lightly floured surface. Knock the dough back (punch it down) gently and then divide it into two pieces, making one piece twice as large as the other.

6 Take each piece of dough in turn and shape it into a plump ball. Place the balls of dough on the prepared baking sheets and cover each with a lightly oiled mixing bowl or with lightly oiled clear film (plastic wrap).

7 Leave in a warm place for about 20–30 minutes, or until both balls of dough have almost doubled in size.

8 Cut a cross, about 4cm/1½in across, in the top of the larger piece of dough. Brush the surface with water and place the smaller round on top.

9 Carefully press the handle of a wooden spoon through the centre of both pieces of dough. Cover the loaf with oiled clear film and leave it to rise for 10 minutes.

10 Meanwhile, preheat the oven to 220°C/425°F/Gas 7. Put the salt and water for the glaze in a bowl, stir to mix, then brush the mixture over the top of the bread.

11 Using a sharp knife, make eight long slashes around the top of the bread and 12 small slashes around the base. Dust the top of the bread lightly with white bread flour.

12 Bake for 30 35 minutes, or until the bread is golden and sounds hollow when tapped on the base. Turn the loaf out on to a wire rack to cool.

SMALL BREADS

Muffins, baps and teacakes are all easy to make with the aid of a bread machine. Preparing the dough doesn't take very long and cooking time is considerably shorter than when a full-size loaf is in the oven, so these small breads, like others in this chapter, are perfect candidates for afternoon tea. Also in this chapter are rolls of various shapes and sizes. Mixed Grain Onion Rolls are very flavoursome. The recipe makes twelve, so you can freeze the surplus, ready for serving with soup at your next dinner party. Ring the changes with Ricotta and Oregano Knots, which are enriched with soft cheese. Or, for a change, try making Italian Breadsticks. They taste so much nicer than the ones you can buy, and will stay fresh for a few days in an airtight container.

WHOLEMEAL ENGLISH MUFFINS

After a long walk on a wintry afternoon, come home to warm muffins, carefully torn apart and spread thickly with butter.

MAKES 9

INGREDIENTS
350ml/12fl oz/1½ cups milk
225g/8oz/2 cups unbleached white bread flour
225g/8oz/2 cups stoneground wholemeal (whole-wheat) bread flour
5ml/1 tsp caster (superfine) sugar
7.5ml/1½ tsp salt
15g/½oz/1 tbsp butter
7.5ml/1½ tsp easy-blend (rapid-rise) dried yeast
rice flour or fine semolina, for dusting

COOK'S TIP
If you don't have a griddle, cook the muffins in a heavy frying pan. It is important that they cook slowly, for the full time stated.

1 Pour the milk into the bread machine pan. If the instructions for your bread machine specify that the yeast is to be placed in the pan first, then reverse the order in which you add the liquid and dry ingredients.

2 Sprinkle over each type of flour in turn, making sure that the milk is completely covered. Add the caster sugar, salt and butter, placing each of them in separate corners of the bread pan. Then make a small indent in the centre of the flour (but do not go down as far as the liquid underneath) and add the dried yeast.

3 Close the lid. Set the machine to the dough setting, choosing the basic dough setting, if available on your machine Press Start. Sprinkle a baking sheet with rice flour or semolina.

4 When the dough cycle has finished, remove the dough and place it on a floured surface. Knock back (punch down) gently. Roll out the dough until it is about 1cm/½in thick.

5 Using a floured 7.5cm/3in plain cutter, cut out nine muffins. If you like, you can re-roll the trimmings, knead them together and let the dough rest for a few minutes before rolling it out again and cutting out an extra muffin or two.

6 Place the muffins on the baking sheet. Dust with rice flour or semolina. Cover with oiled clear film (plastic wrap) and leave to rise in a warm place for 20 minutes, or until almost doubled in size.

7 Heat a griddle over a medium heat. You should not need any oil if the griddle is well seasoned; if not, add the merest trace of oil. Cook the muffins slowly, three at a time, for about 7 minutes on each side. Serve warm.

WHOLEMEAL BAPS

There's nothing nicer than waking up to the aroma of fresh baked bread.
The wholemeal flour adds extra flavour to these soft breakfast rolls.

MAKES 10

INGREDIENTS
140ml/5fl oz/scant ⅔ cup milk
140ml/5fl oz/scant ⅔ cup water
225g/8oz/2 cups stoneground wholemeal (whole-wheat) bread flour, plus extra
   for dusting
225g/8oz/2 cups unbleached white bread flour
7.5ml/1½ tsp salt
10ml/2 tsp caster (superfine) sugar
5ml/1 tsp easy-blend (rapid-rise) dried yeast
milk, for glazing

1 Pour the milk and water into the pan. Reverse the order in which you add the wet and dry ingredients if necessary.

2 Sprinkle over the flours, covering the liquid. Add the salt and sugar in separate corners. Make a shallow indent in the centre of the flour (but not down as far as the liquid) and add the yeast. Close the lid. Set the bread machine to the dough setting, choosing the basic dough setting (if available). Press Start.

3 When the dough cycle has finished, remove the dough from the machine and place it on a lightly floured surface. Knock back (punch down) gently, then divide it into 10 pieces and cover these with lightly oiled clear film (plastic wrap).

4 Take one piece of dough, leaving the rest covered, and cup your hands around it to shape it into a ball. Place it on the lightly floured surface and roll it into a flat oval measuring 10 × 7.5cm/4 × 3in.

5 Repeat with the remaining dough so that you have 10 flat oval dough pieces. Lightly oil two baking sheets.

6 Place the baps well apart on the prepared baking sheets. Cover with oiled clear film (plastic wrap), and leave to rise in a warm place for about 30 minutes, or until the baps have almost doubled in size. Meanwhile, preheat the oven to 200°C/400°F/Gas 6.

7 Using your three middle fingers, press each bap in the centre to help disperse any large air bubbles. Brush the baps with milk and dust lightly with wholemeal (whole-wheat) flour.

8 Bake for 15–20 minutes, or until the baps are lightly browned. Turn out on to a wire rack and serve warm.

PIKELETS

Pikelets are similar to crumpets, and have the same distinctive holey tops, but the cooking method is different. Crumpets are thicker and are cooked inside a ring, which supports them while they set. Serve pikelets warm with preserves and butter. They are also excellent with soft cheese and smoked salmon.

MAKES ABOUT 20

INGREDIENTS
140ml/5fl oz/scant ⅔ cup water
140ml/5fl oz/scant ⅔ cup milk
15ml/1 tbsp sunflower oil
225g/8oz/2 cups unbleached white bread flour
5ml/1 tsp salt
5ml/1 tsp caster (superfine) sugar
7.5ml/1½ tsp easy-blend (rapid-rise) dried yeast
1.5ml/¼ tsp bicarbonate of soda (baking soda)
60ml/4 tbsp water
1 egg white

1 Pour the water into the bread machine pan, then add the milk and sunflower oil. If the instructions for your bread machine specify that the yeast is to be placed in the pan first, reverse the order in which you add the liquid and dry ingredients to the pan.

2 Sprinkle over the white bread flour, ensuring that it covers the liquid completely. Add the salt and caster sugar, placing them in separate corners of the bread pan. Make a shallow indent in the centre of the flour (but not as far down the liquid) and add the easy-blend (rapid-rise) dried yeast.

3 Set the breadmaking machine to the dough setting, choosing the basic dough setting if available. Press Start. Lightly oil two baking sheets.

4 When the dough cycle has finished, carefully lift the bread pan out of the machine and pour the batter for the pikelets into a large mixing bowl.

5 Dissolve the bicarbonate of soda in the remaining water and stir it into the batter. Whisk the egg white in a grease-free bowl until it forms soft peaks, then fold it into the batter.

6 Cover the batter mixture with oiled clear film (plastic wrap) and leave the mixture to rise for 30 minutes. Preheat the oven to 140°C/275°F/Gas 1.

7 Lightly grease a griddle and heat it gently. When it is hot, pour generous tablespoonfuls of batter on to the hot surface, spacing them well apart to allow for spreading, and cook until the tops no longer appear wet and have acquired lots of tiny holes.

8 When the base of each pikelet is golden, turn it over, using a metal spatula or a palette knife, and continue to cook until pale golden.

9 Remove the cooked pikelets and layer them in a folded dishtowel. Place in the oven to keep them warm while you use the remaining batter to cook more pikelets. Serve the pikelets immediately.

Yorkshire Teacakes

These fruit-filled tea-time treats are thought to be a refinement of the original medieval manchet or "handbread" – a hand-shaped loaf made without a pan. Serve them split and buttered, either warm from the oven or toasted.

MAKES 8–10

INGREDIENTS
280ml/10fl oz/1¼ cups milk
450g/1lb/4 cups unbleached white bread flour
5ml/1 tsp salt
40g/1½oz/3 tbsp caster (superfine) sugar
40g/1½oz/3 tbsp lard (shortening) or butter
5ml/1 tsp easy-blend (rapid-rise) dried yeast
50g/2oz/¼ cup currants
50g/2oz/⅓ cup sultanas (golden raisins)
milk, for glazing

COOK'S TIP
If you forget to add the fruit when making the dough, don't worry. Just knead it in when you knock the dough back before shaping it.

1 Pour the milk into the bread machine pan. If the instructions for your machine specify that the yeast is to be placed in the pan first, then simply reverse the order in which you add the liquid and dry ingredients to the pan.

2 Sprinkle over the flour, ensuring that it covers the milk completely. Add the salt, sugar and lard or butter, placing them in separate corners of the bread machine pan. Make a small indent in the centre of the flour (but do not go down as far as the liquid underneath) and pour in the yeast. Close the lid.

3 Set the bread machine to the dough setting, choosing the basic raisin dough setting if available. Press Start. Add the currants and sultanas when the machine beeps. If your machine does not have this facility, simply add the dried fruits 5 minutes before the end of the kneading period.

4 Lightly grease two baking sheets. When the dough cycle has finished, remove the dough from the machine and place it on a lightly floured surface. Knock it back (punch it down) gently.

5 Divide the dough into eight to 10 portions, depending on how large you like your Yorkshire teacakes, and shape each portion into a ball. Pat down each ball to flatten it out into a disc about 1cm/½in thick.

6 Place the discs on the prepared baking sheets, spacing them about 2.5cm/1in apart. Cover them with oiled clear film (plastic wrap) and leave in a warm place for 30–45 minutes, or until they have almost doubled in size. Meanwhile, preheat the oven to 200°C/400°F/Gas 6.

7 Brush the top of each teacake with milk, then bake for 15–18 minutes, or until golden. Turn out on to a wire rack to cool slightly.

8 To serve, split open while still warm and spread with lashings of butter, or let the buns cool, then split and toast them before serving.

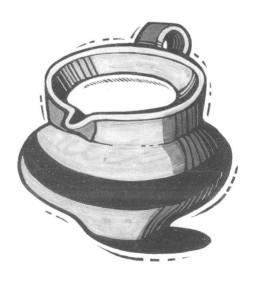

Mixed Grain Onion Rolls

These crunchy rolls, flavoured with golden onions, are perfect for snacks, sandwiches or to serve with soup. If the latter, warm them first.

Makes 12

Ingredients
50g/2oz/¼ cup butter
1 large onion, finely chopped
280ml/10fl oz/1¼ cups water
280g/10oz/2½ cups unbleached white bread flour
115g/4oz/1 cup Granary (whole-wheat) bread flour
25g/1oz/¼ cup oat bran
10ml/2 tsp salt
10ml/2 tsp clear honey
7.5ml/1½ tsp easy-blend (rapid-rise) dried yeast
maize flour (cornmeal), for dusting
30ml/2 tbsp millet grain
15ml/1 tbsp coarse oatmeal
15ml/1 tbsp sunflower seeds

> **Variation**
> *If time is short you can omit the cutting in step 9 and cook as round shaped rolls.*

1 Melt half the butter in a frying pan. Add the chopped onion and sauté gently for 8–10 minutes, or until softened and lightly browned. Set aside to cool.

2 Pour the water into the machine pan. If the instructions for your machine state the yeast is to be placed in the pan first, reverse the order in which you add the wet and dry ingredients.

3 Sprinkle over the white bread flour, Granary (whole-wheat) flour and oat bran, ensuring that the water is completely covered. Add the salt, honey and remaining butter, placing them in separate corners of the bread pan. Make a small indent in the centre of the flour (but not down as far as the liquid) and add the easy-blend (rapid-rise) dried yeast.

4 Close the lid. Set the bread machine to the dough setting, choosing the basic raisin dough setting if available. Press Start. Lightly oil two baking sheets and sprinkle them with maize flour.

5 Add the millet grain, coarse oatmeal, sunflower seeds and cooked onion when the machine beeps. If your machine does not have this facility, add these ingredients 5 minutes before the end of the kneading cycle.

6 When the dough cycle has finished, remove the dough from the bread machine and place it on a surface that has been lightly floured. Knock the dough back (punch it down) gently, then divide it into 12 equal pieces.

7 Shape each piece into a ball, making sure that the tops are smooth. Flatten them slightly with the palm of your hand or a small rolling pin. Place the rolls on the prepared baking sheets and dust them with more maize flour.

8 Cover the rolls with oiled clear film (plastic wrap) and leave them in a warm place for 30–45 minutes, or until doubled in size. Meanwhile, preheat the oven to 200°C/400°F/Gas 6.

9 Using a pair of lightly floured sharp scissors snip each roll in five places, cutting inwards from the edge, almost to the centre. Bake for 18–20 minutes, or until the rolls are golden. Turn them out on to a wire rack to cool.

ITALIAN BREADSTICKS

These crisp breadsticks will keep for a couple of days if stored in an airtight container. If you like, you can refresh them in a hot oven for a few minutes before serving. The dough can be made in any breadmaking machine, regardless of capacity.

MAKES 30

INGREDIENTS
200ml/7fl oz/⅞ cup water
45ml/3 tbsp olive oil, plus extra for brushing
350g/12oz/3 cups unbleached white bread flour
7.5ml/1½ tsp salt
7.5ml/1½ tsp easy-blend (rapid-rise) dried yeast
poppy seeds and coarse sea salt, for coating (optional)

COOK'S TIP
If you are rolling the breadsticks in sea salt, don't use too much. Crush the sea salt slightly if the crystals are large.

1 Pour the water and olive oil into the bread machine pan. If the instructions for your machine specify that the yeast is to be placed in the pan first, reverse the order in which you add the liquid and dry ingredients.

2 Sprinkle over the flour, ensuring that it covers the water completely. Add the salt in one corner of the pan. Make a small indent in the centre of the flour (but not down as far as the liquid) and add the dried yeast.

3 Close the lid. Set the bread machine to the dough setting, choosing the basic dough setting if available. Press Start.

4 Lightly oil two baking sheets. If your baking sheets are small, you may need to use three or four. Preheat the oven to 200°C/400°F/Gas 6.

5 When the dough cycle has finished, remove the dough from the machine, place it on a lightly floured surface and knock it back (punch it down). Roll it out to a rectangle measuring 23 × 20cm/9 × 8in.

6 Cut the dough into three 20cm/8in long strips. Cut each strip widthways into 10 sticks. Roll and stretch each stick until it is 30cm/12in long.

7 Roll the breadsticks in poppy seeds or sea salt if you like. Space well apart on the baking sheets. Brush lightly with olive oil, cover with clear film (plastic wrap) and leave in a warm place for 10–15 minutes.

8 Bake the breadsticks for 15–20 minutes, or until they are golden, turning once. Transfer to a wire rack to cool.

Ricotta & Oregano Knots

The ricotta cheese adds a wonderful moistness to these beautifully shaped rolls. Serve them slightly warm to appreciate fully the flavour of the oregano as your butter melts into the crumb.

Makes 12

Ingredients
60ml/4 tbsp ricotta cheese
225ml/8fl oz/scant 1 cup water
450g/1lb/4 cups unbleached white bread flour
45ml/3 tbsp skimmed milk powder (non fat dry milk)
10ml/2 tsp dried oregano
5ml/1 tsp salt
10ml/2 tsp caster (superfine) sugar
25g/1oz/ 2 tbsp butter
5ml/1 tsp easy-blend (rapid-rise) dried yeast

For the topping
1 egg yolk
15ml/1 tbsp water
ground black pepper

1 Spoon the cheese into the bread machine pan and add the water. Reverse the order in which you add the liquid and dry ingredients, if the instructions for your bread machine specify this.

2 Sprinkle over the flour, ensuring that it covers the cheese and water. Add the skimmed milk powder and oregano. Place the salt, sugar and butter in separate corners of the bread pan. Make a small indent in the centre of the flour (but not down as far as the liquid) and add the yeast.

3 Close the lid. Set the bread machine to the dough setting, choosing the basic dough setting if available. Press Start. Lightly oil two baking sheets.

4 When the dough cycle has finished, remove the dough from the machine and place it on a lightly floured surface.

5 Knock the dough back (punch it down) gently, then divide it into 12 pieces and cover these with oiled clear film (plastic wrap).

6 Take one piece of dough, leaving the rest covered, and roll it on the floured surface into a rope about 25cm/10in long. Lift one end of the dough over the other to make a loop. Push the end through the hole in the loop to make a neat knot. Repeat with the remaining dough.

7 Place the knots on the prepared baking sheets, cover them with oiled clear film and leave to rise in a warm place for about 30 minutes, or until doubled in size. Meanwhile, preheat the oven to 220°C/425°F/Gas 7.

8 Mix the egg yolk and water for the topping in a small bowl. Brush the mixture over the rolls. Sprinkle some with ground black pepper; leave the rest plain.

9 Bake for about 15–18 minutes, or until the rolls are golden brown. Turn out on to a wire rack to cool.

SOURDOUGH & GRAIN BREADS

One of the novel ways of using a bread machine, and one which is unlikely to be mentioned in your manufacturer's manual, is for making the starter for a sourdough. There are many different types of sourdough bread, but all share a similar tangy flavour, which endears them to their many fans. Making sourdough bread sounds like a bit of a fiddle, as it involves the action of airborne yeast spores rather than baker's yeast in a progression that takes several days. If you let the machine handle the process, however, the actual work is minimal. Experiment with San Francisco-style Sourdough. This chapter also introduces a variety of different grains, including rye and oatmeal, and shows how honey, maple syrup and malt extract can be used as sweeteners.

SAN FRANCISCO-STYLE SOURDOUGH

This tangy, chewy bread originated in San Francisco, but the flavour will actually be unique to wherever it is baked. The bread is made without baker's yeast, instead using airborne yeast spores to ferment a flour and water paste.

MAKES 1 LOAF

INGREDIENTS

FOR THE STARTER
25g/1oz/¼ cup plain (all-purpose) flour
15–30ml/1–2 tbsp warm water

1ST REFRESHMENT FOR THE STARTER
30ml/2 tbsp water
15ml/1 tbsp milk
50g/2oz/½ cup plain (all-purpose) flour

2ND REFRESHMENT FOR THE STARTER
90ml/6 tbsp water
15–30ml/1–2 tbsp milk
175g/6oz/1½ cups white bread flour

FOR THE DOUGH
100ml/3½fl oz/7 tbsp water
175g/6oz/1½ cups white bread flour

1ST REFRESHMENT FOR THE DOUGH
100ml/3½fl oz/7 tbsp water
175g/6oz/1½ cups white bread flour
50g/2oz/½ cup wholemeal (whole-wheat) bread flour
7.5ml/1½ tsp salt
5ml/1 tsp granulated sugar
unbleached white bread flour, for dusting

1 Place the flour for the starter in a bowl and stir in enough water to make a firm, moist dough. Knead for 5 minutes. Cover with a damp dishtowel. Leave for 2–3 days until a crust forms and the dough inflates with tiny bubbles. Remove the hardened crust and place the moist centre in a clean bowl. Add the water and milk for the 1st refreshment.

2 Gradually add the flour and mix to a firm but moist dough. Cover and leave for 1–2 days as before. Then repeat as for the 1st refreshment, using the ingredients for the 2nd refreshment. Leave for 8–12 hours in a warm place until well risen.

3 Pour the water for the dough into the bread machine pan. If necessary for your machine, add the dry ingredients first. Add 200g/7oz/scant 1 cup of starter. Sprinkle over the flour, covering the water. Close the lid. Set the machine to the dough setting, choosing the basic dough setting if available. Press Start.

4 Mix for 10 minutes, then turn off the machine. Leave the dough in the machine for 8 hours. Add the water for the 1st dough refreshment to the pan, then sprinkle over the flours.

5 Add the salt and sugar in separate corners. Set the machine as before. Press Start. Lightly flour a baking sheet.

6 When the dough cycle ends put the dough on a floured surface. Knock it back (punch it down) gently and then shape into a plump round ball. Place on the baking sheet; cover with oiled clear film (plastic wrap). Leave to rise for 2 hours, or until it has almost doubled in bulk.

7 Meanwhile, preheat the oven to 230°C/450°F/Gas 8. Dust the loaf with flour and slash the top in a star shape. Bake for 25 minutes, spraying the oven with water three times in the first 5 minutes. Reduce the oven temperature to 200°C/400°F/Gas 6. Bake the loaf for 10 minutes more or until golden and hollow-sounding. Cool on a wire rack.

LIGHT RYE & CARAWAY BREAD

Rye flour adds a distinctive slightly sour flavour to bread. Rye breads can be dense, so the flour is usually mixed with wheat flour to lighten the texture.

MAKES 1 LOAF

SMALL

210ml/7½fl oz/scant 1 cup water
5ml/1 tsp lemon juice
15ml/1 tbsp sunflower oil
85g/3oz/¾ cup rye flour
285g/10oz/2½ cups unbleached white
  bread flour
15ml/1 tbsp skimmed milk powder
  (non fat dry milk)
5ml/1 tsp caraway seeds
5ml/1 tsp salt
10ml/2 tsp light brown muscovado
  (molasses) sugar
3.5ml/¾ tsp easy-blend (rapid-rise)
  dried yeast

MEDIUM

300ml/10½fl oz/1¼ cups water
10ml/2 tsp lemon juice
22ml/1½ tbsp sunflower oil
125g/4½oz/generous 1 cup rye flour
375g/13oz/3¼ cups unbleached white
  bread flour
22ml/1½ tbsp skimmed milk powder
  (non fat dry milk)
7.5ml/1½ tsp caraway seeds
7.5ml/1½ tsp salt
15ml/1 tbsp light brown muscovado
  (molasses) sugar
5ml/1 tsp easy-blend (rapid-rise)
  dried yeast

LARGE

370ml/13fl oz/scant 1⅝ cups water
10ml/2 tsp lemon juice
30ml/2 tbsp sunflower oil
175g/generous 6oz/generous 1½ cups
  rye flour
500g/1lb 2oz/4½ cups unbleached
  white bread flour
30ml/2 tbsp skimmed milk powder
  (non fat dry milk)
10ml/2 tsp caraway seeds
10ml/2 tsp salt
20ml/4 tsp light brown muscovado
  (molasses) sugar
7.5ml/1½ tsp easy-blend (rapid-rise)
  dried yeast

1 Add the water, lemon juice and oil to the bread pan. If your instructions specify that the yeast is to be placed in the pan first, reverse the order in which you add the liquid and dry ingredients.

2 Sprinkle over the rye flour and the white bread flour, ensuring they cover the water. Add the skimmed milk powder and caraway seeds. Add the salt and sugar in separate corners of the bread pan. Make a small indent in the centre of the flour, but not down as far as the liquid, and add the yeast.

3 Close the lid. Set the bread machine to the basic/normal setting and select medium crust. Press Start.

4 Remove the bread pan from the machine at the end of the cycle and transfer the cooked loaf to a wire rack to cool.

BRAN & YOGURT BREAD

This soft-textured yogurt bread is enriched with bran. It is high in fibre and makes wonderful toast. Just the thing for cutting into fingers or "soldiers" for dipping in a lightly boiled egg at breakfast time.

MAKES 1 LOAF

SMALL

150ml/5fl oz/²⁄₃ cup water
125ml/4½fl oz/generous ½ cup natural
   (plain) yogurt
15ml/1 tbsp sunflower oil
15ml/1 tbsp molasses
200g/7oz/1¾ cups unbleached white
   bread flour
150g/5½oz/1⅓ cups wholemeal
   (whole-wheat) bread flour
25g/1oz/⅓ cup wheat bran
5ml/1 tsp salt
4ml/¾ tsp easy-blend (rapid-rise)
   dried yeast

MEDIUM

180ml/6½fl oz/generous ¾ cup water
175ml/6fl oz/¾ cup natural
   (plain) yogurt
22ml/1½ tbsp sunflower oil
30ml/2 tbsp molasses
260g/generous 9oz/2⅓ cups
   unbleached white bread flour

200g/7oz/1¾ cups wholemeal
   (whole-wheat) bread flour
40g/1½oz/½ cup wheat bran
7.5ml/1½ tsp salt
5ml/1 tsp easy-blend (rapid-rise)
   dried yeast

LARGE

230ml/8fl oz/1 cup water
210ml/7½fl oz/scant 1 cup natural
   (plain) yogurt
30ml/2 tbsp sunflower oil
30ml/2 tbsp molasses
375g/13oz/3¼ cups unbleached white
   bread flour
250g/9oz/2¼ cups wholemeal
   (whole-wheat) bread flour
50g/2oz/⅔ cup wheat bran
10ml/2 tsp salt
7.5ml/1½ tsp easy-blend (rapid-rise)
   dried yeast

COOK'S TIP
Molasses is added to this bread to give added flavour and colour. You can use treacle or golden (light corn) syrup instead.

1 Pour the water, yogurt, oil and molasses into the bread machine pan. If the instructions for your machine specify that the yeast is to be placed in the pan first, reverse the order in which you add the liquid and dry ingredients.

2 Sprinkle over both the white and the wholemeal (whole-wheat) flours, ensuring that the liquid mixture is completely covered. Add the wheat bran and salt, then make a small indent in the centre of the dry ingredients (but not down as far as the liquid) and add the easy-blend (rapid-rise) dried yeast.

3 Close the lid. Set the bread machine to the basic/normal setting and select the medium crust. Press Start.

4 Remove the bread pan from the machine at the end of the baking cycle and turn out the loaf on to a wire rack to cool. Serve when still just warm.

MULTIGRAIN BREAD

This healthy, mixed grain bread is one of the most popular loaves there is. It owes its wonderfully rich flavour to honey and malt extract. The slices make very good sandwiches, whether with sweet or savoury fillings.

MAKES 1 LOAF

SMALL
230ml/8fl oz/1 cup water
15ml/1 tbsp clear honey
7.5ml/1½ tsp malt extract
115g/4oz/1 cup Granary
   (whole-wheat) flour
50g/2oz/½ cup rye flour
75g/3oz/¾ cup unbleached white
   bread flour
140g/5oz/1¼ cups wholemeal
   (whole-wheat) bread flour
15ml/1 tbsp jumbo oats
15ml/1 tbsp skimmed milk powder
   (non fat dry milk)
5ml/1 tsp salt
20g/¾oz/1½ tbsp butter
4ml/¾ tsp easy-blend (rapid-rise)
   dried yeast

MEDIUM
300ml/10½fl oz/1¼ cups water
30ml/2 tbsp clear honey
15ml/1 tbsp malt extract
150g/5½oz/1⅓ cups Granary
   (whole-wheat) flour
75g/3oz/¾ cup rye flour
75g/3oz/¾ cup unbleached white
   bread flour

200g/7oz/1¾ cups wholemeal
   (whole-wheat) bread flour
30ml/2 tbsp jumbo oats
30ml/2 tbsp skimmed milk powder
   (non fat dry milk)
7.5ml/1½ tsp salt
25g/1oz/2 tbsp butter
5ml/1 tsp easy-blend (rapid-rise)
   dried yeast

LARGE
375ml/13fl oz/scant 1⅔ cups water
30ml/2 tbsp clear honey
22ml/1½ tbsp malt extract
200g/7oz/1¾ cups Granary
   (whole-wheat) flour
115g/4oz/1 cup rye flour
115g/4oz/1 cup unbleached white
   bread flour
225g/8oz/2 cups wholemeal
   (whole-wheat) bread flour
45ml/3 tbsp jumbo oats
45ml/3 tbsp skimmed milk powder
   (non fat dry milk)
10ml/2 tsp salt
40g/1½oz/3 tbsp butter
7.5ml/1½ tsp easy-blend (rapid-rise)
   dried yeast

1 Add the water, honey and malt extract to the bread machine pan. If the instructions for your machine specify that the yeast is to be placed in the pan first, reverse the order in which you add the liquid and dry ingredients.

2 Sprinkle over all four types of flour, ensuring that the liquid is completely covered. Add the jumbo oats and skimmed milk powder.

3 Place the salt and butter in separate corners of the bread machine pan. Make a small indent in the centre of the flour (but not down as far as the liquid) and add the easy-blend (rapid-rise) dried yeast.

4 Close the lid. Set the bread machine to the wholemeal setting and select the medium crust. Press Start. Remove the bread pan at the end of the baking cycle and turn out the loaf on to a wire rack to allow to cool.

MAPLE & OATMEAL BREAD

Rolled oats and oat bran add texture to this wholesome bread, which is suffused with the delectable flavour of maple syrup. Serve this for afternoon tea, instead of cake, for guests who enjoy a hint of sweetness, but prefer to avoid rich, creamy or iced baked goods.

MAKES 1 LOAF

SMALL
210ml/7½fl oz/scant 1 cup water
15ml/1 tbsp maple syrup
300g/10½oz/2¾ cups unbleached
  white bread flour
50g/2oz/½ cup wholemeal
  (whole-wheat) bread flour
20g/¾oz/¼ cup rolled oats
15ml/1 tbsp oat bran
5ml/1 tsp salt
5ml/1 tsp granulated sugar
25g/1oz/2 tbsp butter
5ml/1 tsp easy-blend (rapid-rise)
  dried yeast

MEDIUM
315ml/11fl oz/1⅓ cups water
30ml/2 tbsp maple syrup
375g/13oz/3¼ cups unbleached white
  bread flour
75g/3oz/¾ cup wholemeal
  (whole-wheat) bread flour
40g/1½oz/½ cup rolled oats
30ml/2 tbsp oat bran
5ml/1 tsp salt
5ml/1 tsp granulated sugar
40g/1½oz/3 tbsp butter
5ml/1 tsp easy-blend (rapid-rise)
  dried yeast

LARGE
410ml/14½fl oz/1¾ cups water
45ml/3 tbsp maple syrup
500g/1lb 2oz/4½ cups unbleached
  white bread flour
115g/4oz/1 cup wholemeal
  (whole-wheat) bread flour
50g/2oz/⅔ cup rolled oats
45ml/3 tbsp oat bran
7.5ml/1½ tsp salt
7.5ml/1½ tsp granulated sugar
50g/2oz/¼ cup butter
7.5ml/1½ tsp easy-blend (rapid-rise)
  dried yeast

COOK'S TIP
Use 100 per cent pure maple syrup. Less expensive products are often blended with cane or corn syrup, and the combination, though tasty, does not have the smooth rich flavour of the real thing.

1 Pour the water into the bread machine pan and then add the maple syrup. If the instructions for your machine specify that the yeast is to be placed in the pan first, reverse the order in which you add the liquid and dry ingredients.

2 Sprinkle over both the white and wholemeal flours, then the rolled oats and oat bran, ensuring that the water is completely covered.

3 Add the salt, sugar and butter, placing them in separate corners of the bread pan. Make a small indent in the centre of the flour (but not down as far as the liquid) and add the yeast.

4 Close the lid. Set the bread machine to the basic/normal setting and select the medium crust. Press Start.

5 Remove the bread pan from the machine at the end of the baking cycle and turn out the loaf on to a wire rack to cool.

MALTED BREAD

A malt and sultana loaf makes the perfect breakfast or tea-time treat. Serve it sliced and generously spread with butter.

MAKES 1 LOAF

SMALL
200ml/7fl oz/⅞ cup water
15ml/1 tbsp golden (light corn) syrup
22ml/1½ tbsp malt extract
350g/12oz/3 cups unbleached white
  bread flour
22ml/1½ tbsp skimmed milk powder
  (non fat dry milk)
2.5ml/½ tsp salt
40g/1½oz/3 tbsp butter
2.5ml/½ tsp easy-blend dried
  (rapid-rise) yeast
75g/3oz/½ cup sultanas (golden
  raisins)

MEDIUM
280ml/10fl oz/1¼ cups water
22ml/1½ tbsp golden (light corn) syrup
30ml/2 tbsp malt extract
500g/1lb 2oz/4½ cups unbleached
  white bread flour
30ml/2 tbsp skimmed milk powder
  (non fat dry milk)
5ml/1 tsp salt
50g/2oz/¼ cup butter
5ml/1 tsp easy-blend (rapid-rise)
  dried yeast
100g/3½oz/generous ½ cup sultanas
  (golden raisins)

LARGE
360ml/12½fl oz/generous 1½ cups
  water
30ml/2 tbsp golden (light corn) syrup
45ml/3 tbsp malt extract
675g/1½lb/6 cups unbleached white
  bread flour
30ml/2 tbsp skimmed milk powder
  (non fat dry milk)
5ml/1 tsp salt
65g/2½oz/5 tbsp butter
7.5ml/1½ tsp easy-blend (rapid-rise)
  dried yeast
125g/4½oz/generous ⅔ cup sultanas
  (golden raisins)

1 Pour the water, golden syrup and malt extract into the bread machine pan. If the instructions for your machine specify that the yeast is to be placed in the pan first, reverse the order in which you add the liquid and dry ingredients.

2 Sprinkle over the flour, ensuring that it covers the liquid. Add the milk powder. Add the salt and butter in separate corners of the bread pan. Make a shallow indent in the centre of the flour (but not down as far as the liquid) and add the yeast.

3 Close the lid. Set the bread machine to the basic/normal setting, choosing the raisin setting if available and selecting the medium crust. Press Start. Add the sultanas when the machine beeps or after the first kneading.

4 Remove the bread pan from the machine at the end of the baking cycle and turn out the loaf on to a wire rack. If you like, glaze the bread immediately after cooking. Dissolve 15ml/1 tbsp caster (superfine) sugar in 15ml/1 tbsp milk and brush over the top crust.

HONEY & BEER RYE BREAD

The flavour of this rye bread is enhanced by leaving the sourdough starter to develop over three days as a prelude to making the dough.

MAKES 1 LOAF

INGREDIENTS

FOR THE STARTER
175ml/6fl oz/ ¾ cup milk
115g/4oz/1 cup rye flour
4ml/ ¾ tsp easy-blend (rapid-rise) dried yeast

FOR THE DOUGH
170ml/6fl oz/scant ¾ cup flat beer
300g/10½oz/scant 2¾ cups unbleached white bread flour
85g/3oz/¾ cup rye flour
15ml/1 tbsp clear honey
7.5ml/1½ tsp salt
2.5ml/½ tsp easy-blend (rapid-rise) dried yeast
wholemeal (whole-wheat) flour, for dusting

1 Mix the milk, flour and yeast for the starter in a large bowl. Stir, then cover with a damp dishtowel. Rest in a warm place for three days; stir once a day.

2 Make the dough. Tip the starter into the bread machine pan and add the beer. If the instructions for your machine specify that the yeast is to be placed in the pan first, reverse the order in which you add the liquid and dry ingredients.

3 Sprinkle over both types of flour, ensuring that the beer is completely covered. Add the honey and salt, placing them in separate corners of the bread pan. Make a small indent in the centre of the flour (but not down as far as the liquid) and add the yeast.

4 Close the lid. Set the bread machine to the dough setting, choosing the basic dough setting if available. Press Start. Lightly oil a 17cm/6½in square pan that is fairly deep.

5 When the dough cycle has finished, remove the dough from the machine and place it on a lightly floured surface. Knock it back (punch it down) gently.

6 Roll the dough into a rectangle about 2cm/¾in thick. It needs to be the same width as the pan and three times as long. Fold the bottom third of the dough up and the top third down, then seal the edges with the rolling pin.

7 Place the folded dough in the prepared pan, cover it with lightly oiled clear film (plastic wrap) and leave in a warm place for 45–60 minutes, or until the dough has risen almost to the top of the pan.

8 Meanwhile, preheat the oven to 220°C/425°F/Gas 7. Dust the top of the loaf with a little wholemeal flour.

9 Using a sharp knife slash the loaf with four long cuts. Repeat with five cuts in the opposite direction to give a cross-hatched effect.

10 Bake the bread for 30–35 minutes, or until it sounds hollow when tapped on the base. Turn out on to a wire rack to cool slightly before serving.

ENRICHED BREADS

As you become more proficient at using your bread machine, you will undoubtedly want to experiment with speciality baked goods. You might be nervous about tackling items like Ham and Cheese Croissants or Devonshire Splits, but knowing that the machine will prepare the perfect dough is a great confidence booster. Enriched breads owe their depth of flavour to extra butter, milk, buttermilk, cheese or chocolate. These ingredients may be an integral part of the dough, or they may be added later, transforming the dough into a flaky yeast pastry. Rich doughs like the one used for Mini Brioche may need a slightly longer proving time than that offered by your bread machine, but the dough can be left in the machine until it has risen sufficiently.

Ham & Cheese Croissants

The crispy layers of yeast pastry melt in your mouth to reveal a cheese and ham filling. Serve the croissants freshly baked and still warm.

MAKES 12

INGREDIENTS
120ml/4fl oz/½ cup milk
30ml/2 tbsp water
1 egg
280g/10oz/2½ cups unbleached white bread flour
50g/2oz/½ cup fine French plain flour
5ml/1 tsp salt
15ml/1 tbsp caster (superfine) sugar
200g/7oz/scant 1 cup butter, softened
7.5ml/1½ tsp easy-blend (rapid-rise) dried yeast

FOR THE FILLING
175g/6oz Emmenthal or Gruyère cheese, cut into thin batons
70g/2½oz thinly sliced dry cured smoked ham, torn into small pieces
5ml/1 tsp paprika

FOR THE GLAZE
1 egg yolk
15ml/1 tbsp milk

1 Pour the milk, water and egg into the bread machine pan. Reverse the order in which you add the wet and dry ingredients, if necessary.

2 Sprinkle over the flours. Place the salt, sugar and 25g/1oz/2 tbsp of the butter in separate corners. Add the yeast in an indent in the flour. Ensure that the indent does not reach the liquid. Set the machine to the dough setting, choosing the basic dough setting (if available). Press Start. Shape the remaining softened butter into an oblong block 2cm/¾in thick.

3 When the dough cycle has finished, place the dough on a floured surface and knock back (punch down) gently. Roll out to a rectangle slightly wider than the butter block, and just over twice as long. Place the butter on one half of the dough, fold it over and seal the edges, using a rolling pin.

4 Roll out again into a rectangle 2cm/¾in thick, twice as long as it is wide. Fold the top third down, the bottom third up, seal, wrap in clear film (plastic wrap) and chill for 15 minutes. Repeat the rolling, folding and chilling twice more, giving the dough a quarter turn each time. Wrap in clear film; chill for 30 minutes.

5 Lightly oil two baking sheets. Roll out the dough to a rectangle measuring about 52 × 30cm/21 × 12in. Cut into two 15cm/6in strips. Using one strip, measure 15cm/6in along one long edge and 7.5cm/3in along the opposite long edge. Using the 15cm/6in length as the base of your first triangle, cut two diagonal lines to the 7.5cm/3in mark opposite, using a sharp knife. Continue along the strip, cutting six triangles in all. You will end up with two scraps of waste pastry, at either end of the strip. Repeat with the remaining strip.

6 Place a pastry triangle on the work surface in front of you, with the pointed end facing you. Divide the cheese and ham into 12 portions and put one portion on the wide end of the triangle. Hold and gently pull each side point to stretch the dough a little, then roll up the triangle from the filled end with one hand while pulling the remaining point gently towards you with the other hand.

7 Curve the ends of the rolled triangle away from you to make a crescent. Place this on one of the baking sheets, with the point underneath. Fill and shape the remaining croissants. Cover with oiled clear film and leave to rise for 30 minutes, until almost doubled in size. Preheat the oven to 200°C/400°F/Gas 6.

8 Mix the egg yolk and milk for the glaze and brush over the croissants. Bake for 15–20 minutes, until golden. Turn out on to a wire rack. Serve warm.

BUTTERMILK BREAD

Buttermilk adds a pleasant, slightly sour note to the flavour of this bread. It also gives the bread a good light texture and a golden brown crust. Buttermilk bread tastes especially delicious when toasted and spread with a little good quality butter.

MAKES 1 LOAF

SMALL
230ml/8fl oz/1 cup buttermilk
30ml/2 tbsp water
15ml/1 tbsp clear honey
15ml/1 tbsp sunflower oil
250g/9oz/2¼ cups unbleached white
  bread flour
125g/4½oz/generous 1 cup wholemeal
  (whole-wheat) bread flour
7.5ml/1½ tsp salt
5ml/1 tsp easy-blend (rapid-rise)
  dried yeast

MEDIUM
280ml/10fl oz/1¼ cups buttermilk
65ml/4½ tbsp water
22ml/1½ tbsp clear honey
22ml/1½ tbsp sunflower oil
350g/12oz/3 cups unbleached white
  bread flour

150g/5½oz/1⅓ cup wholemeal
  (whole-wheat) bread flour
7.5ml/1½ tsp salt
7.5ml/1½ tsp easy-blend (rapid-rise)
  dried yeast

LARGE
370ml/13fl oz/scant 1⅝ cups
  buttermilk
80ml/5½ tbsp water
30ml/2 tbsp clear honey
30ml/2 tbsp sunflower oil
475g/1lb 1oz/4¼ cups unbleached
  white bread flour
200g/7oz/1¾ cups wholemeal
  (whole-wheat) bread flour
10ml/2 tsp salt
10ml/2 tsp easy-blend (rapid-rise)
  dried yeast

COOK'S TIP
Buttermilk is a by-product of butter making and is the fairly thin liquid left after the fat has been made into butter. It is pasteurized and mixed with a special culture which causes it to ferment, resulting in the characteristic slightly sour flavour. If you run short of buttermilk, using a low-fat natural (plain) yogurt and 5–10ml/1–2 tsp lemon juice is an acceptable alternative.

1 Pour the buttermilk, water, honey and oil into the bread machine pan. If your instructions specify that the yeast is to be placed in the pan first, reverse the order of the liquid and dry ingredients.

2 Sprinkle over both the white and wholemeal (whole-wheat) flours, ensuring that the water is completely covered. Add the salt in one corner of the bread pan. Make a small indent in the centre of the flour (but not down as far as the liquid) and add the easy-blend (rapid-rise) dried yeast.

3 Close the lid. Set the bread machine to the basic/normal setting and select the medium crust. Press Start.

4 Remove the bread pan from the machine at the end of the baking cycle, and turn out the loaf on to a wire rack to cool.

CHALLAH

*The flavour of this traditional Jewish festival bread is enhanced by the use of a
sponge starter, which is left to develop for 8–10 hours before the final dough is made.
The dough is often plaited, but can also be shaped into a coil. This shape is favoured
for Jewish New Year celebrations, and symbolizes continuity and eternity.*

MAKES 1 LOAF

INGREDIENTS

FOR THE SPONGE
200ml/7fl oz/⅞ cup water
225g/8oz/2 cups unbleached white bread flour
15ml/1 tbsp granulated sugar
5ml/1 tsp salt
7.5ml/1½ tsp easy-blend (rapid-rise) dried yeast

FOR THE DOUGH
2 eggs
225g/8oz/2 cups unbleached white bread flour
15ml/1 tbsp granulated sugar
5ml/1 tsp salt
50g/2oz/¼ cup butter, melted

FOR THE TOPPING
1 egg yolk
15ml/1 tbsp water
poppy seeds

1 Pour the water for the sponge into the bread machine pan. If the instructions
for your machine specify that the yeast is to be placed in the pan first, reverse
the order of the liquid and dry ingredients.

2 Sprinkle over the flour, ensuring that the water is completely covered. Add the
sugar and salt in separate corners. Make a small indent in the centre of the flour
(but not down as far as the liquid) and add the yeast.

3 Close the lid. Set the bread machine to the dough setting, choosing the basic
dough setting if available. Press Start.

4 When the dough cycle has finished, switch the machine off, leaving the sponge inside. Do not lift the lid. Leave the sponge in the machine for 8 hours. If necessary, transfer to a bowl, cover with a damp dishtowel and set aside.

5 Remove the bread pan from the machine and replace the sponge (if necessary). Add the eggs for the dough to the sponge. Sprinkle over the flour. Place the sugar, salt and melted butter in separate corners of the bread pan. Set the bread machine to the dough setting, choosing the basic dough setting if available. Press Start. Lightly oil a baking sheet.

6 When the dough cycle has finished, remove the dough from the machine and place it on a lightly floured surface. Knock it back (punch it down) gently, then flatten the dough until it is about 2.5cm/1in thick. Fold both sides to the centre, fold the dough over again and press to seal.

7 Using the palms of your hands, gradually roll the dough into a rope with tapered ends. It should be about 50cm/20in long. Coil the rope into a spiral shape, sealing the final end by tucking it under the loaf. Place the coil on the prepared baking sheet. Cover it with a large glass bowl and leave to rise in a warm place for 45–60 minutes, or until almost doubled in size.

8 Preheat the oven to 190°C/375°F/Gas 5. In a small bowl, beat the egg yolk with the water for the topping. Brush the mixture over the challah. Sprinkle evenly with the poppy seeds and bake for 35–40 minutes, or until the bread is a deep golden brown and sounds hollow when tapped on the base. Transfer it to a wire rack to cool before slicing.

MINI BRIOCHE

Rich yet light, these buttery breads have a characteristic fluted shape, which makes them instantly identifiable. They can be eaten with both sweet and savoury foods.

MAKES 12

INGREDIENTS
30ml/2 tbsp milk
2 eggs
225g/8oz/2 cups unbleached white bread flour
2.5ml/½ tsp salt
15ml/1 tbsp caster (superfine) sugar
50g/2oz/¼ cup butter, melted
7.5ml/1½ tsp easy-blend (rapid-rise) dried yeast

FOR THE GLAZE
1 egg yolk
15ml/1 tbsp milk

> COOK'S TIP
> *This is a rich dough and may need more than the standard proving time. If it has not risen very much by the time the dough programme ends, leave the dough in the machine for another 30 minutes, turning off the machine and leaving the lid shut.*

1 Pour the milk and eggs into the bread machine pan. If the instructions for your bread machine specify that the yeast is to be placed in the pan first, simply reverse the order in which you add the liquid and dry ingredients.

2 Sprinkle over the flour, ensuring that it covers the liquid. Add the salt, sugar and butter, placing them in separate corners of the bread pan. Make a small indent in the centre of the flour (but not down as far as the liquid) and add the dried yeast.

3 Close the lid. Set the bread machine to the dough setting, choosing the basic dough setting if available. Press Start. Lightly oil 12 small brioche moulds.

4 When the dough cycle has finished, remove the dough from the machine and place it on a lightly floured surface. Knock it back (punch it down) gently. Slice off a quarter of the dough, cover with oiled clear film (plastic wrap) and set aside. Divide the remaining dough into 12 pieces.

5 Knead each piece of dough into a small round. Place each round in an oiled mould. Divide the reserved piece of dough into 12 and shape each piece into small pear shapes.

6 To shape each mini brioche, make a small hole or cut a cross in the top of each large piece of dough. Place the pear-shaped pieces of dough on top, narrow end down. Cover with lightly oiled clear film and leave in a warm place for 30–45 minutes, or until well risen. Meanwhile preheat the oven to 220°C/425°F/Gas 7.

7 Make the glaze by mixing the egg yolk and milk together. Brush the mixture over each brioche. Bake for 15 minutes, or until the brioche are golden and have risen well. Transfer them to a wire rack to cool. Serve warm or cold.

DEVONSHIRE SPLITS

A summer afternoon, a scrumptious cream tea; Devonshire splits are an essential part of this distinctly British tradition.

MAKES 8

INGREDIENTS
140ml/5fl oz/⅝ cup milk
225g/8oz/2 cups unbleached white bread flour
25g/1oz/2 tbsp caster (superfine) sugar
2.5ml/½ tsp salt
5ml/1 tsp easy-blend (rapid-rise) dried yeast
icing (confectioners') sugar, for dusting

FOR THE FILLING
clotted cream or whipped double (heavy) cream
raspberry or strawberry jam

1 Pour the milk into the bread pan. If your machine instructions specify it, reverse the order in which you add the liquid and dry ingredients.

2 Sprinkle over the flour, ensuring that it covers the liquid completely. Add the caster sugar and salt, placing each of these ingredients in a separate corner of the bread machine pan.

3 Make a small indent in the centre of the flour (do not go down as far as the milk underneath) and pour in the easy-blend dried yeast.

4 Close the lid. Set the bread machine to the dough setting, choosing the basic dough setting, if available. Press Start. Lightly grease two baking sheets.

5 When the dough cycle has finished, remove the dough from the machine and place it on a lightly floured surface. Knock back (punch down) gently, then divide it into eight equal-size portions.

6 Shape each portion of dough into a ball. Place on the prepared baking sheets, and flatten the top of each ball slightly. Cover with oiled clear film (plastic wrap). Leave to rise for 30–45 minutes or until doubled in size.

7 Preheat the oven to 220°C/425°F/Gas 7. Bake the buns for 15–18 minutes, or until they are light golden in colour. Turn out on to a wire rack to cool.

8 Split the buns open and fill them with cream and jam. Dust them with icing sugar just before serving.

Petit Pain au Chocolat

A freshly baked petit pain au chocolat *is almost impossible to resist, with its buttery, flaky yet crisp pastry concealing a delectable chocolate filling. For a special finish, drizzle melted chocolate over the tops of the freshly baked and cooked pastries.*

MAKES 9

INGREDIENTS
125ml/4½fl oz/generous ½ cup water
250g/9oz/2¼ cups unbleached white bread flour
30ml/2 tbsp skimmed milk powder (non fat dry milk)
15ml/1 tbsp caster (superfine) sugar
2.5ml/½ tsp salt
140g/5oz/⅔ cup butter, softened
7.5ml/1½ tsp easy-blend (rapid-rise) dried yeast
225g/8oz plain (semisweet) chocolate, broken into pieces

FOR THE GLAZE
1 egg yolk
15ml/1 tbsp milk

> VARIATION
> *Fill this flaky yeast pastry with a variety of sweet and savoury fillings. Try chopped nuts, tossed with a little brown sugar and cinnamon or, for a savoury filling, thin strips of cheese, wrapped in ham or mixed with chopped cooked bacon.*

1 Pour the water into the bread machine pan. If the instructions for your bread machine specify that the yeast is to be placed in the pan first, then simply reverse the order in which you add the liquid and dry ingredients.

2 Sprinkle over the flour, then the skimmed milk powder, ensuring that the water is completely covered. Add the caster sugar, salt and 25g/1oz/2 tbsp of the softened butter, placing them in separate corners of the bread pan. Make a small indent in the centre of the flour (but not down as far as the liquid) and sprinkle in the yeast.

4 Close the lid. Set the breadmaking machine to the dough setting, choosing the basic dough setting (if available). Press Start. Meanwhile shape the remaining softened butter into an oblong-shaped block, about 2cm/¾in thick.

5 Lightly grease two baking sheets. When the dough cycle has finished, place the dough on a floured surface. Knock back (punch down) and shape into a ball. Cut a cross halfway through the top of the dough.

6 Roll out around the cross, leaving a risen centre. Place the butter in the centre. Fold the rolled dough over the butter to enclose it, then seal the edges.

7 Roll to a rectangle 2cm/¾in thick, twice as long as it is wide. Fold the bottom third up and the top down; seal the edges. Wrap the dough in lightly oiled clear film (plastic wrap). Place in the refrigerator and chill for 20 minutes.

8 Do the same again twice more, giving the dough a quarter turn and chilling it each time. Finally, chill again for 30 minutes.

9 Roll out the dough to a rectangle measuring 52 × 30cm/21 × 12in. Using a sharp knife, cut the dough lengthways and widthways into three strips to make nine 18 × 10cm/7 × 4in rectangles. Divide the chocolate among the dough rectangles, placing the pieces lengthways at one short end.

10 Mix the egg yolk and milk together for the glaze. Brush the mixture over the edges of the dough, then roll up each piece of dough to completely enclose the chocolate. Press the edges together to seal.

11 Place the pastries seam side down on the prepared baking sheets. Cover with oiled clear film and leave to rise in a warm place for about 30 minutes or until doubled in size.

12 Meanwhile, preheat the oven to 200°C/400°F/Gas 6. Brush the pastries with the remaining glaze and bake for about 15 minutes, or until golden. Turn out on to a wire rack to cool just slightly and serve warm.

FESTIVE BREADS

The making and sharing of special foods has always been central to feast days like Christmas and Easter. Families, fragmented for much of the year, come together to share celebration meals at times like these, and there's no better time to prepare a festive treat like Easter Tea Ring or Mocha Panettone. Holidays usually mean that the children are home from school, and might enjoy helping you make Hot Cross Buns. Depending on their age and your patience, they could either pipe the crosses on the buns, using soft dough in a piping bag, or make the crosses from pastry. Equally fun to make is the Finnish Festive Wreath, a loop of braided dough enriched with saffron and cardamom and topped with almonds, sugar, rum and candied lime peel.

Hot Cross Buns

The traditional cross on these Easter buns originates from early civilization and probably symbolized the four seasons; it was only later used to mark Good Friday and the Crucifixion. In this version, the crosses are piped on the buns, but they can be shaped from pastry trimmings if you prefer. This would be a very good way of involving children in the preparation of these traditional treats.

Makes 12

Ingredients
210ml/7½fl oz/scant 1 cup milk
1 egg
450g/1lb/4 cups unbleached white bread flour
7.5ml/1½ tsp ground mixed spice
2.5ml/½ tsp ground cinnamon
2.5ml/½ tsp salt
50g/2oz/¼ cup caster (superfine) sugar
50g/2oz/¼ cup butter
7.5ml/1½ tsp easy-blend (rapid-rise) dried yeast
75g/3oz/scant ½ cup currants
25g/1oz/3 tbsp sultanas (golden raisins)
25g/1oz/3 tbsp mixed chopped (candied) peel

For the pastry crosses
50g/2oz/½ cup plain (all-purpose) flour
25g/1oz/2 tbsp margarine

For the glaze
30ml/2 tbsp milk
25g/1oz/2 tbsp caster (superfine) sugar

Cook's Tip
If preferred, to make the crosses roll out 50g/2oz shortcrust (unsweetened) pastry, and cut into narrow strips. Brush the buns with water to attach the crosses.

1 Pour the milk and egg into the bread pan. Reverse the order in which you add the liquid and dry ingredients if your machine requires this.

2 Sprinkle over the flour, ensuring that it covers the liquid. Add the mixed spice and cinnamon. Place the salt, sugar and butter in separate corners of the pan. Make a shallow indent in the centre of the flour (but not as far down as the liquid) and add the yeast.

3 Close the lid. Set the bread machine to the dough setting, choosing the basic raisin dough setting, if available. Press Start.

4 Add the dried fruit and peel when the machine beeps or 5 minutes before the end of the kneading period. Lightly grease two baking sheets.

5 When the dough cycle has finished, remove the dough from the machine and place it on a lightly floured surface. Knock it back (punch it down) gently, then divide it into 12 pieces. Cup each piece between your hands and shape it into a ball. Place on the prepared baking sheets, cover with oiled clear film (plastic wrap) and leave to rise for 30–45 minutes or until the dough has almost doubled in size.

6 Meanwhile, preheat the oven to 200°C/400°F/Gas 6. Make the pastry for the crosses. In a bowl, rub the flour and margarine together until the mixture resembles fine breadcrumbs. Bind with enough water to make a soft pastry which can be piped.

7 Spoon the pastry into a piping bag fitted with a plain nozzle and pipe a cross on each bun. Bake the buns for 15–18 minutes, or until golden.

8 Meanwhile, heat the milk and sugar for the glaze in a small pan. Stir thoroughly until the sugar dissolves. Brush the glaze over the top of the hot buns. Turn out on to a wire rack. Serve warm or cool.

EASTER TEA RING

This Easter tea ring is too good to serve just once a year. Bake it as a family weekend treat whenever you feel self-indulgent. It is perfect for a mid-morning coffee break or for tea time.

SERVES 8–10

INGREDIENTS
90ml/6 tbsp milk

1 egg

225g/8oz/2 cups unbleached white bread flour

2.5ml/½ tsp salt

25g/1oz/2 tbsp caster (superfine) sugar

25g/1oz/2 tbsp butter

5ml/1 tsp easy-blend (rapid-rise) dried yeast

FOR THE FILLING
50g/2oz/½ cup ready-to-eat dried apricots

15g/½oz/1 tbsp butter

50g/2oz/¼ cup light muscovado (molasses) sugar

7.5ml/1½ tsp ground cinnamon

2.5ml/½ tsp allspice

50g/2oz/⅓ cup sultanas (golden raisins)

milk, for brushing

FOR THE DECORATION
45ml/3 tbsp icing (confectioners') sugar

15–30ml/1–2 tbsp orange liqueur or orange juice

pecan nuts

candied fruits

VARIATION
There is a vast range of dried fruits available in the supermarkets. Vary the sultanas and apricots; try dried peaches, mango, melon, cherries and raisins, to name a few. Just make sure that the total quantity stays the same as in the recipe.

1 Pour the milk and egg into the bread machine pan. If the instructions for your bread machine specify that the yeast is to be placed in the pan first, simply reverse the order in which you add the liquid and dry ingredients.

2 Sprinkle over the flour, ensuring that it covers the liquid. Add the salt, sugar and butter, placing them in separate corners of the bread pan. Make a small indent in the centre of the flour (but not down as far as the liquid) and add the dried yeast.

3 Set the bread machine to the dough setting, choosing the basic dough setting if available. Press Start. Then lightly oil a baking sheet.

4 When the dough cycle has finished, remove the dough from the bread pan. Place it on a surface that has been lightly floured. Knock the dough back (punch it down) gently, then roll it out into a 30 × 45cm/12 × 18in rectangle.

5 Chop the dried apricots into small pieces. Melt the butter for the filling and brush it over the dough. Then sprinkle the dough with the muscovado sugar, ground cinnamon, allspice, sultanas and chopped apricots.

6 Starting from one long edge, roll up the rectangle of dough, as when making a Swiss (jelly) roll. Turn the dough so that the seam is underneath. Curl the dough into a circle, brush the ends with a little milk and seal. Place on the prepared baking sheet.

7 Using a pair of scissors, snip through the circle at 4cm/1½in intervals, each time cutting two-thirds of the way through the dough. Twist the sections so they start to fall sideways. Cover the ring with lightly oiled clear film (plastic wrap). Leave in a warm place for about 30 minutes, or until it is well risen and puffy.

8 Preheat the oven to 200°C/400°F/Gas 6. Bake the ring for 20–25 minutes, or until golden. Turn out on to a wire rack to cool slightly. Meanwhile, make the decoration by mixing together the icing sugar and liqueur or orange juice. Drizzle the mixture over the warm ring, then arrange pecan nuts and candied fruit on top. Cool completely before serving.

SPICED FRUIT KUGELHOPF

Sultanas steeped in spiced rum flavour this brioche-style bread, which is baked in a special fluted mould with a central funnel.

MAKES 1 LOAF

INGREDIENTS
100ml/3½fl oz/7 tbsp dark rum
5ml/1 tsp ground ginger
3 whole cloves
1 cinnamon stick
5ml/1 tsp freshly grated nutmeg
115g/4oz/⅔ cup sultanas (golden raisins)
30ml/2 tbsp milk
5 eggs
500g/1lb 2oz/4½ cups unbleached white bread flour
2.5ml/½ tsp salt
75g/3oz/6 tbsp caster (superfine) sugar
10ml/2 tsp easy-blend (rapid-rise) dried yeast
75g/3oz/6 tbsp butter, melted
75g/3oz/½ cup mixed chopped (candied) peel
icing (confectioners') sugar, for dusting

COOK'S TIP
This bread is best made in a medium or large bread machine as these have longer proving times. If you have a small machine you may need to increase the proving time in the kugelhopf mould.

1 Mix the rum, ginger, cloves, cinnamon stick and nutmeg in a small pan and place over a medium heat until hot, but not bubbling. Remove from the heat, add the sultanas and set aside in the pan for 30 minutes.

2 Pour the milk into the bread machine pan. Add three of the eggs, then separate the remaining eggs, setting the whites aside. Beat the egg yolks lightly, then add them to the milk in the bread pan.

3 Remove the cloves and cinnamon from the rum mixture and discard them (although the cinnamon stick can be dried for re-use later). Place a sieve over the bread pan and drain the sultanas in it so that the juices fall through into the pan. Set the sultanas aside.

4 Sprinkle over the flour, ensuring that it covers the liquid mixture completely. If the instructions for your bread machine specify that the yeast is to be placed in the machine pan first, then simply reverse the order in which you add the liquid and dry ingredients to the pan.

5 Add the salt and sugar to the flour, placing them in separate corners of the bread pan. Make a small indent in the centre of the flour (but not down as far as the liquid) and add the easy-blend dried yeast.

6 Close the lid. Set the bread machine to the dough setting, choosing the basic dough setting if available. Press Start. Mix for 5 minutes, then gradually add the melted butter. Lightly oil a non-stick kugelhopf mould.

7 When the dough cycle has finished, put the dough in a large mixing bowl. In a separate, grease-free bowl, whisk the egg whites to soft peaks.

8 Add the reserved sultanas and cut mixed peel to the dough and fold in, using your hands. Using a metal spoon, fold in the egg whites to form a soft dough.

9 Spoon the dough into the kugelhopf mould in three or four batches, making sure it is evenly distributed. Cover with lightly oiled clear film (plastic wrap) and leave in a slightly warm place for 1–1½ hours, or until the dough has risen and is almost at the top of the mould.

10 Preheat the oven to 190°C/375°F/Gas 5. Bake the kugelhopf for 50–60 minutes or until it has browned and is firm to the touch. You can cover the surface with baking parchment if it starts to brown too quickly. Turn out on to a wire rack to cool. Dust with icing sugar.

Finnish Festive Wreath

This traditional sweet bread, enriched with egg and delicately scented with saffron and cardamom, is called pulla *in its native Finland. For festive occasions, elaborately shaped versions of the bread, like this pretty wreath, are prepared.*

Serves 8–10

Ingredients
5ml/1 tsp saffron strands
200ml/7fl oz/⅞ cup milk
2 eggs
500g/1lb 2oz/4½ cups unbleached white bread flour
5ml/1 tsp ground cardamom seeds
2.5ml/½ tsp salt
50g/2oz/¼ cup caster (superfine) sugar
50g/2oz/¼ cup butter, melted
5ml/1 tsp easy-blend (rapid-rise) dried yeast

For the glaze
1 egg yolk
15ml/1 tbsp water

For the topping
45ml/3 tbsp flaked (sliced) almonds
40g/1½oz/3 tbsp granulated sugar
15ml/1 tbsp rum
15ml/1 tbsp candied lime peel, chopped (optional)

> ### Variation
> *Instead of candied lime peel, other ingredients can be used for the topping, if preferred. Try angelica or candied orange peel instead. Glacé fruits such as cherries or peaches are also good.*

1 Place the saffron strands in a small mixing bowl. Heat half of the milk in a small pan, pour it over the saffron and leave to infuse (steep) until the milk cools to room temperature.

2 Pour the saffron milk into the bread machine pan, then add the remaining milk and the eggs. However, if the instructions for your bread machine specify that the yeast is to be placed in the bread pan first, simply reverse the order in which you add the liquid and dry ingredients.

3 Sprinkle over the flour, ensuring that it covers the liquid completely, then add the ground cardamom seeds. Add the salt, caster sugar and butter, placing them in separate corners of the bread pan. Make a shallow indent in the centre of the flour (but not down as far as the milk and eggs) and add the dried yeast.

4 Close the lid. Set the bread machine to the dough setting, choosing the basic dough setting if available. Press Start. Lightly oil a baking sheet.

5 When the dough cycle has finished, remove the dough from the bread machine pan and place it on a surface that has been lightly floured. Knock the dough back (punch it down) gently, then divide it into three equal pieces.

6 Roll each piece of dough into a rope, about 65cm/26in long. Place the ropes lengthways, next to each other. Starting from the centre, plait (braid) the pieces together, working towards yourself and from left to right. Turn the dough around and repeat the plaiting process. Bring the ends of the plait together to form a circular wreath and pinch to seal.

7 Place the wreath on the prepared baking sheet. Cover with lightly oiled clear film (plastic wrap) and leave to rise for 45–60 minutes, or until it has almost doubled in size. Meanwhile, preheat the oven to 190°C/375°F/Gas 5.

8 Make the glaze by mixing the egg yolk and water in a bowl. In a separate bowl, mix the almonds, sugar, rum and peel for the topping. Brush the glaze over the loaf and sprinkle the almond mixture on top.

9 Bake the glazed wreath for 20 minutes, then reduce the oven temperature to 180°C/350°F/Gas 4 and bake for 10–15 minutes more, or until the wreath is golden and well risen. Turn out on to a wire rack to cool.

MOCHA PANETTONE

Panettone is the traditional Italian Christmas bread from Milan. This tall domed loaf is usually filled with dried fruits; for a change try this coffee-flavoured bread studded with chocolate and pine nuts.

SERVES 8–10

INGREDIENTS
30ml/2 tbsp instant coffee granules or coffee powder
30ml/2 tbsp hot water
140ml/5fl oz/scant ⅔ cup milk
1 egg, plus 2 egg yolks
400g/14oz/3½ cups unbleached white bread flour
15ml/1 tbsp cocoa powder (unsweetened)
5ml/1 tsp ground cinnamon
2.5ml/½ tsp salt
75g/3oz/6 tbsp caster (superfine) sugar
75g/3oz/6 tbsp butter, softened
7.5ml/1½ tsp easy-blend (rapid-rise) dried yeast
115g/4oz plain (semisweet) Continental chocolate, coarsely chopped
45ml/3 tbsp pine nuts, lightly toasted
melted butter, for glazing

> COOK'S TIP
> *The dough for this bread is quite rich and may require a longer rising time than that provided for by your bread machine. Check the dough at the end of the dough cycle. If it does not appear to have risen very much in the bread pan, leave the dough in the machine, with the machine switched off and the lid closed, for a further 30 minutes to allow it to rise to the required degree.*

1 In a small bowl, dissolve the coffee granules or powder in the hot water. Pour the mixture into the bread machine pan. Add the milk, egg and egg yolks. If the instructions for your bread machine specify that the yeast is to be placed in the pan first, reverse the order in which you add the liquid and dry ingredients.

2 Sift the flour and cocoa powder together. Sprinkle the mixture over the liquid, ensuring that it is completely covered. Add the ground cinnamon. Place the salt, sugar and butter in separate corners of the bread pan. Make a small indent in the centre of the flour (but not down as far as the liquid) and add the yeast.

3 Close the lid. Set the bread machine to the dough setting, choosing the basic dough setting, if available. Press Start. Lightly oil a 15cm/6in deep cake pan or soufflé dish. Using a double sheet of baking parchment that is 7.5cm/3in wider than the depth of the pan or dish, line the container so that the excess paper stands up above the rim, creating a collar.

4 When the dough is ready, remove it from the machine and place it on a lightly floured surface. Knock it back (punch it down) gently. Gently knead in the chocolate and toasted pine nuts and shape the dough into a ball. Cover it with lightly oiled clear film (plastic wrap) and leave it to rest for 5 minutes.

5 Shape the dough into a plump round loaf which has the same diameter as the cake pan or soufflé dish, and place in the base of the container. Cover with oiled clear film and leave the dough to rise in a slightly warm place for 45–60 minutes, or until the dough has almost reached the top of the parchment collar.

6 Meanwhile, preheat the oven to 200°C/400°F/Gas 6. Brush the top of the loaf with the melted butter and cut a deep cross in the top. Bake the bread for about 10 minutes, then reduce the oven temperature to 180°C/350°F/Gas 4 and bake the panettone for 30–35 minutes more, or until it is evenly golden all over and a metal skewer inserted in the centre comes out clean.

7 Leave the panettone in the pan or dish for 5–10 minutes, then turn out on to a wire rack and leave it until it is quite cold before slicing.

INDEX